THE LOVER OF QUEEN ELIZABETH

BEING THE LIFE AND CHARACTER OF

ROBERT DUDLEY, EARL OF LEICESTER

1533-1588

By

MRS AUBREY RICHARDSON

"A Creature of my own."
—ELIZABETH.
" Some noblemen will be men."
—Archbishop PARKER.
' *Of greatest ones, he greatest in his place,*
Sate in the bosome of his Soveraine,
And RIGHT AND LOYALL did his word maintaine.'
—EDMUND SPENSER.

ILLUSTRATED

T. WERNER LAURIE
CLIFFORD'S INN
LONDON
E.C.

Printing Statement:

Due to the very old age and scarcity of this book,
many of the pages may be hard to read due to the
blurring of the original text, possible missing pages,
missing text and other issues beyond our control.

Because this is such an important and rare work, we
believe it is best to reproduce this book regardless of
its original condition.

Thank you for your understanding.

LIST OF ILLUSTRATIONS

THE LOVER OF QUEEN ELIZABETH

CHAPTER I

In the great firmament of human personality, no star shines with a fiercer light than Elizabeth, Queen of England. And of the numerous satellites that revolve about her, radiating an effulgence that is their own and hers, the one whose beams most dazzle star-gazers, is Robert Dudley, Earl of Leicester.

These two were born into an age when the influence of the planets on human destiny and on human character was held to be direct and all-determining. It was the hour when astronomy was hardly ousting astrology from the category of the sciences.

The period of Elizabeth and of Leicester was the renascent period of history. In their time, the spirit of the ancients re-incarnated. Learning, art, and literature came to birth in the modern world. Invention and discovery re-emerged from Time's womb. Science and Religion were reconstructed and reformed. To

A

that birth and to that emergence, to that reconstruction and to that reformation, the Queen of England and her Supreme Favourite contributed not a little. Indeed, they were themselves among the most remarkable products of the Renascence. Their lives and their characters exemplify unmistakably the "new" spirit then breathing on Society. The virtues and the vices of Protestantism and of Paganism were incongruously mixed in their compositions.

To understand the character, and to trace the destiny of Leicester aright, one must examine his heredity, and look into the circumstances of his early life.

His father was that John Dudley who was raised to the peerage as Viscount Lisle, by Henry VIII. His mother was Jane, daughter and heiress of Sir Edward Guilford, to whom the guardianship of John Dudley had been given by the King, upon the execution of his father, Edmund Dudley. This Edmund Dudley, Leicester's grandfather, married Elizabeth, daughter of Edward Grey, and of another Elizabeth who was sister and co-heir of Thomas Talbot, Viscount Lisle, a descendant of the famous Richard Beauchamp, Earl of Warwick. After the death of Edmund Dudley, Elizabeth [Grey] married Arthur Plantagenet, a natural son of Edward IV., who was created Viscount Lisle. Of Edmund Dudley, the great Lord

Bacon said he was "one that could put hateful business into good language." This facility was handed down to his grandson Robert. Edmund was beheaded on Tower Hill. While in the Tower he wrote a book he entitled "The Tree of Commonwealth," in which he insisted on the necessity of piety and of the sense of Christian fellowship in a Prince. The tone of his work was very different from that of another book of instruction for Princes, published in Europe at the same period. It was the doctrine of Nicholas Macchiavelli that it was "convenient" for the mind of a Prince to be "at his command, and flexible to all the puffs and variations of fortune; not forbearing to be good whilst it is in his choice, but knowing how to be evil when there is a necessity."

The teachings of both these instructors of Princes bore fruit in the lives of Edmund Dudley's descendants. His son John began his career in the godliness of purpose, inculcated by his father. But as John grew great, he relaxed hold upon principle, and adopted the Macchiavellian doctrine of convenience. John's son, "the illustrious Prince" Robert Dudley, Earl of Leicester, reversed the order his father observed. In his early manhood he adhered to the maxims of the Florentine; he responded in the end to some of the exhortations of his grandsire. Yet his mind was ever "at his command, and flexible to all the puffs and variations of fortune." He could not have been Elizabeth's favourite, without the sovereign grace of self-control, nor without the, to her, more serviceable attribute of flexibility.

But a closer environment than that of the age in which he grew, and a nearer heredity than that of a grand-parent, shaped the princely temper of Elizabeth's Leicester to the form in which history presents it to us. The Court of England was the home of his nature, and the hot-bed of his genius. The pageantry and the power of palace life had supreme attractions for both his parents. To be high at Court was the greatest good life offered for father and for mother; to be out of favour with the reigning Monarch, the last evil of existence. We learn this of the father in actions of his we become acquainted with in following the career of his son. That the mother of Robert was also set on greatness we are informed by her own telling.

In the last will and testament of "the Right Noble and Excellent Princess Lady Jane," who was "wife to the High and Mighty Prince, John Dudley, late Duke of Northumberland, by whom she had issue eight sons and five daughters," the mother of Leicester wrote in her "very own hand":

"My will is earnestly and effectually that little solemnity be made for me, for I had ever have a thousandfold, my debts to be paid and the poor to be given unto, than any pomp to be showed upon my wretched carcase that has had at times too much in this world, full of all vanities, deceits and guiles; and who ever doth trust to this transitory world, as I did, may happen to have an overthrow, as I had; therefore to the worms will I go as I have before written."

Yet the woman's scorn in dying of the honours dear in life, was only half sincere. Another clause in her will provided for a certain commemoration of her greatness.

" I will . . . have . . . a stone laid upon my grave accordingly as the heralds shall think meet, with the whole arms of father and mother upon the stone graven."

But she declared against the practice of embalming:

"In no wise let me be opened after I am dead. . . . I have not lived to be very bold before women, much more I should be loth to come into the hands of any living man, be he Physician or Surgeon."

In the temperament of the mother who wrote these directions and confessions, we find the key to the character of the Earl of Leicester. We can see whence came the spirit that made him accept honours with a gracious contempt, and take to authority as a duck takes to water. We discern also the source of his self-containment, and discover the root of that reserve which in him, as in her who bore him, was the manifestation of a personal pride too deep to be expressed in vanity.

Leicester was no popinjay and no glutton. It was of design that his array was gorgeous; of intention that he loaded his table with costly viands, and sat long at banquets. From her reign's beginning to his life's end he was the most conspicuous noble of Elizabeth's Court, and for long he was the declared lover of the Queen. It was to do honour to his native country, and to glorify the woman he sought to marry, as much as to gratify his own ambition, that he lived in state and practised in all its details, the Prince's art of deportment.

His training in that art was thorough. He was as rigorously educated as Edward VI. himself. But although grounded in Latin, and schooled in modern languages, in the approved royal fashion of his day, his mind imbibed scientific learning more readily than classical. Roger Ascham praised to him "the ability of inditing that is in you naturally," and Thomas Wilson (a Doctor of Laws and a Master of the Court of Requests), who had "familiar conference" with Leicester from his boyhood, had "sufficient proof" of his "careful mind, even in reading, not only of the Latin, but also of the Italian good and sound writers, to know and understand the best used government and the chief laws that have been made in all ages." Wilson observed also that he who had the mind "thus godly inclined to know" had also a "good mind" to put his knowledge in practice.

Leicester received impressions quickly, and represented them with facility and force. His literary style is excellent. He preferred mathematical to linguistic studies. He never learned to speak French with fluency; but other educations than those of the schoolroom fitted him for his part in life. Manly exercises and sports were included in the curriculum of his training, and in his eighteenth year he began in earnest his apprenticeship to the calling of a favourite.

The Viscount Lisle had been one of the sixteen trustees of the kingdom named in the will of Henry VIII. And when Edward Seymour, Earl of Hertford, the young King's uncle, laid swift hands on the reins of government, Lisle was made Earl of Warwick and Great Chamberlain of England, and given the castle and manor of Warwick, and "divers other great lordships and lands." By 1549, Seymour, who had become Duke of Somerset and Lord-Protector, was in disgrace with the populace and with the nobles. Lord Warwick, the soldier and diplomat, assumed the governorship of Edward, by whom he was later created Duke of Northumberland. With him to Court, Dudley brought his sons, Lord John, Lord Ambrose, and Lord Robert. Robert was at once attached to the person of the young Sovereign. Warwick's next concern—as it was doubtless also the concern of his good Countess —was to marry his likely boys to well-dowered brides. The eldest, by a contrivance of the young King to reconcile Warwick and Somerset, was married to Lady Anne Seymour. Ambrose was given for his bride a daughter of an Attorney-General. And on the 4th of June 1550, at the Royal Palace of Sheen, Lord Robert Dudley became the husband of Amy Robsart. Before the ceremony, the boy-King conferred the honour of knighthood on the bridegroom of eighteen. And Edward recorded the fact of Lord Robert's wedding in his diary curtly, displaying his boyishness by the note:

"After which marriage, there were certain gentlemen that did strive who should first take away a goose's head, which was hanged alive on two cross-posts."

The sports of men are barbarous.

It is unlikely that Lord Robert had any previous knowledge of Amy Robsart, who was the only legitimate child of the Norfolk squire, Sir John Robsart of Siderstern, by his marriage with a widow, whose children by her first husband — one Roger Appleyard, Squire of Stansfield, Norfolk — were separately provided for. In the "good old days," parents made the marriages of their children on approved business lines. Amy was her father's co-heiress, and the owner of considerable property. It has been assumed that her country breeding and simple tastes ill-fitted her for Court life. We may believe she had not been instructed in the classic lore that was the fashionable education for the daughters of the nobles of her time. It is doubtful whether she could write. But the tradition that makes her fair, gentle, and trusting, need not be disbelieved. The Duke and Duchess of Northumberland would not have approved an ungainly or an uncouth bride for their handsome young son. And the fact that, nearly two years after their marriage, the Duke settled Hemsby Manor, near Yarmouth, on "Robert Dudley, Lord Dudley, my son, and the Ladie Amie his wife," and that the Duchess, in her will, left to Amy as to her other daughters-in-law, a Court gown (of "wrought velvet"), are proof that Lord Robert's wife was regarded by her husband's family as a fit mate of his dignity.

The portrait of Amy Robsart, drawn by Sir

Walter Scott, is not so fallacious as is the history he has attached to the portrait. Both the fine novel of " Kenilworth," and the old-time *Ballad of Cumnor Hall*, on which " Kenilworth " was founded, are wholly misleading in regard to the circumstances of her life, and the character of her relations to Lord Robert Dudley.   Amy was certainly not present at the great festival at Kenilworth; and she was never Countess of Leicester.   Her death occurred before the manor of Kenilworth was bestowed on her husband, and before he was ennobled.

Yet the true story of Amy Robsart is as pitiful as the imagined one.   Her marriage with Lord Robert was to him, to his family, and to her relations, satisfactory enough.   The *prestige* and the influence of the Dudleys were advantageous to all the Robsart connections. The Dudleys had the Robsart money, so they were satisfied.

In the early days of their married life, the young couple lived on their Norfolk lands. Lord Robert, however, was much at Court. He was made Master of the Buckhounds for life in 1551, and, in the following year, was appointed one of the six gentlemen of the King's Privy Chamber.

But now the young King's health was failing. He was in rapid consumption, and kept close in his apartments. There could be but one end. Those about him began to consider the fate that would be theirs under a new Sovereign. As a consequence of an earlier enthusiasm, and for more selfish reasons of a later time— Edward VI. was an uncompromising Protestant — Northumberland had identified himself with the Reforming party in England. There would be short shrift for him and his if the Princess Mary followed her brother on England's throne.

An Act of Parliament had given to King Henry the power to dispose by will of the succession to his sovereignty. There were many claimants for Edward's reversion, and much doubt in the minds of the lawyers, though little in that of the people, as to who was entitled to succeed the Prince. Following the dictates of natural affection, and inclining to his people's sense of justice, Henry had named Mary to succeed Edward, should he die without heirs of his body. Elizabeth was to succeed Mary in the like case. After these, the Sovereign appointed the descendants of his younger sister Mary to be his heirs. The line of his elder sister Margaret he passed over. The marriage of Margaret's son, King James V. of Scotland, to a Princess of France—Mary of Guise—had drawn France and Scotland too closely together to make a

Scottish Prince an acceptable Sovereign for the English.

The young King was easily persuaded that his power of demising the crown was equal to his father's. But an Act of Parliament had bestowed on Henry the authority for an unconstitutional proceeding. Edward acted by virtue of his kingship alone; and, boy though he was, acted with all the insistance of an autocrat. Archbishop Cranmer's objections were peremptorily over-ruled. The dying youth set his hand to the testament that put aside the claims of both his sisters, and delegated his regal power to the grandchild of his father's younger sister, who had been Queen of France for a season, and afterwards married Charles Brandon, Duke of Suffolk. The child of this union, the Lady Frances Brandon, had become the wife of Henry Grey, Marquis of Dorset. They had three daughters, Jane, Catherine, and Mary. Edward named the eldest of these three the heiress of his kingdom. Northumberland married his fourth surviving son — Lord Guilford Dudley — to the Lady Jane Grey. And he united, at the same time, the Lady Catherine Grey to the son of the Earl of Pembroke, and gave his daughter, the Lady Catherine Dudley to Lord Hastings, son of the Earl of Huntingdon, a descendant of

George, Duke of Clarence. Then Edward died.

For three days Northumberland kept the fact of the King's death secret, while he made cunning preparation for the securing of the Princess Mary, and the proclamation of "Queen" Jane. Full account of the deceptions practised to attain this end, belongs to another story. This one concerns Lord Robert Dudley, who, at the head of a Company of Horse, rode northward from the capital to meet Mary on her way to her "dying" brother, who was really dead. Lord Robert was to give the Princess "safe" conduct to the Tower. His escort of honour was to be the escort of her fate. But Mary had friends as well as foes at Court. The hunting-lodge at Hunsdon, where Lord Robert expected to seize his prey, was empty. Orders were sent after him to follow the fugitive along any track she might have left, and the Duke despatched also his eldest son, by courtesy Lord Warwick, to scour the country in the likely direction of her flight. Both young men had their father's commands to act as swiftly and as desperately as might be necessary, to prevent the Princess from proclaiming herself the Queen. Lord Warwick and Lord Robert were commissioned to decoy Mary with any lie, and, should she turn defiant, to connive at her assassination. But they never overtook her, and two days later she issued her Proclamation at Keninghall, a house of the Duke of Norfolk.

At this crisis in the Dudley destinies, every member of the family acted without scruple. Faithless to England's Queen by law, they were faithful to one another. In London, the Duchess of Northumberland matched her ambition with her lord's, and worked day and night with him to establish the greatness of their house. Their daughter Mary, Lady Sidney, wife of Sir Henry Sidney in whose arms King Edward had died, also took part in the operations carried on in the name of "Queen" Jane. When it had become evident that Edward had only a few more hours, perhaps only a few more minutes, to live, the Duchess of Northumberland had gone to Suffolk House for her son Guilford's bride. Neither Jane nor her mother would allow that the time had come for the ending of the family arrangement, whereby the young Lord, and Lady Guilford Dudley were to live apart until of riper years for matrimony. Only six weeks had passed since their wedding-day. But, prompted by his mother, Lord Guilford came himself and begged Jane, on her duty to him as her husband, to go with him. The child-wife yielded. She

went with Lord Guilford and his mother to
Chelsea, where they kept her strictly until
Lady Sidney, with the deceptive tale that
her father had for Lady Jane a message of
highest moment from the King, bore her off
to Zion House at Isleworth, where the nobles
and their ladies who supported, or pretended
to support, Northumberland, came to declare
to her Edward's death and his will concerning
her. The surprised and gratified girl, who
believed most sincerely that only a Protestant
was a fit Monarch for England, replied to the
great ones who acclaimed her, that she had
never dreamed of such high destiny, but that
if she were called to reign, she prayed for
grace to act as might be best for God's glory
and His people's good.

On the third day of her "reign," it became
known to her Council that Mary had eluded the
dashing pursuit of Lord Warwick and Lord
Robert, and that nobles and gentlemen from
many counties were flocking to her at Keninghall. With his sons, Lord Ambrose and Lord
Robert, the self-appointed champion of English
Protestantism went to do battle with the
hereditary genius of Roman Catholicism. "All
men crowd to see us, but no man cries God
bless us," said Northumberland gloomily, as he
rode at the head of his troops, between the
silent lines of Londoners, who gathered to

watch his departure. He felt himself to be marching to his doom. Before he came to Keninghall many of his soldiers had deserted.

At first news of Northumberland's approach, Mary left Keninghall for Framlingham, a more formidable stronghold of the Catholic Howards. On her way she only just escaped falling into the hands of Lord Robert Dudley and his Company of Horse. But this Prince of many future good fortunes had not the chance that day to take prisoner his lawful Queen. Had he done so, the history of England, of himself, and of that later Queen who made his greatness, would have to be re-written. The seizing of Mary would have meant the establishment on the throne of Jane. And who knows if the great Elizabeth had ever come by her own?

As things turned out, Mary set her standard flying at Framlingham on the 16th July 1553. On the 31st of the same month she made her triumphal entry into London. Her sister Elizabeth had place in the procession as Princess of England. The train of Mary was sufficiently brilliant although Northumberland and his sons were not included in it. The Duke had been taken at Cambridge by Lord Arundel, his subordinate on the Council that proclaimed "Queen" Jane.

Too late Northumberland threw up his cap and cried, "Hurrah!" for Mary. Lord Robert

Dudley was arrested at Lynn, where he had read in the market-place the Proclamation of " Queen " Jane. The star of his early fortunes had declined. The conjunction of his destiny with that other destiny that was to raise his to all ascendancy, had not yet taken place.

CHAPTER II

I⊤ was a portent that the Tower had never before been so full of prisoners as at the first coming to London of Mary, the Queen.

In the Beauchamp Tower, the Dudley family was lodged — Warwick and Guilford on the middle floor; Robert on the lower; Ambrose and Henry in the "Nuns' Bower"; Jane in the deputy-lieutenant's house; the Duke in the gate-house.

No need to tell of the way by which Northumberland, Lady Jane, and Lord Guilford quitted the gaol of gaols. The lad, Henry, appears to have been early allowed to slip out and join his stricken mother. The four remaining brothers — though all forswore their Protestant faith — were kept prisoners for a year and more.

On the stone wall of the lower room into which Lord Robert first was flung, he carved his name:

ROBERT DUDLEY.

Upon the execution of the unhappy Guilford,

Robert joined Warwick in the upper room, and, to this day, there may be seen the beguilements of the three brothers in their misery. Lord Guilford carved the name JANE. Two bears and a ragged staff surmount the name of Warwick, and around the badges and the name they signify are wreathed symmetrically roses, acorns geraniums, honeysuckles. The initial letters of these flowers stand for Robert, Ambrose, Guilford, and Henry. But other meanings lurk within the blossoms. The rose suggests Ambrose, and the oak Robert. A sprig of oak — the device of Lord Robert — with the letters R. D. appears also on the wall.

During their year of incarceration in the stern chamber they made decorative, Lord Ambrose and Lord Robert were visited by their wives. One need know but a little of the heart of such a woman as was Amy Robsart, to assert that these days were not the least happy ones of her married life. Then, at least, Robert Dudley was all her own. Out in the great world, his fancy was drawn this way and that by many a lode-star. He had so many interests, so many ambitions, so many pre-occupations. Love was of his life a thing apart, and he expected of women that they also should cultivate affection in plots, and make of existence a garden of many interests.

But when that great world was shut out, and Lord Robert was forced to find his interests and amusements within a given space, then all the courtesies and the tendernesses, all the gay humours and the facile sentimentalities that were natural flowers of his being, were for the gathering of the faithful wife whose devotion would be the greater in proportion to the depth of the affliction of the husband to whom she belonged. We may not pity Amy Dudley for the time when her Robert lay in the Tower; we may pity her perhaps in the time before. We must pity her thereafter. But at the moment, it was her woman's glory to console the man to whom she had been given, "for better for worse."

There is no evidence to show that her empire over her husband was disputed, even when, in the progress of events, the Princess Elizabeth became a co-prisoner with Lord Robert. A latter-day calumniator of Queen Elizabeth and the Earl of Leicester has built up a theory of the parentage of the great Lord Bacon, and of the Queen's later favourite, Robert, Earl of Essex, on a cryptographic revelation of the supposed fact of the marriage at this time of Elizabeth and Lord Robert Dudley. But the cypher — if there be one — that reveals this circumstance, cannot have been penned by a co-temporary. All the world knew of Lord

Robert's marriage to Amy, and it is impossible that any union, regular or irregular, could have taken place in the Tower. The Dudley brothers were all closely confined.

After their father's execution, Ambrose received licence to walk on the leads of Cold Harbour and Guilford had the same privilege for Beauchamp Tower. Doubtless to Warwick and to Robert were also allotted certain areas of exercise. Elizabeth's first indulgence was that of sometimes walking in the Queen's lodging in the presence of the Constable, the Lieutenant, and three of Queen Mary's ladies. Later on she was allowed to promenade in the garden, after the shutters of all overlooking windows had been carefully closed. A little boy of four who ran to her with some flowers, as she took exercise, was severely threatened, and his father summoned before the Constable and rebuked. Facilities for love-making between prisoners, were—to say the least—restricted.

And, although Elizabeth was fair, rompish, crafty, and anything but retiring, and Robert Dudley graceful, ingratiating and of "very goodly person," they had both, at the moment, too much to lose, and too little to gain by an association, to have entered into one. It does not square with the nature of either that at this juncture they indulged in even a fanciful regard for one another.

In the month of October 1554, the three brothers were set free. Queen Mary had married Philip of Spain in August, and from the first moment of the new King's coming, the Duchess of Northumberland had laboured to procure, through Spanish influences, the release of her sons. The poor, deprived lady, dying in her only remaining house — a Guilford inheritance—of Hales Owen, bequeathed to the Duchess of Alva her green parrot, "having nothing worthy for her else." She left a small memento—"with commendations for the great friendship" he had shown to her in making her have so many friends about the King's Majesty — to the Lord "Donague Damondesay." Two other Spaniards — the Duke of Salva and the Duke of Mathenon— had tokens demised to them with thanks for having done her sons good, "beseeching them, for God's sake, to continue the good lords to my sons in their needs, and my trust is that God will requite them."

"And my sons all three" is another bequest, "I leave them to the King's Majesty and Her Highness behind me." And the careful Duchess proceeded to provide against royal forgetfulness by bribing the royal attendants :

"I give Mistress Clarencieux my tawny velvet jewel coffer; I give to my Lady Paget my high-backed gown of wrought velvet; to my Lord Paget one of my black enamelled rings I did use to wear; to my Lady Sandys another of them, of the less sort."

One may not wonder at the concern of the dying mother for the future of the three boys, who were the only survivors of the eight she had borne, of the six who had grown to years. For besides her boy Guilford, Lord Warwick had received a death-warrant in the Tower. With Ambrose and Robert, he had passed from his cell to the home of his sister, Mary Sidney, at Penshurst. But within ten days from the time of his liberation he died. Neither he nor his surviving brothers had been restored in blood. They were accounted of no rank, and they could neither reclaim nor inherit property.

In the midst of the lengthy will, in the drawing of which she was at pains to note no lawyer or other man of business helped her, Duchess Jane bethought her suddenly that dispositions to persons attainted of high treason, could not take effect. She had divided her property very equally among her children and her children-in-law, giving only to Ambrose, in whom his father's titles might one day be revived, her real estate and a

larger sum of money than to the others. By
a second disposition, she gave all she possessed
wholly to her executors, of whom her son-in-
law, Sir Henry Sidney, was the first named,
"trusting in their fidelity that they will have
special regard and consideration to the advancement and help of my children as to them
shall seem good."

Praying always for the advancement of her
children, the Duchess laid down her pen at
last, but not before she had pictured faithfully
her worldliness and her womanliness, her brisk
practicality, and her maternal care.

The war in Flanders King Philip waged
against the French, provided the first opportunity the brothers had of fighting for their
own. At the siege of St Quintin, Robert
Dudley was Master of Ordnance. And so
effectually did he display his dash, capacity,
and horsemanship, that he was singled out
by Philip to be his special messenger to his
Queen. During this siege young Henry
Dudley lost his life. Ambrose, Robert, Mary
(Lady Sidney), and Catherine (Lady Hastings,
afterwards Countess of Huntingdon), were all
the Dudleys who remained to profit by the
Act of Parliament (4 and 5 Philip and Mary)
that reversed their attainder, and bestowed
upon them fullest rights to enjoy all lands,

tenements, and hereditaments that should at any time descend upon or revert to them.

When Elizabeth mounted the throne, Lord Robert Dudley stood at her footstool, erect, untainted in honour or in name. It was cause of wonder to the envious and the ungenerous — not at the moment, but after-wards, when favours were multiplied — that the new Queen made him almost immediately her Master of the Horse, and that in the first year of her reign she bestowed on him the Garter. It was forgotten that his elder brother, John, had been similarly distinguished by her brother Edward. The Dudleys, if not through Duke John, through Duke John's mother and through Duchess Jane, were men of high degree. The blood of the Beauchamps, Talbots, Greys, Berkely's and Lisles flowed richly in their veins.

It has been said by a genius among historians that, "with the single exception of Leicester," Elizabeth's sagacity was unerring in her choice of "precisely the right men for the work she set them to do." But did John Richard Green, when he wrote those words, fully consider the purpose for which Elizabeth selected Dudley? It is certain that there was much in the character of Lord Robert bound to prove harshly anti-pathetic to persons of reflection and good morals, bred up in the nineteenth century. It is certain also, that Dudley had qualities prejudicial to him as a Minister of State. But Elizabeth did not choose him for a councillor. She did not ask from him the infinite patience, the unremitting labour, the balanced judgment, and the apprehensive outlook that served her so well in Cecil. She did not throw upon him the responsibilities and the trusts that she heaped on Sir Thomas Smith, on Lord Sussex, and on Sir Francis Walsingham. She made him only her Master of the Horse, her chief of the Court revels—her Favourite. That he became the subtle agent of her variable will, her intelligencer of the dispositions of her people, her negotiator in business speculations, the dispenser of her royal bounties, and her representative and chamberlain in respect of the thousand and one interests, pursuits, arts, sciences, and activities that she shared with and promoted among her subjects, is due to the subsequent developments of his intellect and intentions, not to her anticipations of him. In her heirless household, she created him—in all but name—a Prince. Here was one who, in understanding and in artificiality, was her peer ; a man she could bare her soul to unashamed ; who could speak piously and do impiously ; who could act on a moment's call unfettered by any scruples, impeded by no preconceptions. Their relations were unmoral, not immoral.

Withering experience had blighted in each the more spontaneous feelings. Very little of the primitive man remained in Dudley; almost nothing of the primitive woman in Elizabeth. We shall see how strong was the chain of imagination and design that bound them together; how powerful were the interests and characteristics that drove them apart.

In the meantime, we may take instructive peeps at the bearing and office of Dudley in the beginning of Elizabeth's reign.

On Saturday, 14th January 1559, Queen Elizabeth made her State entry into London. She was crowned on the 15th. Dressed in "a royal robe of very rich cloth of gold, with a double-raised stiff pile, and, on her head, over a coif of cloth of gold, beneath which was her hair," a "plain, gold crown without lace, as a Princess, but covered with jewels," Elizabeth rode in "an open litter, trimmed down to the ground with gold brocade," and carried by two very handsome mules, also covered with gold brocade. A multitude of footmen in crimson velvet jerkins, massively studded in silver gilt, with arms of a white and a red rose on their breasts and backs, and the letters E.R. wrought in relief, surrounded her, while on either hand walked the Gentlemen Pensioners, clad in crimson damask, hammers in hand. Behind this gorgeous *cortége* came Lord Robert

Dudley, mounted on a very fine charger, leading a white hackney with trappings of cloth of gold.

Perhaps it was on this hackney that, within a few weeks of her accession, Elizabeth, "apparelled in purple velvet, with a scarf about her neck," had ridden from Charterhouse to the Tower of London. On that occasion also, "next after her" rode Robert Dudley.

On the 2nd of July following, the City of London, to prove its loyalty, and to accustom its burgesses to campaigning and to the exercise of arms, sent a muster of fourteen hundred men to lie out all night in St George's Fields, and to march early the next morning to Greenwich Park. Elizabeth, accompanied by ambassadors of foreign sovereigns, and attended by many lords and ladies, appeared in the gallery above the gateway of Greenwich Palace about five in the afternoon, when Lord Robert Dudley, with the Marquis of Northampton, the Lord Admiral Clinton, and "divers other lords and knights," rode to and fro among the bands "to set them in array to skirmish" before the Queen.

In their "coats of velvet and chains of gold, with guns, pikes, halberds, and flags," the gunners being "in shirts of mail," the London volunteers must have made an imposing show. The Queen's delight and satisfaction at their turn-out were heartily expressed. Whether Lord Robert's eye for smartness and efficiency was gratified, is not recorded. But either then, or a little later, he became aware of the disinclination among the citizens generally, to "warlike gear." It was thought that "apprentices and handycraftesmen men" having "liberty to be trayned . . . wolde thereby fall into such idleness and insolency that many wolde never be reduced again into any good order or service."

Little Englandism of this kind was detestable to Lord Robert. And when, as Earl of Leicester, he came to be at the head of England's forces, the early exploits of the cockneys in Greenwich Park did not plead with him for London train-bands with which he would have nothing to do, "as knowing what burghers are."

So we see Elizabeth's Master of Horse in attitudes more or less special to his office. Other glimpses of him in the early years of her reign are indicative of the variety of interests that claimed the Favourite of the Queen.

One of the first cares of his more intimate office had been to introduce into the secret councils of his mistress a man of science and of necromancy, whose "calculations" could be relied upon to excite the imagination of the Queen, and lead her to the belief that her destiny and her Favourite's were one.

Dr John Dee, of Mortlake, was a scholar of considerable scientific attainment, but he was also a wonder-worker, a spiritualist, and a prognosticator of fates.   In the time of Mary, he had been cast into prison for calculating the nativities of the Queen, the King, and the Princess Elizabeth, and for endeavouring by enchantments to destroy Mary.   Undoubtedly, his forecasts were flattering to the Princess, though in his " Compendious Rehearsall " of his life, he has denied that there was any treason to the monarchs in his proceedings.

Before the coronation of Elizabeth, " by commandment of Lord Robert," Dee " wrote at large and delivered for Her Majesty's use " what in his judgment, " the ancient astrologers would determine of the election day of such a time, as was appointed for Her Majesty to be crowned in."   And, since it was the chief employment of Dee's professional life to cast horoscopes, it was doubtless also, at this time, and by commandment of Lord Robert, that those calculations of nativity were made that established the belief that Elizabeth and her Favourite were born under planets that determined a " strait conjunction of their minds."   Certain it is that Dr Dee composed a " Book of Astrologie " for the Queen's use —a curious production containing diagrams and designs that may mean anything or nothing, according to the faith and instruction of the reader of them.

And all through the years that the Favourite lived at the side of the Queen, Elizabeth's curiosity concerning the arts and discoveries of Dr Dee, persisted. In 1571, at the instance of Lord Leicester, Dr Dee was despatched to Germany to confer with other doctors concerning an ailment from which Her Majesty suffered.   And on the 10th of March 1575, according to a note in Dr Dee's diary:

" The Queen's Majesty with her most Honourable Privy Council, and other her lords and nobility, came purposely to have visited my library; but finding that my wife was within four hours before buried out of the house, Her Majesty refused to come in; but willed me to fetch my glass so famous, and to show unto her some of the properties of it which I did; Her Majesty (being taken down from her horse by the Earl of Leicester, Master of the Horse, by the Church wall of Mortlake) did see some of the properties of that glass to Her Majesty's great contentment and delight, and so in most gracious manner did thank me."

Elizabeth and her Favourite were then forty-four years of age. Yet if, as the Queen peered into the magic crystal, a vision of romance and of fate rose before her eyes, we may be sure the dark countenance of the Earl of Leicester had a place in it.   Her Master of Horse stood by. He was at her side, too, upon another occasion when the machinations of Dee brought her, presumably, contentment and delight. For when later, in 1577, an image of the Queen with a pin through its heart was found in Lincoln's Inn Fields, Dr Dee was again to the fore, "satisfying the request" of Her Majesty and Council in "godly and artificial manner." His incantations ended, the licensed sorcerer, in company with Mr Secretary Wilson, who had witnessed all his proceedings, declared to the Queen what he had done for her protection from witchcraft; "Her Majesty then sitting without the Privy Garden by the landing - place at Richmond, the Honourable Earl of Leicester being also by."

It was in the third year of Elizabeth's reign that Lord Robert Dudley interceded with her for the "Society of the House" of the Inner Temple, to retain Lyon's Inn, which the fellowship of the Middle Temple was trying to appropriate as a recompense for the loss of Strand Inn, upon the building of Somerset House. We read in a garrulous chronicle, that

"through Dudley's intercession there was a stop made therein, and the Society of the Inner Temple did then enact that no person of their society should ever be retained as

Lord Robert Dudley.

council against Lord Leicester or his heirs, and that the arms of the said Lord Robert should be set up and placed in some convenient place in the Hall as a continual monument of his Lordship's favour to them."

And besides the "continual monument," still to be seen of the curious in the Inner Temple, members signalised their gratitude by making Lord Robert the chief personage of the grand masque and feast with which they celebrated Christmas in the fourth year of Elizabeth. After the grandiloquent fashion of these amusements, Lord Robert was constituted Constable and Marshal of the Court of Merriment, and had bestowed on him the title of *Palaphilos.*

Of *Palaphilos* as he appeared at the lawyers' feast, we have the description that he was "a man of tall personage, a manly countenance, somewhat brown of visage, strongly featured, and thereto comely proportioned in all lineaments of body."

This is an instant account of him in his twenty-ninth year, set down by an ambassador from the Venetian Republic. It corresponds exactly with the tradition of the physical qualities of Elizabeth's favourite that remained in the minds of his countrymen when he had

c

become bald, rubicund, and almost portly.   The same tradition survived when the waxen hue of death had paled his brown visage, and when his glittering black eye had been dimmed for ever.

"A man of a flourishing age and comely feature of body and limbs," wrote Camden. "Tall and singularly well-featured, of a sweet aspect, but high foreheaded, which was of no discommendation," was Naunton's description.

Lord Robert Dudley did not lack what greatness lies in physical strength and beauty. Neither did he fail in the knowledge of how to make a success of his array.   When, at fifty-four years of age, he stepped upon Dutch shores, the protector of the liberties of the boors, the bargemen, and the brewers of Holland, his satins, velvets, laces, jewels, and feathers were astounding.   "Everybody is wondering at the great magnificence of his clothes," wrote a conscientious local reporter of the glory that had descended upon Utrecht.   At all times his garments and his accoutrements were the admiration and the despair of the gilded youth of England, who aspired to copy them.

His horsemanship and athleticism were also most wonderful to foreigners.   The refractory Irish chieftain, Shan O'Neil, when he was the "guest" of Elizabeth in 1562, petitioned Her

Majesty to allow him to attend on the Lord Robert.

" That he might learn to ride after the English fashion, to run at the tilt, to hawk, to shoot and use such other good exercises as the said good lord was most apt unto."

CHAPTER III

THE singular regard of Elizabeth for Lord
Robert Dudley, and his constant attendance on
her both officially as Master of the Horse, and
unofficially as boon-companion of her leisure,
led very early in her reign to the stirring of
many jealousies, and to the circulation of many
scandals. Within a year of her accession,
Elizabeth gave to Lord Robert, a messuage
at Kew, the sites of the monasteries of Watton
and Meux in Yorkshire, the lieutenancy of
Windsor Castle and Forest, and a profitable
licence to export woollen goods free of duty.

Men's tongues were not shortened because
the Queen rapidly restored Lord Ambrose to
forfeited dignities and titles. She made him
chief pantler for coronations in 1559, and Earl of
Warwick in 1561; and quickly appointed Lady
Sidney a Woman of the Bedchamber. But
it was not alone the benefactions his Sovereign
heaped on him, that made Lord Robert
Dudley remarked upon and remarkable. It
was Elizabeth's frank delight in the young man's
company; their caresses and their endearments;
their communications by day and by night,

that, as was natural and as was right, angered
puritans, provoked statesmen, and shocked ambassadors. And of all these things—puritans'
anger, statesmen's annoyance, and diplomatists'
horror — Robert Dudley bore the brunt. It
was the vice of Lord Robert, and his seduction
of the Queen, the pulpits raged against; it
was the persuasions and the oppositions of
Lord Robert, Elizabeth's other ministers complained of; it was the duplicity and the faith-
lessness of Lord Robert, diplomatists declared
would prove the ruin of England. Yet in the
game they played; in the front they presented
to the world; in their true and seeming devotions; in their real and apparent faithlessnesses,
Elizabeth and Lord Robert were one.

The first question on men's lips, when
Elizabeth mounted the throne, was whom
will the Queen marry? The popular mind
was no more prepared at the death of Mary
than it had been at the death of Edward, to
imagine a Queen *sole*. The "device" for the
succession, as dictated by Edward, before it
was touched up by the hand of Northumberland, left the throne to the King's heirs male;
failing these, to the heirs male of the Lady
Jane Grey, of the Lady Catherine Grey *et
sequitur*. A son of the King's cousin was to
take precedence of the King's own daughter.
Edward had not been aware of his near end

when he made the will. He expected to have
a son of his own in due course. Northumberland had known well enough that he was
dying, and had provided a King for England
in his own boy Guilford. There were Catholics
in England who would have preferred the
otherwise unpopular "long lad," Henry Darnley,
to Mary Stuart, as a Sovereign for England,
simply because Darnley was a man. There
were Protestants who would sooner have had
the Earl of Huntingdon for a Monarch, than
either Elizabeth or Jane, for the sole reason
that Lord Huntingdon was a male. With
Catherine de Medici ruling Queen-Mother of
France, with Mary Stuart reigning Queen of
Scotland, and with Elizabeth Tudor on the
throne of England, men yet believed that it
was not in the power of females to grasp
sceptres, and that the government of a woman
was no government.

The marriage of Elizabeth's sister, Mary,
had been most unpopular.

One element of the great rejoicings over
Elizabeth's accession had been delight that
Spanish influence was overthrown. Yet, with
strange inconsistency, no sooner was the new
Queen crowned, than a Spanish match began
to be spoken of for her. Both Lord Robert
and Elizabeth knew that if a marriage had
to be, an English union would be the more

popular one. There existed in their day no
established custom of mating royalty only with
royalty. The Earl of Arundel and Sir William
Pickering, the latter a person of good looks
and "excellent gravity," but of no birth to be
accounted of, were both well-supported suitors
for Elizabeth's hand. Yet the right man was
hard to find.

As for Elizabeth herself, she replied to the
deputation of her first Parliament, who urged
her to take a husband—they did not presume
to name a candidate for the office—that she
had already joined herself to a husband,
namely the Kingdom of England. And she
made clear her determination to devote herself to that husband by many symbols of
phrase and gesture. Taking from her finger
the ring placed there at her Coronation, she
held it up for her "estates" to gaze upon.

"Behold the Pledge of this my wedlock,"
she exclaimed. And after a pause, she pleaded:
"And do not upbraid me with miserable lack
of children; for every one of you, and as many
as are Englishmen, are Children and Kinsmen
to me; of whom, if God deprive me not
(which God forbid), I cannot without injury
be accounted barren." Then after promising to
do nothing prejudicial to the Commonwealth,
but if she entered another course of life to
"take such a husband as near as may be, as

will have as great a care of the Commonwealth as myself," she concluded with the much and variously quoted peroration: "And to me it shall be full satisfaction . . . if when I shall let my last breath, it be ingraven upon my Marble Tomb, *Here lieth Elizabeth which reigned a Virgin and died a Virgin.*"

Elizabeth was twenty-five years of age, handsome, vigorous, popular; the hope of every party in the state. It was known that she was neither a fanatic nor a devotee. It was thought that in Protestantism she would go no further than restoring the non-papal Catholicism of Henry VIII. She had conformed to all the ceremonial re-established by Mary. But it was believed that her early training, and her liberality of thought, would make her a friend to all reformers.

From the moment that it became certain that Queen Mary would have no child, it had been the policy of King Philip to treat the Princess Elizabeth with special favour. By his means she had been set free from the Tower, and allowed to appear at Court as heiress-presumptive of the kingdom.

But Elizabeth was no longer Princess on sufferance. By universal acclamation she was Queen. And she had all the self-sufficiency of her years; those years in which the timidities of girlhood have been outgrown, and the experiences of life have not yet destroyed the illusion of self - importance. It has been questioned whether Elizabeth was ever sincere —even at that moment of triumphant vanity, in which she first found herself England's Queen — in asserting her desire for a maiden life. It is certain that in her declaration to De Quadra, Bishop of Arras (King Philip's ambassador in England), that she wished she had been a nun, she was wholly insincere. There may have been moments when the vacuities and the limitations of a cloistered existence beckoned to her as a blessed alternative from the contentions and perplexities of a regal life; but her nature and her habits were the antitheses of those that go to the making of a religious. A convent was an impossible domicile for the genius of Elizabeth. But it is not therefore certain that in spirit, and by temperament, she was not a votary of the maiden state. The woman who not only rebels against maternity, but who is also without elementary instincts of wifehood; who is sufficient unto herself, and unconscious all her life of any inclination to surrender, is a creature of whose existence the world is but beginning to be convinced. It is not the province of the biographer to discuss the worth or the unworth of the type. The historian of character, as of events, is con-

cerned only with what is. Women of this
kind exist. Potentially, at least, they have
always existed. There are among them those
who make use of their immunity from certain
impulses for a bad end; and those who—all
but disregarding the fact that they are immune
—devote their more specialised powers and
intelligencies to noble endeavour.

Many episodes and circumstances of Elizabeth's history justify the supposition that she
was so immune, and that she used her abnormal
self-containment for definite and precise purposes.
How far those purposes were good for England,
and how far they were bad for Society; how far
they contributed to the material prosperity of
the realm, and how far they militated against
the spiritual well-being of her people, the
readers of the story of her relations to Robert
Dudley may determine.

The first evidences we have of the sincerity
of Elizabeth's ambition to remain husbandless
all her days, are her own activity and Lord
Robert's in starting many marriage projects.
So hardy were the enterprises of Dudley, so
various the proposals he supported, that he
almost betrayed the secret that was between
the Queen and him, which secret was to use
to the utmost the political asset of Elizabeth's
single blessedness, but to use it always, so as
never to impair its value. The Elizabeth who

should be Imperial, who should be England free, unpledged, inviolate, and independent, must not be subservient, must not even be perpetually allied to any foreign influence, to any set of religious ideas, to any political party, to any one man.

The answer to the proposal of Philip was prompter and less equivocal than any answer ever made by Elizabeth, either as Princess or as Queen, to a suitor for her hand. She had nothing to gain in personal safety, and nothing for England's good, by further coquetries with her late sister's widower, and for the marrying of her brother-in-law, the initial step would have had to be the obtaining of a dispensation from the Pope. Now it was a papal dispensation that had been the root of all the trouble of her father's reign; the fount of all the misery she and her half-sister of bitter memory, had drunk of so deeply and so long. Philip was set aside. So also was another candidate in the Spanish interest—the Archduke Ferdinand.

A French aspirant was put forward. But the marriage of the Scottish girl-Queen Mary, to the Dauphin, made the rejection of a French suitor an imperative need. The power of France was paramount in Scotland. Mary of Guise was the Queen-Regent of her daughter's minority in the northern kingdom, and the Dauphin and Dauphiness had audaciously quartered the arms

of England, and were styled in France, King
and Queen of Scotland and England. By all
laws of descent, Scottish Mary was heiress-
presumptive to the English throne. James V.
of Scotland, her father, had been son to
Margaret, elder sister of Henry VIII., by her
first marriage with James IV. In the eyes
of Catholics, Elizabeth was an illegitimate child
of her father, and no Princess; the Queen
of Scots rightful Queen of England. The
position now of Mary Stuart as Consort of
France's future King, was justification enough
of the Act of the English Parliament that
had empowered Henry VIII. to set aside the
line of Margaret. The claims to England's
Queenship asserted for Mary by her French
kin, were indignantly rebuffed by the main
body of the English nation. Not only was
the idea of another Catholic Mary on the throne
unwelcome, but English Elizabeth, "daughter
to old Harry th' Eighth," as men loved to
call her, and she loved to be called—although
Heaven knew old Harry th' Eighth had had his
seasons of unpopularity both with his daughter
and with the country—was the ruler England
wanted, to the exclusion of all Frenchified
misses. If Mary had been Queen instead of
Elizabeth, who had been ruler in England
but the French King? The prejudices and
feuds of centuries could not be quieted in an

hour. It was bad enough that French influence was so dominant in the near land of the Scots. In this opinion there were Scots who shared. Protestantism was making its way in the northern kingdom, and the Protestants of Scotland desired the friendship of their English neighbours.

Sir William Cecil appointed by Elizabeth her Secretary of State, at her first Council at Hatfield, was a man without fanaticism, yet a convinced Protestant. The first business of his administration was the settlement of religion. With a view to the surer establishment of Protestantism, and also with the design of checking French and Spanish power, Cecil conceived the idea of secretly encouraging the dissentients from the Franco-Catholic rule in Scotland, and of promoting a friendship between the Protestants of both countries, by marrying Elizabeth to the Scottish heir - presumptive, the Earl of Arran.

The plan was not discouraged by Elizabeth. Indeed, she joined in it with a zest that raised the highest hopes in Cecil. He had yet to learn that Elizabeth's taste for experiences of the kind was insatiable, and that years would be added to years, before custom could stale the pleasure of receiving attentions, in any way to be construed as amorous. Whether politically or personally, the bringing of men

to her feet was the pastime Elizabeth loved.
The Earl of Arran was smuggled by Cecil
out of France into England; was hidden in
the minister's house for a time, and surreptitiously visited there by the Queen. Arran
was a curious weakling, who subsequently
became pronouncedly insane. His deficiencies
must have proclaimed themselves to Elizabeth
during their clandestine interviews. There is
no touch-stone of the mental strength of a
man, to be compared with that of love-making.
And when the lady wooed is decidedly wide
awake, and all her sighing and simpering of
design to provoke declarations and to test the
quality of the wooer, shortcomings of virility
and intelligence must quickly be discovered.
But had the romantic ardour of a Raleigh,
the fanciful sentimentality of a Hatton, and
the calm audacity of a Leicester, been com-
bined in Arran, he could not have prevailed
with Elizabeth. She had no intention of
attracting the enmity of the Catholic party,
of the French, or of the Queen of Scots, by
identifying herself, as this marriage Cecil
reckoned on would have identified her, with
Protestants, and the disaffected generally. Yet
she coquetted with the idea of it, and let
Cecil think her inclined to it, for some little
time.

Great, therefore, was the grievance of the

Secretary against the Favourite when he discovered that Lady Sidney, on behalf of her brother Lord Robert, had been entertaining De Quadra with professions of the Queen's readiness to marry the Archduke Charles, cousin of Philip, and a younger son of the Austrian Emperor. Lady Sidney told the Bishop that a plot had been formed to murder the Queen and Lord Robert at Lord Arundel's, and that the acuteness of Elizabeth's danger, and the unsettled state of Scotland—where subjects were rebelling against their lawful Sovereign—had so alarmed the Queen, that she had determined to marry. Lord Robert confirmed his sister's story, and announced himself willing to put before Her Majesty the advantages of an Austrian match.

When De Quadra spoke to the Queen herself on the matter, Elizabeth asked that the Emperor would send his son to England for her to see. Other Princesses married for interest; she would marry for love. The Bishop demurred. The Archduke could not come without assurance that Her Majesty would not be displeased. Elizabeth smiled, and said if he had no fear but that, he might come when he would. She added, in affected embarrassment, that she was afraid he might hear things said of her which might not please him.

"Let not your Majesty trouble about that,"

was the reply of De Quadra; "we know too well what really passes in this Court to be moved by idle rumours. Had we given credit to the talk of the world, we would not have desired to see the Archduke here."

This answer seemed to please Elizabeth. On her side, the purpose of the audience had been rather to ascertain the view held by foreign courts of her relations with Dudley, than to bring the match with the Archduke nearer. The Sovereigns of Europe did not yet appear to be scandalised.

De Quadra wrote to his master:

"There are ten or twelve Ambassadors of us, all competing for Her Majesty's hand; and they say the Duke of Holstein is coming next, as a suitor for the King of Denmark. The Duke of Finland who is here for his brother, the King of Sweden, threatens to kill the Emperor's man; and the Queen fears they will cut each others' throats in her presence."

One would believe in the escape of the Court from this sensation, had it not been the Queen who expressed the fear of it. To be the heroine of such a dramatic moment had not been all unpleasant to the young woman whose delight it was to breed follies in men. Yet it was of diplomacy that the Queen coquetted with each suitor in turn. When the time came for Lord Robert to go over from the Spanish to the Swedish interest, De Quadra was not surprised. But he was astounded to hear "from a person who usually gives me true information, that Lord Robert had sent instructions to have his wife poisoned; and that all the dallying with us, all the dallying with the Swede, all the dallying which there will be with the rest, one after the other, is merely to keep Lord Robert's enemies in play, till his villainy about his wife can be executed. I have learnt also certain other things as to the terms on which the Queen and Lord Robert stand to one another, which I could not have believed."

And when the Spaniard reminded the Queen of what Lady Sidney had said to him about the Archduke, Elizabeth, with shameless mendacity, replied: "No doubt Lady Sidney had meant well, but she had spoken without commission." The Bishop "burst out at this," and Elizabeth was "very ill-pleased at being forced so far to declare herself."

Indeed, she had gone so far in the affair, that Lord Paget said she *must* now accept the Austrian marriage. The Duke of Norfolk, who believed that it was on account of Lord Robert that the Queen held back from the Archduke, said that the Favourite should "never die in his bed unless he gave over his preposterous pretensions." A few days later, Lord Robert told the Duke that whoever advised the Queen to marry a stranger was no good Englishman.

D

High words passed. Dudley stood his ground. Norfolk threatened to leave the Court, and to retire to Framlingham.

Little wonder that, as De Quadra noted, Lady Sidney was disquieted, and that she quarrelled with her brother over his retreat from the Spanish negotiations. Lady Sidney remembered the reign of Mary, when Philip's interest was exerted for the Dudleys. She could not blow hot and cold. She could follow well enough the progress of ideas evinced in Elizabeth's refusal of Philip, in her consideration of the suit of Arran, in her revulsion from Protestantism under the fierce pulpit reproaches of her friendship with Lord Robert, and in her entertainment of the match with the Catholic Archduke. She could even—simple woman and fond sister—engage in a manœuvre that had for an objective the confusion of the scandal-mongers. For the fact of Dudley going himself to the Ambassador, and negotiating, on terms, the marriage of Elizabeth with the Archduke, might be supposed to dispel the belief that the Favourite sought to be to his Queen anything more than her confidential adviser for her own and the nation's good. But Lady Sidney could not be false to professions, and neither she nor any other could believe it was the plan of Lord Robert to keep his Queen unwed, and to maintain his rank of supreme favourite of a maiden ruler. She could not yet understand the curious and fascinating office which Dudley's own commanding parts, and the Queen's *bizarre* imagination, had thrust upon him.

But now the inevitable was to happen. The penalty attached to eccentricity, idiosyncrasy, abnormality—call it what one will—is never to be avoided.

Robert Dudley had a wife. His wife—as is the way with many good wives — had little care for or understanding of his greater hopes and larger ambitions. Yet it does not appear that they quarrelled. Indeed, they seem to have been on the best of terms.

We should have much light on the true story of Amy Robsart, and learn more of the true story of the lord, her husband, if we could ascertain precisely, why, after the coming of Elizabeth to the throne, Lady Robert Dudley had no settled home, but journeyed much to and fro; going sometimes to London, though never staying there long. From the carefully kept account books of herself and her husband, one learns that she had command of sufficient money to gratify every change and turn of her woman's fancy in dress, and to have horses always in readiness to take herself and her suite to the next country house she desired to visit. From time to time, at the different places she remained at, she was joined by my

lord, ridden from the Court. He would stay
and dine, play at the cards, perhaps sleep a
night or two, and then, a foot in the stirrup,
and the Master of the Queen's Horse was off
again on his royal mistress's service. The lands
in Norfolk had still to be managed. And on
an occasion, the Lady Robert wrote (or dictated
to her Secretary) a letter that gives just a
glimpse—such a short, cursory glimpse!—into
her home relations with her husband. It was
addressed to an agent of her lord's in Norfolk.

" Mr Flowerdew,—I understand by Gryse
that you put him in remembrance of that you
spake to me of, concerning the going of certain
sheep at Siderstern ; and although I forgot to
move my lord thereof, before his departing,
he being sore troubled with weighty affairs,
and I not being altogether in quiet for his
sudden departing, yet, notwithstanding, knowing
your accustomed friendship towards my lord and
me, I neither may nor can deny you that
request, in my lord's absence, of mine own
authority, yea, and it were a greater matter,
as if any good occasion may serve you to try
me ; desiring you further that you will make
the sale of the wool so soon as is possible,
although you sell it for VI's. the stone, or
as you would sell for yourself; for my lord
so justly required me, at his departing, to see
those poor men satisfied, as though it had been
a matter depending upon life ; wherefore I force
not to sustain a little loss thereby to satisfy
my lord's desire, and so to send that money
to Gryse's house to London, by Bridewell, to

whom my lord hath given order for the payment
thereof.   And thus I end, always troubling you,
wishing that occasion may serve me to requite
you ; until that time I must pay you with my
thanks, and so to God I leave you.

"From Mr Hyde's, this VII of August, your
assured, during life,

"AMYE DUDDLEY."

There is a wifely touch in the phrase, "he
being sore troubled with weighty affairs, and
I not being altogether in quiet for his sudden
departing." The business that troubled Dudley
was, unquestionably, that of the Queen's
marriage. Lady Robert's words convey the
impression—it may have been part of her
loyalty as Dudley's wife deliberately to choose
words to convey it—that she was concerned
with, as well as for her husband. In any case,
matters were reaching a climax at the Court.
And if only stray fragments of the gossip, going
about in town for months past, had been
scattered throughout the country, poor Amy
must have known that men were saying the
Queen would have no husband but my Lord
Robert, and that the design was between
Elizabeth and her Favourite to get rid of the
Lady Amy by the means either of divorce or
of poison.

Men of state, who were also leaders of the
Liberal and Protestant party, heads of noble
houses who desired a return to the "old order"

of society and religion; foreign ambassadors who
had the interests of their several countries to
consider; and men and women of the world who
held that an unmarried woman—not a nun—
must be necessarily immoral, were all anxious
to settle Elizabeth with a husband, who should
serve their cause, insure their greatness, or
restore its lost reputation to the Court. The
refusal of Elizabeth to choose that husband,
and the persistence of her coquetry with a
married man, could breed but one thought—
that she was desperately in love with that
man. Furthermore, when it began to be stated
in the royal circle, that the wife of Dudley
was in poor health, it required no special
malice of invention for men to say, and to
believe, that a plan was in order for the wife's
destruction. It is not, however, beyond the
bounds of possibility that Lady Amy was
afflicted with some special mental or physical
distress. The facts that, although Lord Robert's
purse was at her command and she spent
largely of it, she had not to order the expenses
of a great establishment; that she was indulged
in constant change and excitement of a mild
order; and that Cumnor Hall belonged to a
former Court physician, though let to Sir
Anthony Forster at the time Lady Amy went
there on her last visit, point perhaps to the
conclusion that her health was not good, and

that a special mode of living had been prescribed for it. Before Amy's tragedy overtook her, it was said that she had cancer. After the event, there was a suggestion that she was hysterical, or of unsound mind. That all these things were disbelieved by those who wished to disbelieve them, is matter of course. Yet stranger things are true. It was easier in the sixteenth, than in the twentieth, century, to hold the greatest guilty of foul play. It came naturally enough to people of the time of Lady Amy to take the view that the Queen and her Favourite were conspiring to end her life. Yet it is permissible to believe that they did not so conspire.

The sinister view is at once supported and refuted by a letter from De Quadra to the Duchess of Parma (Philip's regent in the Netherlands), written on 11th September 1560.

" Since my last letter to your Highness, so many and unexpected matters have taken place here that I think it right to give you immediate information of them.

" On the 3rd of this month the Queen spoke to me about her marriage with the Archduke. She said she had made up her mind to marry, and that the Archduke was to be the man. She has just now told me drily that she does not intend to marry, and that it cannot be.

" After my conversation with the Queen, I met the Secretary Cecil, whom I knew to be

in disgrace.   Lord Robert I was aware, was
endeavouring to deprive him of his place.

" With little difficulty I led him to the subject,
and after many protestations and entreaties that
I would keep secret what he was about to tell
me, he said that the Queen was going on so
strangely that he was about to withdraw from
her service.   It was a bad sailor, he said, who
did not make for port when he saw a storm
coming, and for himself he perceived the most
manifest ruin impending over the Queen through
her intimacy with Lord Robert.   The Lord
Robert had made himself master of the business
of the State, and of the person of the Queen,
to the extreme injury of the realm, with the
intention of marrying her; and she herself was
shutting herself up in the palace to the peril
of her health and life.   That the realm would
tolerate the marriage, he said that he did not
believe; he was therefore determined to retire
into the country, although he supposed they
would send him to the Tower before they
would let him go.

" He implored me for the love of God to
remonstrate with the Queen, to persuade her
not utterly to throw herself away as she was
doing, and to remember what she owed to
herself and to her subjects.   *Of Lord Robert, he
twice said he would be better in Paradise than here.*

" I could only reply that I was most deeply
grieved; I said he must be well aware how
anxious I had always been for the Queen's
well-doing.   I had laboured as the King my
master had directed me, to persuade her to
live quietly, and to marry — with how little
effect he himself could tell.   I would try again,
however, as soon as I had an opportunity.

"He told me the Queen cared nothing for foreign Princes; she did not believe she stood in any need of their support. She was deeply in debt, taking no thought how to clear herself, and she had ruined her credit in the city.

"Last of all, he said they were thinking of destroying Lord Robert's wife. They had given out that she was ill; but she was not ill at all; she was very well, and was taking care not to be poisoned; God, he trusted, would never permit such a crime to be accomplished, or allow so wicked a conspiracy to prosper.

"This business of the Secretary cannot but produce some great results, for it is terrible. Many men I believe are as displeased as he, especially the Duke of Norfolk, whom he named to me as one of those most injured by Lord Robert, and most hostile to him.

"The day after this conversation, the Queen on her return from hunting told me that Lord Robert's wife was dead, or nearly so, and begged me to say nothing about it. Assuredly, it is a matter full of shame and infamy, but for all this I do not feel sure that she will immediately marry him, or indeed that she will marry at all. She wants resolution to take any decided step; and, as Cecil says, she wishes to act like her father.

"These quarrels among themselves and Cecil's retirement from office will do no harm to the good cause. We could not have to do with any one worse than he has been; but likely enough a revolution may come of it. The Queen may be sent to the Tower, and they may make a King of Lord Huntingdon who is a great heretic, calling in a party in France [*i.e. the Huguenots*] to help them, because they know that when they aim at injuring religion, they have nothing to hope for from His Majesty [King Philip]. I have my suspicions on both these points. It is quite certain that the heretics wish to have Huntingdon made King. Cecil himself told me that he was the true heir to the crown; Henry the Seventh having usurped it from the House of York. That they may have recourse to the French I dread, from the close intimacy which has grown up between Cecil and the Bishop of Valence. It may be that I am over-suspicious, but with such people it is always prudent to believe the worst. Certain it is they say openly they will not have a woman over them any more; and this one is likely to go to sleep in the palace, and to wake with her lover in the Tower. The French, too, are not asleep. Even Cecil says *Non dormit Judas*. We can be sure of nothing except of revolution and change. If I made up to them, they would trust me and tell me all; but I have no orders what to do, and until I receive instructions I shall listen to both sides and temporise. Your Highness will be pleased to give me directions. I show the Catholics all the attention in my power; and they are not so broken, but what, if His Majesty will give the word, they will resist the machinations of the rest. It is important that His Majesty should know that there is no hope of improvement in the Queen; she will be his enemy and her own to the last, as I have always told him.

"Since this was written, the death of Lord Robert's wife has been given out publicly. The Queen said in Italian that 'she had broken her neck.' It appears she fell down a stair-case."

CHAPTER IV

" IT appears she fell down a stair-case."

Over three centuries have passed since these words were written. Two coroners' inquests, a government enquiry, the comments and criticisms of many generations of historical students, the coming to light by degrees of a number of official despatches and private letters, have not made any clearer the mystery of Lady Robert Dudley's death. We have only inference to guide us in our search after the truth of the matter. It appeared at the time, it appears now, that she fell down a stair-case. How she fell, whether thrown by false hands, whether by her own act of desperation, whether by an accident, is not known.

She was found dead at the stairs' foot. But no testimonies show how she came there.

Suspicion fell on her husband, and on the Queen. Minions of Dudley and of Her Majesty were supposed to have performed the timely act of removing the obstacle of their marriage. It was supposed also that, in despair over the loss of her husband's affection and consideration, she made of herself a rash sacrifice to his advancement. There were few who took the view more charitable to all—that her death came by misadventure.

All the views are supported by possibility. Among all the wild improbabilities of Sir Walter Scott's story of the tragedy, the one, not probability, but possibility, is that the hapless Amy may have been lured on to the stair-case by a simulation of her husband's call. But there is no suggestion in history, for the piteous, pretty tale. And the likelihood does not lie on the side of her death occurring by the order of the husband, or with the connivance of the Queen.

On the strength of all the ugly stories and gruesome anticipations that were Court and common gossip anent the Queen, her Favourite, and the disregarded wife, and for the reason that, on the 9th or 10th of September, Elizabeth told the Spanish ambassador that Lady Robert was "dead, or nearly so," it has been held by some historians that Dudley and Elizabeth were murderers by intention. But it was just the circulation of the ugly stories and of the gruesome anticipations that would have prevented the Queen and Lord Robert bringing about a death by violence for poor Amy, even if it had been in their hearts to wish it for her. Their after words and conduct prove certainly that they felt the event to be the most inopportune that could have happened.

On the day that Elizabeth told De Quadra that Amy was "dead, or nearly so," she *was* dead. News of some disaster to her, though not the full particulars, had already travelled from Cumnor Hall to Windsor Castle, and Lord Robert had already sent a confidential agent, one, "Cousin Blount," to Cumnor to ascertain the details of an event that he knew to be untoward for Amy. To this agent, the following letter from Lord Robert was despatched very shortly after his starting.

"Cousin Blount,—Immediately upon your departing from me there came to me Bowes, by whom I do understand that my wife is dead, and, as he saith, by a fall from a pair of stairs. Little other understanding can I have of him. The greatness and the suddenness of the misfortune doth so perplex me, until I do hear from you how the matter standeth, or how this evil should light upon me, considering what the malicious world will bruit, as I can take no rest. And, because I have no way to purge myself of the malicious talk that I know the wicked world will use, but one which is the very plain truth to be known, I do pray you, as you have loved me, and do tender me any my quietness, and as now my special trust is in you, that you will use all the devices and means you can possible, for the learning of the truth; wherein have no respect to any living person. And as by your travail and diligence, so likewise by order of law, I mean by calling of the Coroner, and charging him to the uttermost from me to have good regard to make choice of no light or slight persons, but the discreetest and [most] substantial men for the juries, such as for their knowledge may be able to search thoroughly and duly, by all manner of examinations, the bottom of the matter, and for their uprightness will earnestly and sincerely deal therein without respect; and that the body be viewed and searched accordingly by them; and in every respect to proceed by order and law. In the meantime, Cousin Blount, let me be advertised from you by this bearer with all speed how the matter doth stand. For, as the cause and the manner thereof doth marvellously trouble me, considering my case, many ways, so shall I not be at rest till I may be ascertained thereof; praying you even as my trust is in you, and as I have ever loved you, do not dissemble with me, neither let anything be hid from me, but send me your true conceit and opinion of the matter, whether it happened by evil chance or by villainy. And fail not to let me hear continually from you. And thus fare you well in much haste; from Windsor this IXth of September, in the evening [1560]. Your loving friend and kinsman much perplexed.

"R. D."

"I have sent for my brother Appleyard, because he is her brother, and other of her friends also to be there, that they may be privy, and see how all things do proceed."

Thomas Blount replied:

" May it please your Lordship to understand that I have received your letter by Bristo, the contents whereof I do well perceive; and that your Lordship was advertised by Bowes upon my departing that my Lady was dead; and also your strait charge given unto me that I should use all the devices and policies that I can for the true understanding of the matter, as well as by mine own travail as by the order of law, as in calling the Coroner, giving him charge that he choose a discreet and substantial jury for the view of the body, and that no corruption be used or person respected. Your Lordship's great reasons, that maketh you so earnestly search to learn the truth, the same with your earnest commandment, doth make me to do my best therein. The present advertisement I can give to your Lordship at this time is, too true it is that my Lady is dead, and, as it seemeth, with a fall; but yet how or which way I cannot learn. Your Lordship shall hear the manner of my proceeding since I came from you. The same night I came from Windsor I lay at Abingdon all that night; and because I was desirous to hear what news went abroad in the country, at my supper I called for mine host, and asked him what news was thereabout, taking upon me I was going into Gloucestershire. He said there was fallen a great misfortune—within three or four miles of the town; he said my Lord Robert Dudley's wife was dead; and I axed how; and he said by a misfortune, as he heard, by a fall from a pair of stairs; I asked him by what chance; he said, he knew not: I axed him what was his judgment, and the judgment of the people; he said some were supposed to say well and some evil. That is your judgment? said I. By my troth, said he, I judge it a misfortune because it chanced in that honest gentleman's house; his great honesty, said he, doth much curb the evil thoughts of the people."

So much for the capacity and for the methods of the agent Lord Robert employed in the delicate and most anxious matter of ascertaining the impression created immediately and locally by the event that synchronised too closely with the forecasts of Lord Robert's enemies, not to be a disastrous one for him as well as for the poor victim of his greatness.

The story of the last hours of hapless Amy, pieced together from the statements of several members of the Cumnor Hall household, and verified by the oaths of a Coroner's Court, is as follows: It was the day (Sunday) of Abingdon Fair. Lady Robert rose very early and announced her desire that all the household should go to the Fair. Her own suite of attendants was, apparently, considerable. There were other servants in the house in the employ of Sir Anthony Forster. So insistent was she that all the servants, from the lowest to the highest, should have the day out, that she was "very angry" with "any of her own sort that made reason for tarrying at home," and gave vent to her annoyance in a loud complaint to a Mrs Odingsells, a widow who lived in Sir Anthony Forster's house, and who was sister to that William Hyde with whom Amy had been staying in the previous year, when she wrote the letter about her lord being " sore troubled with weighty affairs."

Although a gentlewoman, and no dependent of the Dudleys, the Lady Robert wished to send Mrs Odingsells also to the Fair. But the widow said it was no day for a gentle-woman to go; the morrow would be a better day. At this, Amy showed more temper, saying Mrs Odingsells " might choose and go at her pleasure, but all her's should go." Her insistence appeared unreasonable to those about her, and she was asked " who should keep her company if they all went ? " She replied that Mrs Owen should dine with her. Now, Mrs Owen was the wife of the retired physician, from whom Sir Anthony Forster rented Cumnor, and with whom, it has been supposed, Amy was placed on account of his cunning in the use of medicines. But if Amy were " taking care not to be poisoned," it is evident that she was not exercising her precautions against the Owens. Nor could she have had any fear of Sir Anthony Forster, who was in the house, and whose going to the Fair she did not suggest. Unless, indeed, " the strange mind in her " led

E

her, believing that poison was to come, to plot deliberately that it should come quickly.

One, Pirto — probably Amy's maid — "who doth dearly love her," scouted the idea that her mistress sought self-destruction. "She was a good and virtuous gentlewoman," so Pirto answered Blount, when he suggested the theory of suicide, "and daily would pray upon her knees." And "divers times," good Pirto added, the Lady Robert had been heard to pray to God to "deliver her from desperation." But Pirto was insistent that there was no insanity in her lady's mind. "No, good Mr Blount," she urged, "do not judge so of my words; if you should so gather, I am sorry I said so much." But Blount had his ideas; "truly the tales I hear of her maketh me to think she had a strange mind in her, as I will tell you at my coming," was his comment to Lord Robert on the evidence of Pirto. And if we may consider the statements of Pirto to be quoted by Blount without travesty or exaggeration, it seems that the faithful maid protested just a thought too much. By her faith, she did judge the death of her lady to be "very chance, and neither done by man nor by herself." Yet why was Pirto so sure? If done by man, those who loved the lady thus "piteously slain" would have desired the culprit to be brought to punishment. If by her own act she rushed upon her doom, these same devoted ones would swear that it came upon a chance.

In any case, Blount was able to assure Lord Robert that, already — 11th September — and before his coming, the most of the jury were chosen and they were, in his judgment, " as wise and as able men to be chosen upon such a matter as any men, being but country - men, as ever I saw." He added he had good hope they would " conceal no fault if any be; for as they are wise, so are they, as I hear part of them, very enemies to Anthony Forster."

It was all to the good for the carriage of justice that Forster was not popular in his immediate neighbourhood. His doings would be the more thoroughly searched. Yet the innkeeper at Abingdon had told Blount that he judged the tragedy a " misfortune, because it chanced in that honest gentleman's house; his great honesty," mine host asserted, " doth much curb the evil thoughts of the people."

But evil thoughts were rampant, and Lord Robert at his house at Kew was in deepest anxiety. " Until I hear from you again how the matter falleth out in very truth, I cannot be in quiet," he wrote to his " Cousin Blount " on September 12th, and again affirmed his desire that the jury shall " according to their duties, earnestly, carefully, and truly deal in this matter, and find it as they shall see it fall out."

A circumstance held by enquirers of our own day, to place Lord Robert under deep suspicion, was his remaining at Court, and neither immediately flying to Cumnor, nor subsequently attending the ceremonious funeral of his wife at Oxford. But, apart from the facts that attendance at the inquest and personal direction of the disposition of Lady Robert's body ι nd affairs would have caused suspicion of his influence militating against the course of justice, and that the "chief mourner" at State funerals in those days was always a deputy, and of the same sex as the deceased, it was impossible for him to go upon a journey. Upon the receipt of definite news of his wife's death, the Queen had ordered Lord Robert into seclusion. From what spot—whether the Tower or an apartment of some palace where Elizabeth was not—he wrote the letter to Cecil that proves him to have been in disgrace and his liberty curtailed, is not known. But this is clear, the perspicuous but angered Secretary who, in his recent speech with the Spanish Ambassador, had brought railing accusation against Dudley, visited the suspected man in durance, and came away persuaded of his innocence.

If it were possible for an Elizabethan states-

man to feel any self-reproach for actions of
self-interest and treachery to colleagues, Cecil,
during his interview with Lord Robert, may
have felt some pangs of remorse for his earlier
conference with De Quadra. It is true, that
while Cecil had been absent upon State affairs
in Scotland, Lord Robert had made a throw
for the leadership of the Protestants, and the
Secretary, upon his return, had found himself
no longer the unchallenged head of the national
party. These facts and the absorption of the
Queen's time and interest by Lord Robert,
were natural goads to Cecil to make friends
with Spain, and to widen the breach between
Lord Robert and the Philipians. The news
of a catastrophe at Cumnor precipitated his
action. With a celerity that marks his genius
for affairs, Cecil provided at once for all
contingencies. Should the bad news from
Cumnor be confirmed, Elizabeth and Lord
Robert might find themselves so condemned
of popular opinion as to make their future
conduct of public business impossible. In that
case, Cecil, by dissociating himself from the
event before it could be supposed he had known
of its happening, gained credit of the party
that must come to power if Protestantism lost
favour. On the other hand, if the reputation of
Queen and Favourite remained unscathed, the
support of the Catholics and of Spain would

be a needed strength to the Secretary, now that he had lost influence through Dudley's greatness. The ability of the Favourite to convince him of a loyalty to their Queen, different in character from any that would be dreamed of by one of the Cecil temperament, brought about an understanding between the two men of opposite natures, who, for good or for ill, were the councillors who exercised the most potent influence over the mind and actions of Elizabeth of any of her advisers.

This is the letter of Lord Robert Dudley to Sir William Cecil, sent from the writer's retreat after the recipient had visited him.

"*September,* 1560.

"SIR,—I thank you for your being here, and the great friendship which you have shown towards me I shall not forget. I am very loath to wish you here again, but I would be very glad to be with you there. I pray you let me hear from you what you think best for me to do. If you doubt, I pray you ask the question, for the sooner you can advise me thither, the more I shall thank you. I am sorry so sudden a chance should breed me so great a change; for methinks I am here all this while as it were in a dream, and too far— too far from the place where I am bound to be; when methinks also this long idle time cannot excuse me from the duty I have to discharge elsewhere. I pray you help him that sues to be at liberty out of so great bondage. Forget me not though you see me not, and I will remember you and fail ye not, and so wish you well to do. In haste this morning, R. DUDLEY."

" I beseech you, sir, forget not to offer up the humble sacrifice you promised me."

Unless this letter were written of the deep design to convince Cecil of an alienation which did not really exist, but which was assumed of Elizabeth and Lord Robert in order to divert every breath of suspicion from the Queen, it is very direct evidence that Her Majesty highly disapproved of the Lady Robert's death, occurring at the time and in the manner that it did.

The missive of the Favourite under arrest has in it a ring of distress too genuine to have been assumed, and we have the touch of poetry that is in all natural expression, in the words "methinks I am here all this while as it were in a dream and too far—too far from the place where I am bound to be." Was that place Cumnor Hall or Windsor Castle? Those who know what manner of man was Dudley, will answer unhesitatingly, Windsor Castle. In his history of Elizabeth's reign, Mr Froude quotes this letter, yet says in condemnation of its writer, " a husband on receiving an account of the sudden and violent death of a lady, in whom he had so near an interest, might have been expected to have at least gone in person to the spot." The saying is fatuous, yet the worst that Froude believed of Dudley was that followers of his, with the idea of rendering their patron a signal service, used the murderous method of removing from his path the obstacle to his elevation to regal power, and that Dudley and the Queen—both too happy in the prospect thus opened before them — connived at the event, *after its happening*, by not insisting on a particular investigation into the circumstances of Amy's death.   But Dudley's letters to his "Cousin Blount," and the Queen's actions immediately upon hearing of the catastrophe, do not support the theory of connivance, although the anterior conduct of Elizabeth and her Favourite provoked the suspicions entertained of them.

Elizabeth marked the restoration to favour of her Master-of-the-Horse, by announcing her intention of bestowing a peerage on him. The patent was drawn up and brought to her for signature. But with a parade of temper, she slashed the parchment and cut it in pieces before the eyes of the anticipator of ennoblement. She would not make a peer, she declared, of the son and the grandson of traitors. Thus she brought him high ; then sent him low. Yet she gave promise to him of eventual raising. His reproaches of her captiousness met with a clap on the cheeks, and a "No, no, the bear and the ragged staff is not so soon overthrown."

The effect of poor Amy's death had not been to subdue the levity of Elizabeth, and all over Europe shocking tales of the Queen and Lord Robert were being repeated. "I hear," said the youthful Queen-Dauphine [Mary Stuart] cynically, "the Queen of England is to marry her Horse-keeper, who has done away with his wife to make room for her." This remark, and others like it, flying round in Paris, roused in the English Ambassador — Sir Nicholas Throckmorton—the most fearful anxieties for the repute of England and of England's Queen. He was frenzied with indignation against the audacious lordling, whose devotions were so compromising to Elizabeth, and, failing to get any re-assuring letter from England, he sent from France a subordinate of his embassy to remonstrate with Her Majesty. Elizabeth provoked, quizzed, and wordily belaboured the plucky emissary. "She would an' she would not" say if a marriage with my Lord Robert was in prospect. It was the same when courtiers asked her to marry my lord. She would "pup with her lips" and declare that she would not marry a subject, "men would come and ask for my lord's grace." They told her she could make her husband a King, but "that she would in no wise agree to." Neither would she agree to orders being given in the Court that were contradictory to her own.

"God's death, my Lord, I have wish'd you well," she said to "Sweet Robin," on an occasion when he presumed to assert authority, "but my favour is not so confin'd to you that others shall not share it with you. I will have but one Mistress here and no Master."

Year by year Lord Robert was made to know himself, though always the first of them but one of a crowd of votaries at the Queen of England's shrine.

"I have many servants," she told him in the hearing of the Court, "to whom I will show countenance, and resume my regards at pleasure."

CHAPTER V

THE Protestant pulpits that had been loud in criticism of the "greatness" of Lord Robert Dudley with Elizabeth while his wife lived, were louder still in denunciation of the understanding between the Queen and her Master of Horse, after Lady Amy's death.

Elizabeth had favoured the Reformers, and she hated Rome. But the zeal for morality in the Protestant preachers became an offence to her. The pendulum of Reform had swung too far. There was need for more "order" in religion. The Queen put candles on the altar of her chapel, and permitted vestments to her priests. Since the indulgence which, under pressure from Cecil, she had extended to the "gospellers," was being so hatefully abused, she would show the conventicles and her Chief Secretary that she could make to herself friends of the Mammon of Catholicism.

The emissary of King Philip was again approached. This time, Sir Henry Sidney— the Lord Robert's brother-in-law—was spokes-

75

man.   No Sovereign had ever a more hard-
working, a more conscientious, or a worse
requited servant than Sir Henry.   In politics
he followed the practices of the times.   He
could negotiate and intrigue like his colleagues.
But, no more than the Lady Mary, his wife,
was he double by nature.   Such tortuous
mazes of duplicity, as the Queen and her
Favourite walked in, Sir Henry did not
tread.   If he could follow their involutions, he
possibly doubted the ultimate wisdom even
the expediency of them.   The proposal he
took to De Quadra gained sincerity from the
reputation of the bearer.   It differed from
that which the Lady Mary had first made to
the Ambassador.   This time the Dudley-Sidney
" combine " was not to promote the candidature
for Elizabeth's hand of a foreign Prince.   Spain
was asked to give support to the pretensions
of Lord Robert himself.

" The marriage," Sir Henry told De Quadra
in January 1561, " is now in everybody's mouth."
The Queen, herself, was anxious for it.   Sir
Henry was surprised the Ambassador did not
seize an opportunity to gain Lord Robert's
good - will.   The King of Spain would find
Lord Robert as ready to obey him as would
he one of His Majesty's own vassals.   " The
Queen and Lord Robert were lovers," so De
Quadra reported Sir Henry's words, " but they

intended honest marriage, and nothing wrong
had taken place between them which could
not be set right with His Majesty's help."
As to Lady Dudley's death, "Sidney averred,
he had examined carefully into the circumstances, and he was satisfied that it was
accidental." He frankly admitted, however,
that the circumstances were suspicious, and
acknowledged that there were many who did
not share his view.

Not knowing how Philip would take the
formal suggestion of Dudley's marriage with
the Queen, the Ambassador met the overtures
of Sidney haughtily. Sir Henry was reminded
of all that had passed between De Quadra and
Lady Sidney in the affair of the Archduke,
and of how Her Majesty had deceived both
her Lady-in-Waiting and the Ambassador of
Spain. Sidney was of opinion that Elizabeth's
personal interest in Lord Robert would lead
her to treat these negotiations with more
seriousness than she had bestowed on the
advances of the foreigner. He represented
that the Queen's maidenly instincts prevented
her from introducing the subject, but that she
awaited only the King of Spain's consent to
conclude the marriage. Lord Robert would
offer his services to Philip to the extent of
his power; especially he would assist in restoring *the religion.* He would support the policy

of a General Ecclesiastical Council. De Quadra
—as a good bishop should—said religion ought
not to be complicated with love matters.
"Whether married, or wishing to be married,
if the Queen were a Christian, she would take
religion to be between God and herself."
Lord Robert, however, was determined to
keep religion well to the front in his negotiations. At an interview he himself had with
De Quadra, he declared that rather than that
England should not be represented on the
General Council there was then talk of hold- ·
ing, he would attend it himself.

Communications with Spain were slow in
the sixteenth century, and Philip was a
deliberate correspondent. Though intelligent
and ingenious, his diplomacy failed because
his decisions always came too late. This was
good for England. It was good also for Lord
Robert. Dudley had the design of marrying
Elizabeth, if he could. He meant to remain
her Favourite if he could not. But he did not
really intend to take her as his bride from the
hand of Spain. His professions to De Quadra
were made with the object of gaining time,
and of giving a knock to the Puritans who
opposed his union. In spite of all treacheries
and of all defections, the reliance of Dudley,
as of Elizabeth, was ultimately on the loyalty
and on the patriotism of the English people.

De Quadra had not yet received instructions from his master when — a month after his interview with Sir Henry Sidney—he had a conversation on the matter broached, with Elizabeth herself.   In this audience the Queen fancifully told the Ambassador " after much circumlocution," that she would make him her ghostly father, and he should hear her confession.   The confession was that " she was no angel."   She had a high regard for the many excellent qualities she saw in Lord Robert. She had not resolved to marry either him or any one ; only every day she felt more and more the want of a husband.   She thought her own people would like to see her married to an Englishman.   Then she asked De Quadra —and by her question revealed what in her own mind was the crux of the matter of an English marriage — what His Majesty would think " if she married one of her household, as the Duchess of Suffolk had done, and the Duchess of Somerset whom she used to laugh at ? "

It is seen that Elizabeth's determination was forming—if not already formed—not to marry an inferior, and in particular not to render wifely submission to one she had — it is her own phrase—" raised from the dust."   She was, however, to be flattered by flatteries of her Robin.   In reply to her remarks about the kind of marriages made by her aunt, the French Queen-Dowager, to Charles Brandon, Duke of Suffolk, and by the widow of the Lord - Protector—Edward Seymour, Duke of Somerset—with plain Mr Francis Newdigate, the Bishop said he had never spoken on the subject with the King of Spain. But, marry with whom she would, His Majesty would be pleased. He well knew the high character which was borne by the Lord Robert.

Sails were trimming indeed! It was not so very long since De Quadra had described Lord Robert as "the worst and most procrastinating young man I ever saw in my life, heartless, spiritless, treacherous, and false." But that was when the worst young man was opposing a Spanish marriage, and not in a position to negotiate with Spain for his own. The courtly words of the Ambassador pleased the Queen. "With an air of much satisfaction," De Quadra stated, "she said she would speak to me again, and meanwhile she would promise to do nothing without your Majesty's sanction. She evidently wished that I should say more, but I refrained for fear of making a mistake, and because she is—what we know her to be."

What was this? A woman "possessed with a hundred thousand devils?"

In those words De Quadra had once described the young Queen. He also, upon an occasion, gave it as his opinion that Elizabeth was quite insane.

The impression he carried away from this audience appears to have been that England's Queen was an undisciplined young woman, wholly infatuated with a man there were difficulties about her marrying. The Bishop left with her a hope of the Power of Spain and of the Church Catholic being on the side of a match with Dudley.

" Carried away by passion as she is, she may fly into some opposite extravagance," he wrote to Philip. " The heretics are full of energy ; they have intelligence with Germany, France, and Scotland. Your own Low Countries are in no safe condition ; and if we let this woman become desperate, she may do something that may fatally injure us, although she destroy herself at the same time."

But infatuated with Lord Robert in the ordinary meaning of the phrase, Elizabeth was not. Both she and Dudley, though priming De Quadra with every hope of their reversion to the Romish religious system, and with every belief that their marriage was impossible without the aid of Spain, were determined, both of them, that by no folly of their own would they destroy themselves. Rather was it by their follies that they saved themselves. And that they did emerge triumphant, with their policies and with their loyalties to their country and to

F

the reformed religion intact, is evidenced by De Quadra's own statements.

Early in April, the Court went to Greenwich, where, it was believed, a Nuncio was to be received. Greenwich was chosen in order that the papal emissary might not be exposed to dangers to his person by a progress through Protestant London. But it was soon made clear to De Quadra that no Nuncio was to come. "The Queen had changed her mind, and would act like a woman, and the blame would be thrown upon Lord Robert," said Lord Robert's brother-in-law, Sir Henry Sidney. Lord Robert did indeed devotedly perform for England the function of receiving much of the blame of the Queen's frequent changes of mind and policy. In any case, blame had to be thrown on some one now. Sir Henry pitched it on to Elizabeth. De Quadra laid it at the door of Cecil and the Queen's Council. The Catholic nobles of England, ignoring what the Favourite had effected for their peace, cast the onus on Dudley.

At the meeting of the Knights of the Garter, on St George's Day, the Earl of Sussex proposed an address to the Queen, recommending the Lord Robert to her for her husband. The elder peer had no love for the lordling he called "the gipsy," but he wanted Elizabeth to "follow so much her own affection as by the

looking upon him whom she should choose,
omnes ejus sensus titillarentur, which shall be
the readiest way with the help of God to bring
us a blessed Prince."

And Sussex believed that Robert Dudley was
the man by whom alone Elizabeth's womanhood
was stirred.

The Duke of Norfolk, the Earl of Arundel,
and Lord Montague promptly refused their
assent. In the end, an address was presented
recommending marriage, without naming a
bridegroom. The Queen was angry. "When
she married she would consult her own pleasure,
not that of her Council."

For all her anger, the reply was as non-
committal as her remarks in general. A
favourite response of hers to any urging of
Dudley by name came to be that she would
marry Lord Robert "when she chose," or, better
still, "when she decided to do so." The nearest
approach to self-committal was, perhaps, six
months later, when she told De Quadra (according to the account of De Quadra himself) that
she knew no one better, fitter to be her husband
than Lord Robert, she would be grateful, therefore, if the Princes, her allies, and especially His
Majesty of Spain, would recommend him to her,
that she might be able to say she was acting
with the advice and the approval of her friends.
As the statement did not draw from the wily

Bishop the pledge the Queen hoped for, she broke out in a pet with "whether His Majesty consented or not she would marry Lord Robert when she chose, but if it were done without His Majesty's help, Lord Robert would be little obliged to him." The Bishop laughed, and said she had better make no more delays or excuses. Let her give Lord Robert what he wanted, and she might rest assured the King would be well pleased.

In the meantime, His Majesty was anything but "well-pleased" with the course affairs were taking in England, and his Ambassador, for many reasons, had serious fault to find with the Favourite, and definite quarrels to pick with the English Government.

On the 27th of April, De Quadra wrote to Lord Robert a long letter, carefully composed and formally signed, in which he declared, with some heat, his innocence of participation in any plot among Catholics to murder the Queen. Rumours of conspiracies to kill Elizabeth, and with her the Lord Robert, were rife. Some among the many stories circulated, directly accused De Quadra of the foul intention. This accusation he sought to rebut. But his principal reason, as he said, for writing the letter was to repeat *seriatim* all the promises Dudley and others had made concerning a General Council of the Church. He thought the repetition of them to their chief enunciator would provoke the English Government to give a favourable answer about the coming of the Nuncio from the Pope to patronise Elizabeth, and to reconcile England once more with Rome.

In this letter, De Quadra said concerning the accusation of his designs on the Queen's life:

"I should have wished to satisfy the world publicly with respect to it, the defamation having been public, but considering that I cannot do this at the present time without prejudice to your Lordship and your affairs which I have in hand" — these affairs were the marriage of Lord Robert with the Queen —"I have decided to keep silent for the present, and only justify myself to your Lordship that you may inform Her Majesty, as it is probable the counsellors will have given to both of you the information disseminated by the public voice."

The Queen read and re-read this letter which narrated all the dealings between the Sidneys, Lord Robert, and De Quadra. But the writer's hopes of it, in the matter of the Nuncio, were not realised. When De Quadra spoke with Elizabeth two days afterwards, he "found in her no more decision than usual." She complained that some of the imprisoned bishops, and other papists in London, were spreading the report that she had promised to turn Catholic at the instance of Lord Robert, and were saying that they received their information from men of De Quadra's household. The object of the prisoners in publishing such statements, Elizabeth averred, was to disturb the Protestants, and make them take arms against her. And the Queen asked De Quadra if it were true that the Spanish King had promised Lord Robert his friendship on condition of the restoration of religion. The Ambassador said Philip had promised nothing, but, on hearing of Lord Robert's "good-will" towards religion, His Majesty had ordered his Ambassador to thank him, praise his good intentions, and promise him continuation of the favour ever shown him. Elizabeth said she did not think Lord Robert had ever promised religion should be restored, but the Ambassador reminded her of his professions about a General Council.

Elizabeth's official reply to Philip's demands for her representation on a General Church Council, and for her reception of a Nuncio, were in the negative. England could not attend the Ecclesiastical Parliament of which the Pope of Rome was to be not merely a president but a dictator. A Nuncio could not be admitted to the country since it was against the laws and good policy of the realm to welcome a papal emissary. This then was practically the conclusion of the whole matter of Lord Robert's negotiations with Rome and Spain for his marriage with Elizabeth. Fitfully, for some years, the subject cropped up again. There was no finality in the mind of Dudley, or in that of his royal mistress. But what sincerity there had been in the advances on either side was now eliminated. In a despatch to King Philip, on the 3rd of June, De Quadra passed this verdict on the "recent negotiations":

"I have come to the conclusion that the foundation of it was to prevent the Queen of Scots from marrying into your Majesty's family, as they knew that with that claim, and the Catholic party with you as well as your Majesty's own forces, a great change could suddenly be brought about here. To check this, and to get time to provide against emergency, they thought necessary to make a great show of wishing to amend their ways as regards religion, and subject themselves to the devotion and protection of your Majesty, from which intention the Queen herself probably was not averse, particularly if she saw herself driven in a corner by this business of the Queen of Scots."

What "this business of the Queen of Scots" was, and how Lord Robert was concerned in it, will be told in another chapter. In this one is described the character of the overtures to Spain and to Rome, in making which Lord Robert has been deemed false to his country and to the Protestant faith. The view of the wily Ambassador that all the negotiations were to "get time to provide against emergency," sums them up very justly. Yet in spite of the perspicuity of his judgment, De Quadra still went on bandying words with Elizabeth and the Favourite, as if he still believed their advances and their professions to be sincere. In any case, the persistent cleric meant to obtain, if he could, better treatment for the "bishops and other papists" who had recently been committed to the Tower, and for certain priests who, because of the good theory of Elizabeth's rule that no one should suffer for their opinions, had been "exposed on the pillory as conjurers and necromancers." The priests had been found "making a figure of the nativities of the Queen and Lord Robert, with I know not what other strange things," and they had fallen into the hands of men "glad to make priests ridiculous."

De Quadra took the opportunity, when invited to a river-party given by the Lord Robert on Midsummer Day, to ask the Queen whether she thought her Ministers had done good to their country by making a laughing-stock of Catholics, and he told her she should look better to them, and not allow headstrong, violent men to guide her in so serious a matter as religion. "She listened patiently," the Bishop wrote, but was not to be drawn into argument. Indeed, her mood was sportive and, with Lord Robert, she baited the grave Spaniard. In the afternoon, on the gallery of Lord Robert's barge, the Ambassador found himself alone with the Queen and his splendid young host, who " began to talk nonsense." They "went so far"—the words are the Bishop's—"that Lord Robert at last said as I was on the spot there was no reason why they should not be married if the Queen pleased."

Elizabeth took up the ball thus tossed. Perhaps the Bishop did not understand sufficient English !

"I let them trifle in this way for a time," remarked the worthy Churchman. Then he spoke solemnly. If Dudley and the Queen would be guided by him, they would shake off the tyranny of the men who oppressed the realm, *i.e.*, the Protestants—and restore religion and good order. Then they could marry when they pleased, and gladly would he be the priest to unite them.

Truly a glorious prospect! A Roman wedding ceremonial for the Protestant Queen of England, with a Spanish Bishop to administer the sacrament !

Let the heretics complain if they dared, the ecclesiastic told the sportive pair before him ; with the Majesty of Spain at her side the Queen might defy danger. At present, he complained, "it seemed she would marry no one who displeased Cecil and his companions."

Heedless of the sunny irresponsibility of a Thames Regatta Day, although the mood of those he lectured actively reflected it, the Bishop "enlarged on this point." He confided later to his King and Master, the reason of his tediousness.

". . . unless I can detach her and Lord Robert from the pestilential heresy with which they are surrounded, there will be no change. If I can once create a schism, things will go as we desire. This, therefore, appears to me the wisest course to follow. If I keep aloof from the Queen, I leave the field open to the heretics. If I keep her in good humour with your Majesty there is always hope—especially if the heretics can be provoked into some act of extravagance. They are irritated to the last degree to see me so much about the Queen's person.

"Your Majesty need not fear that I shall alienate the Catholics. Not three days ago, those persons whom your Majesty knows of sent to me to say that their party was never so strong as at this moment, nor the Queen and Council so universally abhorred."

There are informations in this letter not intended to be conveyed; and evidences also of the scope and of the limitations of the Bishop's vision.

It was true that little could be done in the Catholic interest until the Queen and her Favourite were detached from the "pestilential heresies " of England.   But from those heresies, neither Lord Robert, nor the woman he served, intended to be detached.   Even while Dudley kept the Bishop in tow, and gained the countenance of Spain for the suit he pressed, or affected to press, he was offering to the Huguenots of France the support they desired from England, if they would aid his cause with England's Queen.   The Bishop discovered his defection, and taxed him with it.   Lord Robert, unabashed, declared he was but " practising " with the French Protestants, and that both he and the Queen were as anxious as ever to receive one another from the hands of Philip.   The Bishop did not accuse Lord Robert of " practising " with him, but there were always reservations in the opinions of the Spaniard.   Bolstered by the hopes of the sanguine Catholic party, De Quadra believed that only by the help of Spain could Elizabeth safely become the wife of her Favourite. He believed also that it was the infatuated desire of the Queen to marry Dudley.   In these beliefs he was wrong.   Yet the rejection by Elizabeth of all other suits had brought even Cecil to the point of requesting the Spanish Ambassador to ask his Master, in his turn, to request of Elizabeth that she would marry an Englishman. Cecil had not desired to have Dudley named by Philip, but he had admitted that to ask the Queen to marry a countryman of her own, was tantamount to asking her to take Lord Robert. Now, if the thought of this marriage had been so odious to the English Protestants as De Quadra represented, Cecil would never have gone even so far in promoting it.   Again the statements of the Bishop himself disclose some causes of Puritan disaffection, which did not proceed directly from the conduct of the Lord Robert and the Queen.

"There is always hope — especially if the heretics *can be provoked* into some act of extravagance," are words that betray many secrets.   The "heretics" had undoubtedly been provoked already, and provoked, moreover, by "these persons whom your Majesty knows of."

Who were those persons ?

Upon the coming to her own of "Bloody Mary," Elizabeth had ridden into London at her sister's side acknowledged, tacitly, Princess of England.   Later, in the reign of that Queen, the sister she desired to trust, but could not, was acknowledged—again tacitly—the heiress-presumptive.   But in the intermediate time, and for a considerable period, a Princess of the Blood — the Lady Margaret Douglas, afterwards Countess of Lennox — had been led by the Queen's favours, to believe herself Mary's successor on the throne.   This Princess, the daughter of Margaret, elder sister of Henry VIII. (Queen-Dowager of Scotland), by her second marriage with the Earl of Angus, was reputed to have urged Elizabeth's execution upon Mary. She had certainly offered to Elizabeth, in Mary's time, some unforgettable insults. Yet Elizabeth had received her at her Court, and had given her there the precedence of her rank.

The tolerance of Elizabeth had not, however, won over the Lady Margaret. She did not forget that her boys—Lord Darnley and Lord Charles Stuart—were of both Scottish and English blood-royal. Lord Darnley had been early taught to count himself a near heir to the crowns of England and of Scotland, and the castle of Lord Lennox in Yorkshire was a rallying place of the rebels of the North. "Under colour of her conscience," Lady Lennox continued to use "her beads, auricular confession, and the pinning of idols and images above her bed, and the bed of the Lord Darnley," long after these things had been forbidden by the law of England. In the Lennox household, Elizabeth was spoken of as a "bastard," and the Lady Margaret's fool was allowed "to rail at the Queen and Lord Robert." Francis Yaxlee, a Gentleman (?) of the Bed-chamber, furnished Lady Lennox with constant intelligence of the "goings on" —only the vulgar expression denotes the vulgar view of the proceeding—of Elizabeth and her Favourite. We may be sure the informer put the worst construction, as is the practice of informers in all ages and in all societies, on the dealings of the most talked of personages in the realm. "She herself," the statement is De Quadra's, "did set forth the Queen of Scots' title, declaring what it were to have both realms in one, meaning the conjunction of her son to the Scottish Queen, who should be King both of Scotland and of England."

All these treacheries were not known to Elizabeth at the time. In her desire to propitiate and to manage all parties, she had overlooked Lady Lennox's past offences. No one was quicker to understand than the Queen of many practices, how under one regimen, a person, for reasons, may blow hot, and under another, may blow cold.

But Lady Lennox had other occupations than that of currying favour with the Sovereigns to whom she owed allegiance. She was a definite agent of the Court of Rome, and a pronounced ally of Spain. The spread of much of the foul gossip concerning the Queen and the Lord Robert was due to an organised plan of action, whereof the Lady Margaret was the instigator. The letters of De Quadra give good indication that not only did Lady Lennox and her party continually beseech the active interest of Spain in the Catholic interest, but they spared no pains to circulate among the Protestants just those tales of, and insinuations against, the Queen that would be most detestable to Puritan consciences, and which, in their reaction, through the indignation of the preachers, would afford the greatest perplexity and annoyance to a maiden ruler.

Here, then was, a volcanic England, over which it was Elizabeth's task to hold sway! Had she at once been aware of all the ramifications of treachery about her, she had perhaps walked more circumspectly in the beginning. And yet one doubts. The courage and the defiance of the Tudors rose as danger threatened.

In splendid defiance of interfering foreign powers, and of the insubordination of home subjects, Elizabeth Tudor and Robert Dudley took the path of their own demarcation. They almost persuaded the Spaniards and the Papists of their desire to re-establish " order " in religion, and, by these persuasions, they delayed the conjunction of Spain with the Catholic party in England. They kept France at bay by negotiations with the Huguenots, with the Protestant and Patriotic party in Scotland, and with this same powerful Spain whose alliance with England was the veritable bogey of the French nation. And, despite all they had to endure from " hot-gospellers," they showed themselves intrepidly English by making common cause with Cecil in his suppression of the Mass, and in his rejection of the Pope's offer to send a Nuncio to England to deal with the Queen for a settlement of religion.

CHAPTER VI

THE persuasions of Catholic Spain and the requests of Protestant English lords alike, were powerless to make Elizabeth give herself to Lord Robert as his wife. There grew in her a dislike of marriages for all members of her Court, whether women or men. Yet, all the year past, she had been busy matchmaking for her "good sister," the Queen of Scots.

In December 1560, the young King of France was gathered to his fathers, and Mary Stuart, who had boasted of a triple crown—of Scotland, France, and England—made graceful surrender of one kingdom. Though never Queen of England, she was "by the laws of all nations" heiress-presumptive to the English crown. And she was a focus for the plans, and a figure-head for the party of the English Catholics, compared with whom Lady Lennox was but the shadow of a shade.

Another heiress-presumptive, to whom the parliamentary Act and the testamentary disposition of Henry VIII. gave her right, was the

Lady Catherine Grey, the beloved sister of Lady Jane. Elizabeth had taken Lady Catherine to live at Court, and had allowed her a certain precedence as Princess of the Blood, but had never treated her with any kindness. Her position was different from that she had been accorded in the late Queen's reign. The Catholic inclinations of Lady Catherine had insured her a consideration from both Mary and Philip. And when Elizabeth refused two Archdukes in succession, and it began to be doubted whether she had any intention of marrying at all, a scheme was set afoot to match Lady Catherine with an Austrian Prince. "I keep on good terms with Lady Catherine. She promises me, for her part, not to change her religion, and not to marry without my consent," wrote the Ambassador for the nonce of Philip, in March 1559. But infidelity to promises was a Tudor characteristic, and some of the Protestantism of the family of Grey survived in Lady Catherine.

In little more than a year from the time Spain was reassured concerning her, she made a secret marriage—in furtherance of a purely English, if not a wholly Protestant, design—with Lord Hertford, the son of the late Protector Somerset, and the hereditary enemy of the Dudleys. We have the declaration of Queen Elizabeth in September 1561, that "there had been great practices and purposes," and that "many persons

G

of high rank were known to have been privy to the marriage." It was supposed that in a moment of disgust with the Queen, because of the negotiations between the Sidneys and De Quadra for the marriage of Lord Robert, Cecil conceived the plot. Lord Arundel—the "White Horse," it was the hope of some, Elizabeth might marry in preference to her "Horse-keeper," the Earl of Bedford—Lord St Lo, his wife the famous "Bess of Hardwick," and a few others were concerned in it. The manœuvre had been intended as a provision, not as a menace, and had been so secretly managed that it was hard, even in its revelation, to convict any save the chief parties. Lady Catherine and her husband paid the full penalty of their rashness. The Archbishop of Canterbury, for the cause of Lady Catherine's earlier marriage in form to Lord Herbert, at the time of Northumberland's great throw for power, pronounced her marriage in fact with Lord Hertford null, and her child to be born illegitimate. The unfortunate mother of the babe defamed, never again tasted the sweets of liberty. Lady Catherine languished for seven years in captivity, and then died. Lord Hertford was kept in the Tower until after her death, and, even then, was subjected to a semi-imprisonment for some years longer.

In the meantime, there were high words at

Court. Lord Robert spoke insolently to Arundel. Arundel let fly with reminders of dark happenings at Cumnor. The effect of the sensation, generally, was to clear the way for the acknowledgment of Scottish Mary as heiress to Elizabeth's throne. She had a right to it Elizabeth herself could not gainsay. But the days were not yet for the English Queen to put aside hope of an heir of her own body. And to proclaim an heiress-presumptive so unequivocally Catholic, of such prominence and so befriended as was Mary, was for Elizabeth to put a premium on her own assassination. Yet, if Mary would relinquish absolutely the title of Queen of England, during Elizabeth's lifetime, Elizabeth agreed to *consider* her claim as heiress-presumptive. But Mary would not divest herself of the regal name, unless, by an Act of the English Parliament, she should be declared next in succession after Elizabeth and her children.

It was against all the principles and policies of Elizabeth's rule to give the pledge Mary's sagacity demanded. The two Queens were now opposed; in battle array, if with flag of truce flying, they were set over against one another to strive for dominance. The duel had begun, of which the last prick and final thrust were delivered at Fotheringay, twenty-six years later.

And if Elizabeth had the strength, the resolution, and the faith in herself, which finally prevailed over all Mary's enthusiasms and graces, Mary had equal skill in parry, and practised the greater variety of strokes. It was Mary who desired, and who almost obtained by her persistence, a meeting with Elizabeth. Who knows, if the Queens had ever met, how matters would have fared?

Elizabeth would not risk the face-to-face and hand - to - hand conflict. She designed, however, to clip the wings of Mary's o'er-topping ambition by giving her in marriage to a creature of her own.

The first candidate naturally thought of, was the fifteen-year-old Lord Darnley, but the Catholic proclivities and intriguing pro-pensities of his mother prevented Elizabeth from putting him forward. The man, she finally and definitely proposed, was Lord Robert Dudley.

At certain stages of the negotiations for this marriage Elizabeth had a real desire to see her favourite joined to the heiress-presumptive, and the crown settled on his children. The whole story of Elizabeth's life confirms her frequent statements that she had no disposition for marriage. It was also true, as she often took occasion to remark, that there might arise circumstances compelling her to a politic union.

At this time, there was no reason to be called pressing for her own marriage, except that of despoiling Mary of her claims.

But if she could render those claims innocuous by marrying her to a safe man, and, at the same time, could confer the greatest honour possible, next to marriage with herself, on him who owed his distinction to her selection of him, and was therefore, to the mind of Elizabeth, distinguished indeed, Elizabeth felt she would be performing at once a *tour de force* of politics, and a highly benevolent act. She had moods in which she could not contemplate the loss of the companionship of Lord Robert. In those moods, she persuaded herself, and endeavoured to persuade others, that she was making a costly sacrifice of her own happiness for that of her "sister" and her "brother." Preferably to the only available Prince of the Blood—Lord Darnley—who had claims of his own to kingship of the Isle, and who was in the Catholic interest, she would give a "most illustrious Prince" of her own instituting, whose affections were towards Protestantism, and who had, of himself, no pretensions whatever to England's or to Scotland's sovereignty.

About this time appeared a book upholding the claims on the succession of the Lady Catherine, whose popularity had been increased by her giving birth, in the Tower, to a second child by the Earl of Hertford. In the publication of this book Cecil had had a hand, and Lord Robert, by messages sent through Roger Ascham; and by his own "using" of Hales, the author, at Windsor, had shown himself as agreeable as Cecil to the book's argument. This argument was, that the birth of the Lady Frances Brandon, Marchioness of Dorset, had been legitimate, although the first wife of her father had been yet alive when he married Mary Tudor. It was not an argument agreeable to those who desired a Catholic succession in England. King Philip wrote to his Ambassador—the successor of De Quadra:

"I have read what you say of the book on the succession; of the Queen's anger; and of the suspicions indicated to you by Lord Robert, that Cecil was at the bottom of it. I avail myself of the occasion to tell you my opinion of that Cecil. I am in the highest degree dissatisfied with him. He is a confirmed heretic; and if, with Lord Robert's assistance, you can so inflame the matter as to crush him down and deprive him of all further share in the administration, I shall be delighted to have it done."

But though Lord Robert practised the regal habit of excusing himself by throwing the blame on others, he never could have been so false to England and to his Queen as to attempt to crush down Cecil, even had such a task been as possible as the lethargic Monarch of Spain imagined. And aggravated as Cecil often was by Lord Robert's cunning, and by the graces and the wiles of him that were the supposed impediments to the Queen's acceptance of a royal suitor, the sagacious Secretary seems always to have regarded the Favourite as "safe" in the Liberal and non-papal interests. This opinion was fully justified by the after career of Lord Robert. His dealings with Spain and Rome, so strongly condemned by ultra-Protestant and free-thinking historians, were only dealings. And they were the complements and extensions of Elizabeth's own political practices.

On the 2nd of July 1564, De Silva (for this was the name of the rather inferior substitute for the clever De Quadra, who had died the year before), wrote to Philip:

"Lord Robert is more pressing than ever in offering his assistance to your Majesty. The gentleman of whom I spoke tells me that Lord Robert has still hopes of the Queen, and that, if he succeeds, the Catholic religion will be restored. Again cautioning me to be secret, he informed me that Lord Robert was in communication with the Pope about it, and had agents continually residing at the Papal Court. . . . I suspect the French have been trying to make use of Lord Robert. His father, people tell me, had large French connections."

Not only were the French trying to make use of Lord Robert, but Lord Robert was making use of the French. Yet in the Spano-Romish negotiations, the Favourite continued to play up to his royal mistress with an histrionic skill equal to her own. At Richmond, in July, the two acted their little comedy to perfection. De Silva was received by the Queen with "pointed kindness." She took him aside (she was in the garden with her ladies on his arrival), and kept him for an hour, talking the whole time of the King, his master. "After supper," De Silva related, "she had more conversation with me, and as it was then late I thought it time to take my leave; but the Queen said I must not think of going; there was a play to be acted which I must see. She must retire to her room for a few minutes she said, but she would leave me in the hands of Lord Robert. The Lord Robert snatched the opportunity of her absence to speak of his obligations to your Majesty, and to assure me that he was your most devoted servant. She returned almost immediately, and we adjourned to the theatre." De Silva adds in regard to the performance that followed this one, "the piece was a comedy . . . the plot as usual turned on marriage." But he had not eyes for the "*lever de ridean*" which had been the true drama of the evening. Could one expect "eyes" for deep-seeing from the gentleman who stated that the Queen spoke with "unaffected sincerity"? When De Silva had been four months in England he began to see through things a little better.

In the meantime, the design of Lord Robert's marriage with the Scottish Queen was much discussed, although all hint of it was studiously withheld from De Silva. To avoid making any promises on behalf of Mary, her envoy, Sir James Melville, suggested to Elizabeth that the matter of his mistress's marriage—whether to Archduke Charles, Lord Darnley, Lord Robert, or another—should be referred to a commission to be composed of the Earl of Murray and Secretary Maitland on behalf of Scotland, and to the Earl of Bedford and Lord Robert on behalf of England.

"Ah, you make little of Lord Robert, naming him after the Earl of Bedford!" exclaimed Elizabeth haughtily. "I mean to make him a greater Earl, and you shall see it done. I take him as my brother and my best friend."

So it came about that Lord Robert Dudley was created Earl of Leicester—a title appertaining to the progeny of Kings of England in virtue of their rank as Dukes of Lancaster —on Michaelmas Day 1564. His supporters were the Earls of Sussex, Huntingdon, and Warwick. He had previously been invested as Baron of Denbigh; the Lords Hunsdon, Clinton, and Strange accompanying him to the Presence.

The Earl of Leicester received his initiation to his new honours with becoming gravity. He took the belt and collar "sitting upon his knees" before the Queen; the Scottish Envoy and the French Ambassador standing on either hand to witness the fulfilment of Elizabeth's promise. The solemnity of the men of state, as of the Court darling, fitted the occasion. But the frolicsome Queen must needs tickle her "dear brother" in the neck as she performed the investiture. In his account of the scene, no particular surprise at the action was expressed by the sententious Melville. He had already seen Elizabeth dance "high and disposedly," and had been skittishly slapped and pushed by the august lady on an occasion when it had been her pleasure to consider herself *surprised* by him while playing on her virginals.

The patent of nobility, for some time dangled before the eyes of her Favourite, was now definitely bestowed. Elizabeth had contrived the matter so that it should be without prejudice to her own reputation, and without undue flattery to the man ennobled. She made him a peer to fit him for marriage with another Queen.

As for the new - made Earl, although his

peerage had been bestowed upon him by a somewhat invidious method, his purposes were well served. He had gained a prize, and at the same time had supported, as he always supported, the designs of the woman he hoped to keep in the "good tune" of marrying with himself. Yet Lord Robert was careful not to be too deeply involved in the meshes of the net wherein Elizabeth hoped to drag Mary of Scotland in the wake of English interests.

When the time came for Sir James Melville to leave the English Court, he was invited by Leicester to "sail in his barge down the water of Thames to London, which was ten miles from Hampton Court." On the way, the consummate courtier told Mary's emissary that he was so well acquainted with him by report that he dared to be so homely as to ask what the Queen of Scots thought of the bridegroom and of the marriage that had been proposed. Melville answered coldly, as he had been by his Queen commanded. Whereupon Leicester began "to purge himself of so proud a pretence as to marry so great a Queen . . . alleging the invention of that proposition to have proceeded of Master Cecil, his secret enemy." Said English Leicester, as translated by Scotch Melville: "Gif I should have seemed to desire that marriage, I should

have tint the favour of baith the Quenis."
And he prayed that it would please her
Scottish Majesty not to impute unto him,
but unto the malice of his enemies, the
"lourd" fault. When Melville finally went
north, he bore "writings" from the Earl of
Leicester to the Earl of Murray, to excuse
him at the Queen's hands.

After Mary had been informed, "at great
length," of all the "handling" of Sir James
in England, she asked him whether he thought
Elizabeth meant as truly towards her in her
heart as she did outwardly in her speech.
Melville replied that in his judgment there was
neither plain dealing nor upright meaning, and
having already hindered Mary's marriage with
the Archduke, Charles of Austria, Elizabeth
was now offering Leicester, whose acceptance
she desired as little as that of the other.
Mary gave Melville her hand, and vowed she
would never marry the "new - made Earl."
Albeit, a short time after, as Melville himself
has related, Lord Murray and Lord Bedford
met at Berwick to "treat upon the marriage
with Leicester," which treaty was entered into
on the English side with "slenderer offers and
less effectual dealing than was looked for."
Meanwhile the Earl of Leicester had written
"so discreet and wise letters unto my Lord
Murray for his excuses, that the Queen [Mary]

appeared to have so good liking of him that the Queen of England began to fear and suspect that the said marriage might perchance take effect."

What a reflex of Elizabeth's own art were these machinations of her Favourite! He had his way with both women. While making a certain bid for the Scottish Queen's favour, he kept within bounds of loyalty to his own Sovereign, and helped forward the true English policy of delaying a marriage for Mary with a foreign potentate, and of preventing an immediate junction — through a union of Darnley and Mary — of the interests of the Scottish and English Catholics.

" The gentleman sent hither from the Court of Scotland has returned, and this Queen has written by him to say that for various reasons there will be no Parliament this year. The succession question therefore will be allowed to rest. She says she is not so old that her death need be so perpetually dragged before her.

" Cecil has intimated to the heretical bishops that they must look to their clergy; the Queen is determined to bring them to order, and will no longer tolerate their extravagances."

These words that tell their own tale are from a letter from De Silva to his King on 9th October. The faithful scribe continued:

" He desires them to be careful how they proceed against the Catholics; the Queen will not have her good subjects goaded into sedition by calumnies on their creed, or by irritating enquiries into their conduct. I am told that the bishops do not like these cautions.

"Cecil understands his mistress, and says nothing to her but what she likes to hear. He thus keeps her in good humour, and maintains his position. Lord Robert is obliged to be on terms with him, although at heart he hates him as much as ever. Cecil has more genius than the rest of the council put together, and is therefore envied and hated on all sides.

"The Queen, happening to speak to me about the beginning of her reign, mentioned that circumstances had at first obliged her to dissemble her real feelings in religion; but God knew, she said, that her heart was sound in His service; with more to the same purpose: she wanted to persuade me she was orthodox, but she was less explicit than I could have wished.

"I told her (she knew it already) that the preachers railed at her in the most insolent language for keeping the cross on the altar of her chapel. She answered that she meant to have crosses generally restored throughout the realm.

"Again and again she has said to me, 'I am insulted both in England and abroad for having shown more favour than I ought to the Lord Robert. I am spoken of as if I were an immodest woman. I ought not to wonder at it: I have favoured him, because of his excellent disposition, and for his many merits; but I am young and he is young, and therefore we have been slandered. God knows, they do us grievous wrong, and the time will come when the world will know it also. *I do not live in a corner—a thousand eyes see all I do, and calumny will not fasten on me for ever.*' "

These are the words of Elizabeth, as translated from the Spanish of De Silva, by the emotional historian, Mr James Anthony Froude. A later decipherer of the Simancas Manuscripts, of more critical temper, renders the same phrases:—" *My life is in the open, and I have so many witnesses that I cannot understand how so bad a judgment can have been formed of me.*"

The version of Mr Martin A. S. Hume is undoubtedly the most exact—yet the spirit that was in Elizabeth concerning these calumnies is not too theatrically expressed by Mr Froude. In six months the Queen was again emitting the same note of virtuous indignation.

" There is a strong idea in the world," said Elizabeth this time, " that a woman cannot live unless she is married, or at all events if she refrains from marriage, she does so for some bad reason, as they said of me that I did not marry because I was fond of the Earl of Leicester, and that I would not marry him *because he had a wife already.* Although he has no wife alive now, I still do not marry, notwithstanding that I was spoken to about it, even on behalf of my brother the King [of Spain]. But what can we do? We cannot cover every one's mouth, but must content ourselves with doing our duty and trust in God, for the truth will at last be made manifest. *He knows my heart which is very different from what people think, as you will see some day.*"

These words from the Spanish Calendar are as sentimental and as emphatic as any Mr Froude has put into the mouth of his admired Elizabeth. And, whatever else they indicate, they show that it had become the policy of Elizabeth and of Leicester to assert their freedom from any personal bonds to one another.

About this time Lady Lennox was told, by Leicester himself, that all thought of a marriage was now given up, and De Silva noted that the Favourite was "now attending to affairs carefully, which was different from what he used to do." This announcement was significant, if belated. Two years had passed since Leicester — as Lord Robert Dudley — had surprised the world by his capacity for, and understanding of, work. In 1562, the Queen had had a severe attack of small-pox. Lying on what she believed to be her death-bed, she had protested that "although she loved, and had always loved, Lord Robert dearly, as God was her witness, nothing improper had ever taken place between them."

On recovering from the crisis of her illness,

she had begged the Council to make Lord Robert Protector of the Realm, with a title and £20,000 a year. This could not be. Lord Robert was, however, put into the Council to despatch all business for the Queen, and, on account of her disfigurement, all audiences were to Lord Robert—except a few to the Duke of Norfolk. Since then, his industry in affairs had been remarkable, and, although Elizabeth quickly became herself again, his position and power had grown daily. After Court receptions, and at other seasons of royal entertainment, ambassadors and all guests of distinction were invited to sup with the Earl of Leicester. His expenses for feasts and pageants were great. No wonder, therefore, that the Queen bestowed on him treasure in the shape of lands, monopolies, patents, and licences. As Leicester himself remarked at another time, "the least war being admitted, cannot be maintained without great charge."

In that prolonged battle of scheme and counter - scheme with the powers of Europe, in which the Queen appointed Leicester Captain - General of her diplomatic forces, treasure had to be expended, and there is no justice in pelting the Favourite with abuse, because, in the provision of the treasure, Elizabeth adopted the means of her day, and, in spending it, Leicester considered the

H

demands of political and social circumstance. The administration of Elizabeth was remarkable for its economy. If it had not been for the few wars she undertook, she might never have called for any parliamentary subsidies, and it is universally admitted that her statecraft prevented many wars. In that statecraft, Leicester, by the peculiarity of his position in Elizabeth's favour, as well as by his own inclination, was a coadjutor more forceful than any. Even at this time, he had the character of being an advocate of peace. "I believe he desires to please everybody, as he seems well-disposed, and has no inclination to harm," was the opinion of De Silva after he had begun to see through many of the "tricks" the Queen and Leicester were so fond of playing.

It is descriptive of the Favourite and of his methods that, at this period, he was at once consulting amicably with Cecil in regard to the Scottish Queen's marriage; aiding Archbishop Parker in the establishment of Protestant Church methods; interceding with the Queen for the abandonment of certain Catholic "reforms" in the matters of the marriages of the clergy and the wearing of distinctive ecclesiastical "gowns"; sending out as spies, throughout Europe and to Rome, renegade Catholics of whom it was given out that they were leaving England for the better exercise of their Catholicism abroad; and professing a continued devotion to the Spanish King.

"The Lord Robert, whom they now call Earl of Leicester" (wrote De Silva at the same time that he recorded Elizabeth's disavowal of her intention of marrying her Favourite), "has been with me again, repeating his protestations of a desire to be of use to your Majesty. He mentioned particularly the troubles in the Low Countries, and the necessity of taking steps to pacify them.

"I assured him of the confidence which your Majesty felt in his integrity, and of the desire which you entertained for his advancement. I repeated the words which the Queen had used to me about religion; and I said that now when she was so well disposed there was an opportunity for him which he should not allow to escape. If the Queen could make up her mind to marry him, and to re-unite England to the Catholic Church, your Majesty would stand by him, and he should soon experience the effects of your Majesty's good-will towards him; the Queen's safety should be perfectly secured, and he should be himself maintained in the reputation and authority which he deserved.

"He answered that the Queen had put it off so long that he had begun to fear she would never marry him at all. He professed himself very grateful for my offer, but of religion he said nothing. In fact he is too wanting in skill in such matters to take a resolute part on either side, unless when he has some other object to gain.

"I told him the dependence of the Catholics

was wholly on the Queen and himself. To him they attributed the preservation of the bishops and of the other prisoners, and I said that by saving their lives he had gained the good-will of all Christian Princes abroad and of all the Catholics at home, who as he well knew were far more numerous than those of the new religion. The heretics notoriously hated both him and his mistress, and had not the Catholics been so strong would long ago have given them trouble; the Queen could see what was before her in the book on the succession, which after all it appeared she was afraid to punish.

"His manner was friendly, but I know not what he will do. Had the Catholics as much courage as the heretics, he would declare for them quickly enough, for he admits that they are far the larger number; things are in such a state that the father does not trust his child."

De Silva's four months' experience of the "sincerities" of Elizabeth and her Leicester had taught him many things. He was already doubting — as De Quadra had so decidedly doubted—the good intentions of the Queen and her Favourite for the restoration of the Pope's sway. Lord Robert's concern for the pacification of the Netherlands was a concern the emissary of Philip was bound to consider superfluous if not insidious. No political development was so much dreaded of Spain, as an understanding between England and the Low Countries. In both of these countries Protestants abounded. De Silva's surmise that "had the Catholics as much courage as the heretics," Leicester "would declare for them" is only a surmise. And by his own statement he admitted that the Protestants were the sturdier community. He admitted, also, that the Queen's "orthodoxy" was a dubious matter, in spite of her resolution to have crosses in the churches. It was hard for the Latin mind to understand the forces alive in England, which the English Queen and the English Leicester understood so well; though, indeed, the professions of the two to Spain were shockingly insincere.

Among all the shifts and prevarications of her speech, the words in which Elizabeth gave impassioned denial to the calumnies of herself and Lord Leicester have a ring of sincerity. These words, De Silva told his Monarch, she had repeated to him again and again. Yet they were words the Spanish King and his Ambassador were little concerned to hear. What did they, as men of the world, and as quite unmoral, if not immoral, practisers of statecraft, care about the secret relations of the English Queen and her Favourite? It was rather the personal sense in Elizabeth, of wrong inflicted by malicious tongues, that made her cry aloud for those who ran to hear: "*I do not live in a corner—a thousand eyes see all I do, and calumny will not fasten on me forever!*"

CHAPTER VII

ELIZABETH did not attract Leicester by any purely womanly attributes of a higher kind. Yet there is no evidence that the lower allurements of sex called to him in her. She was always dominant, always Queen, despite her grotesque coquetries of action, and her homely indelicacies of speech. And he, studying her, sought to stir her imagination, to excite her pity, to propitiate her temper, to abet her politics, and to aid her plans. He provided constant food for her fancy, constant opportunities for her self-display, and constant occasions for the exercise of her statecraft. And he pleased her supremely by affecting to be dazzled by her physical charm, her personal beauty, her compelling womanhood. He interpreted and presented her to a line of favourites, and the devotions always due to Queenship forever prevented the dispelling of her maiden dream that it was satisfaction enough for any man, who worshipped her beauty and her talent, simply to be allowed to worship.

More and more, as her isolation became confirmed, her attractions turned to repulsions through their self-consciousness. And Leicester's assaults of flattery, though undoubtedly the only means by which any kind of capitulation could be obtained, were largely responsible for the peculiar development that took place in her character. This development, inhuman and diabolic as it seemed in some aspects, was yet a development that preserved the life of Elizabeth, and established the integrity of her realm.

And the incomparable Leicester, though he would complain now and again, for political purposes, of this one and of that one—particularly of Cecil — who influenced the Queen against marriage with himself, knew all the time that the influence that brought them together, yet kept them still apart, was the influence of Elizabeth's self. He had many methods of assailing the virginity of her spirit. One was her diversion with mask and pageant; another the delivery to her, through stage characters, of homilies of greater or less length, on the advantages of, and necessities for, matrimony.

At an entertainment given by the Favourite to his Queen in March 1565, a masque was enacted, in which advices to marry were pointed. Juno and Diana contended with each other anent the blessedness of the single and married states. Jupiter himself appeared, heard the arguments on both sides, summed up the respective claims of the goddesses, then gave the palm to Juno. "This is against me," said Elizabeth good-humouredly to the Spanish Ambassador, who was making at the time one of many efforts to gain her hand for Archduke Charles. And the oft-chronicled allegorical and topographical pageant with which Leicester entertained Elizabeth at Kenilworth in July 1575, should—in the design of her host—have been concluded with a device of goddesses and nymphs entitled "The Masque of Zabeta," by the Court poet Gascoigne.

Zabeta was a nymph of Diana, who became a great queen. She resisted the beguilements of Juno, and remained "in constant vow of chaste, unspotted life." The descriptions of her nymph, given by Diana, leave no doubt as to what great Queen is signified.

"My sister first, which *Pallas* hath to name,
　　Envied *Zabeta* for her learned brain.
My sister *Venus* feared *Zabeta's* fame,
　　Whose gleams of grace her beauty's blaze did stain.
Apollo dread to touch an instrument,
　　Where my *Zabeta* chanced to come in place :
Yea, *Mercury* was not so eloquent,
　　Nor in his words had half so good a grace,
My stepdame *Juno*, in her glittering guise,
　　Was nothing like so heavenly to behold. . . . "

Iris, sent by Juno, implored this Virgin Paragon to "consider all things by the proof," and then she shall find "much greater cause to follow Juno than Diana."

In conclusion, Iris delivered the following prophecy:

> "Where you now in Princely port
> Have passed one pleasant day,
> A world of wealth at will
> You henceforth shall enjoy
> In wedded state, and therewithal
> Hold up from great annoy
> The staff of your estate;
> Oh Queen, oh, worthy Queen,
> Yet never wight felt perfect bliss
> But such as wedded been."

But the planned diversions of the "one pleasant day" were not completed. A careful reporter of the proceedings has left it on record that he could not attribute the cause of the omission of the "device" to "any other thing than to a lack of opportunity and seasonable weather." A recent writer[1] has advanced the theory that "Her Majesty preferred not to be so directly courted in similitudes." Yet, neither in similitude, nor in earnest, did Elizabeth at any time prefer not to be courted. We may presume that greater causes than the exigencies of the weather prevented the delivery of the exhortations put into the mouth of Iris. So far back as 1566, Leicester's hopes of marriage with Elizabeth had appeared to be dead. But the minds of both Queen and Favourite were so curiously elastic, that the cutting short

[1] Mr Felix E. Schelling in "The Queen's Progress, and other Elizabethan Sketches."

of a project of either, did not always result in the project's destruction. Rather did the severance serve as a process of fissure, whereby two or more separate plans, each bearing some resemblance to the original thought — entity, started into being. Yet, since their aims coalesced, and their methods matched, it is likely that Leicester withdrew the masque from the programme of the day, for fear the direct suggestion of "Iris" might prove an offence to some other lover then being kept in play. The masque was suppressed, but Leicester had propitiated and enlivened his Elizabeth by the surprises, tiltings, mock - fights, bear-baitings, rustic bridals, declamations of comic and mythological apparitions, swimming of grotesque monsters of the deep, and whatnot of frolic and scenic representation, that formed the memorable pageant of Kenilworth.

And Leicester further assailed the fortress of his Queen's completeness by constituting himself her partner in display of her linguistic accomplishments, in assertions of her erudition, and in exercises of her wit. The visits of the Queen to Cambridge in August 1564, and to Oxford in 1566, were triumphs almost as great for Leicester as for Elizabeth. Upon the advice of their Chancellor, Sir William Cecil, the authorities of Cambridge University, some time before the coming of the Queen, directed letters to Lord Robert, the High Steward of the University, humbly desiring his honour to "commend all their doings to the Prince, and to be a mean that all should be taken in good part." In a long letter, Lord Robert replied that they need be in no fear that the exercises designed for the Queen's entertainment would not by her be taken in good part, and he promised in every way to further the exertions of the University, "with my purse to assiste and spend with youe; and myne owne selfe att your commandment."

Early on the day of the Queen's arrival in Cambridge, Sir William Cecil, the Vice-Chancellor, and all the Heads, received the Favourite "at the King's College then called the Court." Leicester rode thither from the town bounds, "all the Bedells going before him bareheaded." "And there, after he had saluted Sir William Cecyl, he first did peruse the Queen's lodging, and after the Church, and the way that the Queen should come to the same."

Within a few months of the date of this Cambridge visit, Leicester was made Chancellor of the University of Oxford. He found learning and discipline at a very low ebb there, and lost no time in instituting a better order for "the advancement of true religion, virtue, and learning."

In an important note sent to the University in July 1565, he marvelled and was sorry that his "well-devised orders" had been ill observed and kept; marvelled "at the minds of men so soon altered from their own device and purpose"; and was sorry "for the evident hurt of that University, which hath heretofore been counted the right eye of England, and a light to the whole realm." He assured the learned men he wrote to, that he would be "loath to see the University fall any wise in decay," so long as his charge continued over it. Therefore his letter was to pray, and to require the authorities to "look more straightly" to their own orders, in particular to those which directly touched "Learning and Religion, as Sermons, public Exercise and Disputations, whereby all Universities stand and keep their name; not neglecting either such inferior orders as are appointed necessary." And Leicester showed his determination to have the reforms he prescribed carried out, by an ultimatum:

"Else shall the want of your good conformities herein (being for your own benefits) cause me for want of being able to do good, as willingly release the charge I have, as I did with very good mind toward you all, carefully receive it for the well discharging my duty therein."

The internal evidence of this letter is

sufficient to prove that Leicester had a very real sense of the importance to a nation of good learning and exact religion. In the reply of the University, while defending themselves against some misrepresentations of complainants to Leicester, the authorities promised to guard against abuses, and that nothing thereafter should be committed that might justly be offensive to his Lordship. They entreated the continuance of his protection, and acknowledged gratefully his recent defence of their privileges in obtaining the transference of an action brought in the Court of Common Pleas to the Court of the Chancellor of the University, where it was an ancient privilege to have suits against Masters of Colleges— which this one was—tried.

The intercession of Leicester, on behalf of University privileges, recalls the earlier intervention of his in favour of the rights of the Inner Temple against the Middle Temple. His interests were quick and many in regard to the learned bodies and the responsible institutions of the country. He was genuinely and most patriotically concerned for the encouragement of Art and Learning. He maintained a troop of actors, and "Leicester players" were the first "stock" company to give dramatic performances in England. At the head of his company was James Burbage, the father of the original representative of Hamlet.

These domestic activities and concerns of his were hardly perceived, and certainly not understood by the foreign ambassadors, whose letters are now too much relied upon for data of Leicester's life and character. The informations of the envoys were derived mainly from the disaffected and the designing of the Court circle. The feeling and condition of the country at large could not be known to them. Other archives than those of Simancas and of Venice furnish the world with elucidations of the character of Leicester. They are the records of the English seats of learning, of the English Church, and of the English Government; contemporaneous biographies of colleagues and associates of Leicester; and whole volumes of correspondence of Leicester himself, and of others of Elizabeth's men of state. There are the records also of the lives of the poets, historians, and adventurers, of whom Leicester was the patron. One must search them all to estimate aright the character of him, Edmund Spenser sung of as

> "A mightie prince, of most renowned race,
> Whom England high in count of honour held,
> And greatest ones did sue to gain his grace,
> Of greatest ones, he greatest in his place,
> Sate in the bosome of his soveraine,
> And *right and loyale* did his word maintaine."

And these records reveal Leicester to us a man of many weaknesses, but of great parts, of some vices, though not destitute of virtues;

a man for all his "practices" and dissemblings, single-hearted in his devotion to England, and unaffected in his admiration of England's Queen; a man who, above all, was sumptuous in his views of life, and magnificent in his designs for Society. All that was best and most resplendent in intellect, in talent, and in achievement, were the "properties" he sought out for decoration of the daily scene of existence, whether for himself, for his Queen, or for that country of his, which his efforts and his ambitions assisted to make great.

Yet there was a sinister aspect to his activities. "A most accomplished Courtier, free and bountiful to soldiers and students," he was yet "a cunning Time-Server and Respecter of his own advantages," and "he preferred Power and Greatness . . . before solid Virtue."

A year after Leicester sent his admonitory letter to the Oxford dons, the Queen, on progress, made her famous visit to the University, and it was shown to Leicester that lectures, disputations, and public exercises formed part of the curriculum. We have no record of any speech by Leicester on the occasion although, accompanied by Cecil, he made his own State entry into the town two days before Her Majesty's arrival. But the Greek and Latin orations of Elizabeth were fully reported, as well as her gibe to Dr Humphreys, who had objected to the ecclesiastical habit she desired to impose upon the clergy. As in scarlet robe and hood, the learned doctor approached to kiss the hand of Majesty, this bolt flew at him: "That loose gown becomes you mighty well, Mr Doctor, I wonder your notions should be so narrow."

Leicester had the toil of the Oxford reception; the Queen, as was fitting, the glory. Yet the noise of the visit—as of the one to Cambridge—redounded to the fame of Leicester also. People began to recognise in him a true encourager of learning, and of much of what a philosopher of later time has designated "sweetness and light."

In "the spacious times of great Elizabeth," Leicester was certainly one who enlarged the interests of the people, and raised high the national ideals. He laboured also to convince Elizabeth of the true power and independence that were hers. He believed that everything that assisted the development of the mind of man contributed to national and to individual greatness. Of the value of moral character, he had not a proper sense. His services to the Universities—especially to Oxford—were real, although undertaken, in part, with the design of establishing his own importance and proclaiming the celebrity of his Queen as the great patroness of learning—the true Minerva of her age.

Leicester further established his influence over Elizabeth by giving himself — after the sentimental and mystical fashion of the day— a name that was a symbol of his devotion to, and of his care for, her. To be symbolical in dress, in gesture, and in speech, was the delight of Elizabethans. The Queen's own tastes in allegory are commemorated by the many fanciful portraits that exist of her. Chief among these, and most interesting, is the picture by Zucchero at Hatfield, which has the motto, "*Non sine Sole Iris*," and in which Elizabeth— the sun of many iridescent reflections—bears a rainbow in her hand. Twisted on her sleeve and in her hair are jewelled serpents — emblems of wisdom. Within her ruff is hung a miniature glove of mail. She had the courage of a warrior when she list. And over her under-dress, flower-embroidered, she wears a cloak studded with human eyes and ears. That this cloak was a marvel of needlework is evident by the painter's reproduction of it ; and it was marvellous in other ways. In this curious — even horrifying garment — Elizabeth presented herself to her subjects with ever-open ears and eyes — all-knowing, all-seeing. The omniscience of her regality was her chief conceit.

And even as the Queen listened for the first faint reverberations of an alarm of the national peace : even as she surveyed her people's best achievements with satisfaction, and discerned

I

their faults with censure, so also were the eyes
of her Favourite ever watching for and over
her. Leicester called himself the "eyes" of
Elizabeth. He was the "look-out" man of the
ship of State, the Queen's clear-visioned deputy,
the guardian with and for her of the national
welfare and the national quiet.

"Your great favour thus oft and so far to
send to know how your poor 'eyes' doth"—
Leicester drew the symbol, he did not write
the words—"is greatly beyond the reach of his
thanks that already for 1,000 benefits stands
your bondman," are lines of a letter to Elizabeth
written most probably in 1571. He gave also
in this letter an assurance that he who watched
over the Queen's interests had also a regard
for the woman who was the Queen. After
giving an account of an ailment from which
he suffered, and for which he had found relief
in "the commodity of a bath," he told her:
"Meantime it shall be most comfort to your
poor 'eyes' to hear that you continue your
health." And further: "Nothing is better for
your health than exercise, and no one thing
has been a greater hindrance thereto, than your
overlong abode in that corrupt air about the
city."

Again, in 1575, shortly after the conclusion
of the successful Kenilworth revels, Leicester
wrote two letters in which concern for the

"perfect health" it was his "continual prayer" for Elizabeth to enjoy, and anxiety for his own return to "the wonted place of comfort, our heaven in earth," to be again witness of the "good and blessed state" of "the joy and life of us all," were explicitly stated, while his loyal devotion was implicitly declared by repeated introduction of his symbol õ õ (eyes). Ingenuity in device was a sure passport to Elizabeth's favour. Leicester's ingenuity, as also his affection, are exemplified in the following phrases, occurring in two letters:

"I most humbly thank my mõõst gracious lady for her great comfort showed toward her absent õ õ, by the testimony of her own sweet hand, which never yieldeth less joy than greatest contentation both to body and mind. And as it is not possible hereby to express the least part of those comforts it brings, so do I now haste me to be a further partaker of those greater joys (the only upholder of life and all), which is your blessed presence. . . . Your Majesty's most faithful and most bounden õ õ,
"R. LEYCESTER."

And the device of eyes is further, and most curiously, inserted in the capital letter of the word Queen, thus: "My gracious ." The second letter terminates "Your Majesty's mõõst humble and most bond,
"R. LEYCESTER."

Few things in a man are so gratifying to the woman he pays homage to, than his having eyes to see the shifts and turns of her health, and the sympathy or the art to suggest to her the remedies she most delights in. The common taste in Leicester and in Elizabeth for exercise, their joy in horsemanship, their eagerness for the chase, rendered them good company for one another. Others of her nobles and gallants were sportsmen besides her Master of the Horse, but not all of them, if any, were concerned to give her a comrade's share in their pastimes.

Whether Leicester rode beside the Queen, as they journeyed from country-house to country-house, "hunting by the way," or whether she looked on as he held the lists against all comers, tilted in the jousts, or played at tennis, it was always Leicester's way to associate her, the woman, with himself, the man, in the sports both loved.

The incident of Leicester carelessly snatching the Queen's kerchief to mop his brow when he was "sweaty" in the tennis court, and the other event of Elizabeth, disguised as her maid's maid, stealing past her guard to behold Lord Robert "shooting a match in the Park" with Lord Windsor, though counted by "old" nobles as an action of *lèse - Majesté* on the part of Leicester, and a movement of indecorum on the part of Elizabeth, are evidences truly that the Favourite could pay Her Majesty the dear compliment of treating her as a sportswoman, and forgetting she was a Queen.

CHAPTER VIII

IT was an indication of the national temper that at Cambridge an eulogy on virginity had been included in the exercises that celebrated Elizabeth's visit; and at Oxford one of the subjects of disputation had been the necessity of a Sovereign declaring his or her successor. A debate was held on the relative advantages of hereditary and elective monarchy. The Queen, by her comments, appeared to favour the elective principle. Elizabeth always believed her unequivocal title to the throne to lie in the suffrages of her people. This belief Leicester studied to conserve in her. On this principle, his own title to kingship, and in particular his right to the office of King Consort, was as good as anybody's.

It had ever been a notion of the Dudleys that the King should be the "canning," the able man. But Leicester's abilities were not quite great enough, or of the right order, to prevail over other qualities in him that inevitably raised prejudices in the popular mind.

It was now six years since his poor Amy's

terrible fall, yet Cecil noted in a Minute-paper of this year, 1566, that her death " had infamed " the Favourite. And in 1566, the nation—as shown by the Oxford orations, by an infinity of Privy Council notes, and by a strongly worded petition of Parliament—was again pressing to know its heir. Of all that had previously offered, the Archduke Charles, and my Lord of Leicester, were the only two suitors now to be counted on.

The arguments for and against these two, were drawn up by the exact and contemplative Cecil in some tables that are sufficiently curious, and sufficiently informing for one of them to be copied here.

It is seen that the chief objections Cecil had to Leicester, are precisely the qualifications that, in pursuance of their joint policy, the Queen and and her Favourite reckoned as points in his favour. To mate with any Prince of Europe would have joined her indissolubly either to Catholic or to Protestant interests, and while giving her a friend, would have raised up for her some formidable enemies. The peace of England could not have been preserved, as it was preserved for many years, by Elizabeth's superb craft, and by Leicester's devotion to her methods, had Elizabeth yielded to the supplications of her councillors, and, either in 1566, or at any earlier or later period, given herself

CONVENIENT PERSON.	CAROLUS.	EARL OF LEICESTER.
In birth . .	Nephew and brother of an Emperor	Born son of a Knight, his grandfather but a squire
In degree . .	An Archduke born	An Earl made
In age . .	Of —— and never married	Meet
In beauty and constitution .	To be judged of	Meet
In wealth . .	By report 3,000 ducats by the year	All of the Queen and in debt
In friendship .	The Emperor, the King of Spain, the Dukes of Saxony, Bavaria, Cleves, Florence, Ferrara, and Mantua	None but such as shall have of the Queen
In education .	Amongst Princes always	In England
In knowledge .	All qualities belonging to a Prince, languages, wars, hunting, and riding	Meet for a courtier
In likelihood to bear children .	His father Ferdinando hath therein been blessed with multitude of children. His brother Maximilian hath plenty. His sisters of Bavaria, Cleves, Mantua, and Poland have already many children	'Nuptiæ steriles.' No brother had children and yet their wives have —— Duchess of Norfolk. Himself married and no children
In likelihood to love his wife .	His father Ferdinando *et supra*	Nuptiæ carnales a lætitia incipiunt et in *luctu terminantin*
In reputation .	Honoured of all men	Hated by many. His wife's death

in marriage to a member of a reigning House of Europe.

In 1566, negotiations for her marriage with the young King of France had been begun. The Queen - Mother, Catherine de Medici, sent ambassadors with a present of a state coach and two camels to Elizabeth, and the Order of St Michael for two nobles of her appointment. Elizabeth designated the Earl of Leicester, who, on grounds that are still obscure, asked the Queen to allow him to refuse the decoration. She insisted on his acceptance of it, and had to be very emphatic also in commands to the Duke of Norfolk to be a recipient with Leicester of the French Order. Norfolk had the "old" nobles' grudge against the "new." But the Queen was determined that the St Michael should go to Leicester as to one of the two chief nobles of her Court, and not as to her one favourite. When the proposals of the French King were withdrawn, Leicester obtained from the ambassadors a recommendation of his own pretensions for Elizabeth's hand. These pretensions were not now serious, but the recommendations of foreign powers put Leicester into a more assured position for future negotiations for his Sovereign, both at home and abroad.

While the *pourparlers* with the French went on, Elizabeth had continued to press Leicester on Mary Stuart. But, in 1565, Mary married

Queen Mary and Lord Darnley.

Darnley, and, in the early days of 1566, it was known that her child was to be born.

In this situation, those opposed to a Stuart rule, and to a Stuart claimancy, felt more strongly than ever that the only hope for England lay in the speedy marriage of the English Queen to a foreign Prince. By their words and actions, Leicester and Elizabeth appeared to share the feeling of the Council, the Parliament, and the Nation. But it was policy, not affection, that led the Queen and her Favourite — they two against the world — to decide that there should be no marriage with the Archduke or with another.

Leicester was now chief minister of state. His diligence in affairs became marked. He kept his distance, and sought applause for his disinterestedness. There were special reasons at the moment for the display of self-sacrifice in the patriotic cause. The question of his connivance at the death of his wife was again disturbing men's minds.

John Appleyard, who had come to be in greatly reduced circumstances, made an attempt to extort blackmail from Leicester by the assertion that the jury of the inquest on the Lady Amy's death had been suborned. Being examined by the Council, he made a written admission of his "mistake," and an acknowledgment that in the copy of the verdict supplied to him by the Council, he not only found "such proofs, testified under the oaths of fifteen persons, how his late sister by misfortune happened of death, but also such manifest and plain demonstration thereof as hath fully and clearly satisfied him."

Even if the ghost of Leicester's past had not walked inopportunely, it is doubtful whether the old make-believe of an intention to wed Leicester would have been assumed by Elizabeth. She wanted to prove to Mary, to Darnley, and to their following that she had friends—and Catholic friends—to her power. She desired to persuade her people that a greater Prince than he to be born in Edinburgh, would soon spring to being, on English soil.

Leicester took his part aptly in the game Elizabeth played. He joined with her in deceiving her nobles and statesmen, as to her willingness to yield to their representations and requests, and in hoodwinking the Spaniards as to her readiness to further the papist cause, by allowing the Archduke to hear Mass when he came to England as her husband.

The envoy, De Silva, who, on his first coming to England, had been so ingenuous, and had taken Elizabeth and Leicester to be as guileless as himself, was not now convinced of the Favourite's disinterestedness. Like many originally simple-minded people, De Silva had been brought to the point of confusing imagination with discernment. A few months earlier, he had evolved the idea that Elizabeth and Leicester had been for some time married. He said Lady Northampton, who was no partisan of Leicester, bore herself towards him in such a way—presumably with such respect —that it could only be conceived that his relations with the Queen were not so irregular as had been supposed. "It is nothing to Princes to hear evil without giving cause of it," was his compassionate comment. And, when the negotiations for the Austrian marriage were reopened, De Silva had to be specially assured by personages "in the know," that Elizabeth was free to contract herself. Yet, with inconsistency, the Spaniard noted that, in opposition to Leicester, Lady Northampton encouraged Elizabeth to marry the Archduke. By good chance, rather than by good judgment, the divining one hit on the fact that Leicester's furtherance of the Archduke's cause, as well as a coolness that was observed about this time between him and the Queen, were all "artfulness," and a blind to deeper purposes.

It was on the 4th of February 1566 that the little play began. De Silva went to Greenwich Court in reference to the Austrian marriage under discussion, and found the Queen and Lord Leicester "walking in the lower gallery of the garden." Leicester drew aside to allow the Ambassador's approach, and Elizabeth praised her Favourite to De Silva, and told him that, at the very moment of his appearance, Leicester had been "persuading her to marry for the sake of the country and herself, and even on his account, as every one thought he was the cause of her remaining single, which made him unpopular with all her subjects."

To convince the world and Philip's Ambassador that he was not influencing the Queen against a marriage of state, Leicester left the Court a few days later; "the rumour being he was going to his own home." But he went no further than Lord Pembroke's house, Baynard's Castle; and the Queen, in disguise, but accompanied by the Lord High Admiral Clinton and Lady Clinton—it must have been a very transparent disguise, resembling perhaps the travelling titles of modern royalties — followed him next day, and dined with him and the others at Lord Pembroke's house. "After dinner," De Silva noted with exactness, "the Queen returned to Greenwich, Lord Pembroke went to his estates, and Lord Leicester retired to his house."

In this absence of the Favourite a despatch from Elizabeth's commissioner (for her marriage) at Vienna, was put before the Queen for signature. In it she had to promise " if the Arch-duke will come to England to marry him, unless there be some apparent impediment."

Sir Nicholas Throckmorton, the Minister who at the beginning of the reign had been loudly denunciatory of the relations of Elizabeth and Lord Robert, had now become an attached follower and good friend of Leicester. It was he who sent to the absent Minister full account of the contents of the despatches intended for the Archduke. His letter concluded with the words: " I did understand Her Majesty had deferred the signing . . . until your Lordship's coming." How fertile was the genius of Elizabeth of causes for putting matters off! Cecil was another who wrote to Leicester of the state of affairs. His Lordship replied:

" I heartily thank you, Mr Secretary, for your gentle and friendly letter, wherein I perceive how far Her Majesty hath resolved touching the matter she dealt in on my coming away. I pray God Her Highness may so proceed therein as may bring but contentation to her-self, and comfort to all that be hers. Surely there can be nothing that shall so well settle her in good estate as that way—I mean her marriage, whensoever it shall please God to put her in mind to like and to conclude. I know Her Majesty hath heard enough thereof, and I wish to God she did hear that more that here abroad is wished and prayed for. Good-will it doth move in many, and truly it may easily appear necessity doth require of all. We hear ourselves much also when we be there, but methinks it is good sometimes that some that be there should be abroad, for that is sooner believed that is seen than heard; and in hope, Mr Secretary, that Her Majesty will earnestly intend that which she hath of long time not yet minded, and delay no longer her time, which cannot be won again for any gift, I will leave that with trust of happiest success, for that God hath left it the only means to redeem us in this world."

In this letter, written by Leicester to the man who had more power than any to discredit his influence with the Queen, and who was, at the moment, opposing Elizabeth's inclination for him, there were many insincerities. But it was genuine, as an expression of Leicester's conviction, that what he had heard "abroad" (that was without the Court circle in ordinary paths of English life) made it necessary for him, for the present, to follow the policy of promoting Elizabeth's marriage with the Archduke. The general political situation was inspiration of the view that "God had left" the marriage "the only means to redeem us in this world." To marry the English Queen to the cousin of Spanish Philip and son of the Austrian Emperor, was the one sure way of escape from the dangers of the heirship to England of Mary and Darnley. But in view of the events that went before, and that followed after, one may accept the opinion of De Silva that in all they said and did in this matter, Elizabeth and Leicester were feigning.

The need for feigning was destroyed by a sudden event. On the 9th of March, not long after Leicester's return to Court, Rizzio, the much-favoured Secretary of Mary, Queen of Scots, was slain in her cabinet at the instance of her husband, Darnley. The discredit cast by the foul deed on the Stuart party, made for the security of Elizabeth on her throne. Mary and her Consort had to bend their wits to keep their Scottish crowns. No force was left in them to scheme for English ones.

But before news of the northern tragedy reached Greenwich a southern comedy had begun, which the all too penetrating De Silva took to be played entirely in set scene and given phrase. We who may follow the text of the playlet, with a commentary of surrounding and subsequent facts not known to De Silva, find in the speeches and actions of the characters more spontaneity than was discovered by the Spaniard to whom the "dissembling English way" was often befogging.

One of the causes for Leicester espousing the cause of the Archduke — so De Silva asserted — had been that he had proved to himself, by a trick, that Elizabeth had no longer any affection for him. He had been advised to the course, so De Silva asserted, by Throckmorton, "who rules Leicester." The plan was for Leicester first to pretend to fall in love with one of the Queen's ladies, and then to ask leave to go to his country-house, as other nobles did. In the first experiment, Leicester chose Lettice (Knollys) Viscountess Hereford, described by the Spaniard as "one of the best-looking ladies of the Court, and daughter of a first cousin of the Queen, with whom she is a great favourite." It is well to remember how and when one first hears of Lettice in connection with Leicester. But even as "the lover of Queen Elizabeth" made profession of a new attachment, Elizabeth herself —we do not know if hers were the provocative or the retaliatory act—threw looks of favour on a certain Heneage, "who served in her chamber."

This development was not part of the plan of Leicester and Throckmorton, and the Favourite forgot dignity, and entered into a "dispute."

In dudgeon, at the preferment of Heneage, Leicester asked leave to go to his house. The Queen turned on him furiously, upbraided him for his quarrel with Heneage, and with his attentions to the Viscountess. It was Heneage who left the Court. Leicester retired only as far as his own apartments, where he sulked for three or four days. Then the Queen sent for him. Cecil and Sussex intervened to smooth over the affair; both Elizabeth and Leicester shed tears, and he returned to his former favour. One does not know why the enemies of the Favourite interceded for him. Probably there was no getting the Queen to do any business with Leicester absent from the Council Board. The first act of Leicester on his restoration, was to bring Heneage back "to avoid gossip," and Cecil told De Silva: "Leicester held his ground as usual. The Queen made a show of it for her own purposes." King Philip, on hearing the whole relation, passed the judgment that it was evident the Queen was in love with Leicester, and it was no good to press any other suitor on her.

Presuming that the events occurred exactly as related by De Silva, which is dubious, what were the "purposes" of the Queen in playing off Heneage against Leicester, and then in soundly rating Leicester for paying attention to the Viscountess? Did she seek only to teach the lesson that her royal amusements must never be interfered with, and that her favours could never be distributed for her? Or was the purpose deeper, and did Leicester

K

aid it with the subtlety that was his? In any case, the King of Spain had been convinced that the affections of Elizabeth were fixed, and that the Queen of England, secure in an undivided Council, was strong in her own dominions. And it is certain that at this time the French were urging upon Elizabeth a marriage with Leicester, and Leicester was informing Cecil that the Queen would never marry any one but himself.

It is a greater tribute to the genius for dissimulation and misrepresentation in the two, that in only a few weeks' time the arrangements for the Austrian marriage were once more being seriously considered at Vienna and at Madrid, and that, as the new year (1566) broke, it was believed that Leicester was in disgrace at Court. How deep was this "disgrace," it is for those who follow the relations of the Queen and Favourite from beginning to end to judge. Certainly Heneage was presuming on Elizabeth's continued kindness, and on Leicester's dislike of scenes.

It was Twelfth Night, and the festive lords and ladies were gathered round the Queen, playing forfeits. It was the turn of Heneage to cry a penance for my Lord of Leicester, and he put into the mouth of the Favourite, to ask the Queen, this question: "Which is the stronger, an evil opinion instilled by an informer, or jealousy?" Leicester "played the game," and without comment put the question haughtily. The Queen replied, probably with intention, that both were powerful, but, in her opinion, jealousy had the greater force.

Next day Leicester was very angry with the upstart in Elizabeth's grace, but the affair cooled again, and Leicester remained the trusted adviser of Her Majesty, whom the impertinences of her parlour pets could not permanently disturb. Yet one must believe that his anger on the occasion was real. It was Leicester's first encounter with a rival in the fondness of Elizabeth. He was to learn by experience how, himself, to attract those bright particles to whom the iridescence of the Queen's gay fancy imparted a changeable lustre and a variable influence.

Another "affair" followed speedily on that with Heneage. When Leicester returned to the Court after that ostentatious absence of his in February, Lord Ormonde — "an Irishman, of good position, thirty years old, and a great friend of Heneage"—was a new favourite. And when, in March, Leicester went away again, it was supposed that he left out of pique, and that he thought a few more days of absence would bring the Queen to her senses. But it was known that he went to visit his sister, Lady Huntingdon, who was ill; and we have the evidence of extant letters to show that he and the Queen corresponded amiably while he was absent, and that business about exchange of lands kept him employed at Kenilworth. He was also at Oxford labouring for some of those reforms he was to see carried out there on the occasion of his visit with the Queen to the University in the ensuing summer.

Nevertheless, Elizabeth had some grounds of offence against him, and his plans did work to "bring her to her senses." Shortly after his departure the Queen said to Lord Hunsdon, in the hearing of her Court: "My lord, it hath been often said that you should be Master of the Horse, but it is now like to prove true." Yet before Leicester came back in April it was believed that the letter the Queen sent, and her messages delivered by a Gentleman of the Chamber, contained entreaties for his return, and that when he wrote at last, begging for fifteen days more grace, she refused them, and ordered him back at once.

But De Silva noted that on Leicester's return Lord Ormonde was still in favour, and on July 1st, nearly three months later, he painted vividly a scene at a "supper, masquerade, and ball" given by the Earl of Sussex to celebrate the marriage of his sister. At this feast, Elizabeth, by way of showing herself still "in" with the Austrian marriage, made much of De

Silva, but she "greatly praised" to him the "talent and good parts of Lord Ormonde" while she displayed affection for Leicester. "She is a great chatterer, and the people, even the aristocracy, are offended at her manner of going on, but everything is put up with," was the Spaniard's comment on her behaviour at Lord Sussex's party.

Yet De Silva knew that "everything" was not "put up with." In May it had been known to him, as to others, that the Archbishop of York [Thomas Young], a friend of Leicester, had admonished the Queen in regard to her conduct, and had told her that people were speaking ill of her favour to Lord Ormonde. The Queen had turned on the prelate in one of those royal rages, for which she is famous, and with "great roughness and hard words," had "threatened to prosecute him." The matter ended "at the instance" of Leicester. And after the Queen's impartial display of endearments to both Ormonde and Leicester at the Sussex marriage-feast, De Silva noted: "Leicester and Ormonde are friends, though Leicester does not want a rival, and Ormonde aspires to be one." And again: "The Queen greatly favours Leicester's party, but all her near relatives, whom she esteems, are on the other side."

These relations would be Lord Hunsdon,

the Duke of Norfolk, and Lady Hereford—
all cousins, of the Boleyn blood, of Queen
Elizabeth. The "other side" was the side
of Cecil, Sussex, and Arundel. De Silva's
discernment was not altogether at fault when
he commented on his own statement: "It
must be all a trick to retain them both."

And a "trick" of Leicester being now
and then in disgrace was also played. In
August the Queen was captious about a projected visit to Kenilworth, her first visit to
this castle which had been in the possession
of Leicester since 1563, when also the manor,
lordship, and castle of Denbigh, and lands in
Lancashire, Surrey, Rutland, Carmarthen, York,
Cardigan, and Brecknock were conferred on
him. Since then some twenty other estates
had come into his hands, and, in 1565, he
had had granted to him a licence to retain
one hundred persons, and was made Chancellor
of the County Palatine of Chester.

One of Elizabeth's excuses for not going to
Kenilworth, after she had planned to do so,
was that she did not wish to throw upon
Leicester the expense of her visit. It was
unusual for the Queen to be thoughtful in
this way, but Leicester only thanked her
for her consideration. His gratitude had the
effect that he intended. Her Majesty set out
for Kenilworth towards the end of August,

proceeding thence on her already recorded progress to Oxford. Yet we find Cecil, in this month, writing to France that Leicester was not a person of so much consequence as formerly.

The cloud that obscured the consequence of Leicester was a passing one. He was the elect of Elizabeth for his lifetime; only in this year of chop and change in their relationship, something happened to start both—though with ever such a fine dividing line between them—on separate courses. The individual in each had received a certain impulse of development by which the other was untouched.

The evidences are that during Leicester's short absence from the Court in February, he had, by his hearing and seeing of things not to be heard or perceived in the palace of the Queen, come to a decision as to the policy England, as distinct from Elizabeth, needed. His later and longer absence in March and April did not lead to that decision's undoing. Leicester had been "abroad"; he had escaped from the atmosphere of intrigue, pretence, and dissimulation, which had become the breath of Elizabeth's life. His eyes had been turned from continual watching of the checks and counter - checks of the European chess - board; and he had been shown that there were "powers that be" in popular wills and consciences, as well as in the authorities of sovereigns.

On the other hand, Elizabeth had learned in his absence that he was not the only lord in England who could be amusing. There were others, striplings and bearded men, who had attractions and parts that were a joy to contemplate, and a delight to see exercised for her entertainment and her honour. A lull in the anxious businesses of her reign enabled her to take her pleasure for a time; and she desired to put off declaring an heir, and to sport and to divert herself without regard to that subject — matrimony — which was the death's head at all her feasts.

But Leicester returned to Court full of the keen, popular desire for the naming of a successor. The appointment of an heir was a political necessity upon which all parties were agreed. There was no need to defer the appointment for Elizabeth's select purpose of balancing parties. The hour was come when the claim of Mary could be set aside with little offence to any. The visit to his sister may be an indication that Leicester had some hope of the naming of Lord Huntingdon. But the Lady Catherine Grey was still alive, and she had sons. In any case, Leicester was one of the group of noble lords who, in November, strongly supported the petition from Parliament praying to know the crown's heir.

Elizabeth was very angry with the courtiers of hers—nobles all—who joined in this attempt to force her hand. And she stood up to them in a manner that was her own. The Duke of Norfolk, she called to his face, a traitor and a conspirator. And when the Earl of Pembroke told her it was not right to treat Norfolk badly, since he and the others were considering the good of the country, and giving her advice which, if she did not adopt, it was their duty to offer; she told him shortly he talked like a swaggering soldier. To Leicester she said she had thought that if all the world abandoned her, he would not have done so. He vowed he would die at her feet. "That has nothing to do with the matter," she snapped. Then she turned on Lord Northampton. It was his present countess who had attempted covertly to separate Elizabeth and Leicester, and to gain Her Majesty for the Archduke. But he had had another countess who had been put away with legal formulas to make room for the one Elizabeth favoured.

Now the ingenuities of Northampton made him fair quarry. His advices were contemptuously pooh-poohed. He had better bring up the arguments that had been used for his marrying again, when he had a wife living, and not mince words with his Queen. Her tirades ended with a declaration that she would order them all under arrest. But she did not carry out her threat. They were, however, commanded not to appear before her again until they received permission, and in the loss of so many of her advisers, she went to De Silva for sympathy. Him she told that all these lords were against her, and asked him what he thought of the ingratitude of Leicester, after she had shown him so much kindness and favour that her honour had suffered. Cecil, she said, was her only friend. One does not know by what wiles Cecil got himself excluded from the general disgrace. Perhaps because he pressed on her her marriage rather than her appointment of a successor.

In December, though the Queen was still complaining of Leicester's part in the affair, she was saying she thought he had acted for the best, and was deceived. She was certain he would sacrifice his life for hers, and, if one of them had to die, he would willingly be the one. So his somewhat irrelevant protest about dying at her feet had not been unavailing with the woman he knew so well.

In the New Year — 1567 — Leicester was known to be returning to the Queen's good graces.

CHAPTER IX

IT has been seen that the time had come for the aims of the Queen and her Favourite to diverge, and for their characters to develop along lines that, from being at first only not quite parallel, became more and more removed. Yet for twenty - two years longer, we may trace Leicester's career as councillor, and mark him—even in his unique and unapproachable rank of Favourite—acting with Cecil as first minister of the realm; busy with affairs, civil, military, and ecclesiastical; maintaining his self-appointed office of Her Majesty's "Eyes"; plying his craft as a physician of the national ills; identifying himself with causes; and working for reforms. From time to time, he followed ideas and projects, and men called him a traitor; he defined, while he widened the path of religious reformation, and it was thought that all he did was of hypocrisy; he gave of his strength and his wealth unsparingly to his country and to his Sovereign and he was styled a minion and a *debauchee*. It is not contended that Leicester's methods were superior to the methods of his period and

155

class. All the leading Ministers of Elizabeth's government, received bribes from foreign rulers, though, as has been said by a present - day examiner of records, for many of the "presents" given, small value was received. Traffic in places under Government, and in offices in the Church, was more or less openly carried on by nearly all statesmen, and the fashion of spoliating ecclesiastics for the benefit of the laity—above all of the aristocratic laity—was a "good old custom," started by "bluff King Hal," that was not all iniquitous, though one does not wish to see it revived. It is true that Leicester received bribes from the Spanish and the French kings, and that commissions on various kinds of deals—financial, political, religious, literary, and educational — were charged by him for licences, patents, charters, orders in Council, secretaryships, guardianships, and what not. But then commissions of the kind were part of the very system of Society in his day, and Leicester was not the only Minister who distributed his interests "on agency lines."

But Leicester is said to have exceeded them all in the rewards he took for promoting to bishoprics. In a "Brief View of the State of the Church," Sir John Harington tells the "pretty tale" of a Bishop of Winchester of his day, being in "pleasant talk" with the Archbishop of Canterbury. Winchester compared his revenue with that of Canterbury: "Your Grace's will show better in the rack, but mine will be found more in the manger," said he. A courtier, who was present, replied, "It might be so *in diebus illis.*" He added, "The rack stands so high in sight, that it is fit to keep it full, but that may be since that time some have with a *provideatur* swept some provender out of the manger." Sir John Harington commented: "And because this metaphor comes from the stable, I suspect it was meant by the Master of the Horse."

Leicester was certainly not less mercenary or less business - like than others, who were nobles of Elizabeth's Court, and Councillors of Elizabeth's Board. On the contrary, he was more grasping and more speculative than most. It was a ceaseless endeavour of his to put money in his purse. Whether he ever made the least attempt to prevent it running out again, is a doubtful matter. He did not share his Queen's fault of niggardliness. He was always in debt, because he always spent freely. He entertained royally, not always because he wanted to do so, but because the duties of his office and his Queen's gracious condescension in visiting him, and in allow-ing him to receive England's visitors on her behalf, obliged him to be royal in hospitality. It was impossible for him to be satisfied with such incomes as flowed towards him. He had to tap currents of supplies. He was forced to devise and to manipulate various sources of wealth. That is to say, he had to do these things in a pushing world, and with a close employer, if he desired to maintain his greatness, together with the greatness of the tasks he undertook and of the aims he followed. That he did so desire, was not altogether to the disadvantage of the England of Elizabeth, neither was it to the disadvantage of the England of to-day.

In 1567 there was talk of the Earl of Sussex going to Vienna to take the Garter to the Emperor, and to arrange preliminaries of a marriage between Elizabeth and the Archduke Charles — that marriage that was never to get beyond "preliminaries"! De Silva, in his correspondence with Spain, noted that Leicester's party was persuading against the mission. The talk and the persuasions went on for six months before Lord Sussex finally departed. With him — it was said by the direction of Leicester, who wished to have a friend on the spot to put spokes into the wheel of negotiation—went Lord North.

Leicester, in whom eye-opening experiences of life beyond Court circles, had impressed a

Thomas Radclyffe, Earl of Sussex.

deep sense of the value of Protestantism as a separate religious system, was now at cross-swords with Cecil, Sussex, and Norfolk, who advocated the Austrian alliance. Between Sussex and Leicester there had never been any love lost. Sussex had sounded the top-note of his patriotism when he had advocated Leicester's marriage with Elizabeth in 1561.

Much water had flowed beneath London Bridge in the six years since then. Sussex had been in Ireland for Her Majesty. There, his weakness and his want of faith had assisted disastrous policies. These, upon his return, were criticised by Leicester. A quarrel took place at the Council Board. Sussex approached Leicester, and complained that some one had told the Queen that he had helped the Irish against the Queen's own people. By his indeterminate action this was exactly what he had done, but, of course, not of intention, and Sussex flung out at Leicester that "whoever said so lied," and he could prove it. Leicester made no reply in the Queen's presence. But Her Majesty rapped out a sharp rebuke of the uncourtly manners of my Lord of Sussex. After the Council, Leicester's friends gathered round him, telling him he ought to take further notice of the matter.

The next day the Favourite asked Sussex for

an explanation of his conduct. Sussex was not of those who stand up to their opposers with persistence, and he had been enjoined by the Queen to make friends with Leicester, so he replied that his words had been intended only for the persons who had accused him. The matter ended, and both noblemen made show of being on their former terms, but thenceforward, for some time, the followers of the two took care to go armed, and to keep close in groups for their own and their master's protection. The opinion Sussex ever held of Leicester may be known from the circumstances that, in 1565, the "old" noble said of the "new" that he had only two ancestors, a father and a grandfather, and both of them were traitors; and that in 1583, when Sussex lay upon his death-bed, his words of warning to the gentlemen of his party gathered round him were: "Beware of that gipsy, for he shall be too hard for any of you!"

Certainly Leicester was too hard for Sussex —as for Cecil, Norfolk, and their adherents among peers and commons—in the early months of 1567. And the fates aided Leicester in his hardness.

In the first days of January, the embassy to Vienna had been the most pressing State necessity. Elizabeth herself told the nation she was resolved to marry, and by the line she took in religious matters, she indicated the direction in which her hand was to be given. The Archduke was supposed to be a Liberal Catholic. There were yet Protestants in England and elsewhere—Cecil among them— who believed, even at the epoch of the Great Schism, that a Liberal Catholicism was possible.

Is Leicester to be judged the lesser patriot, and the more hypocritical religionist, because he opposed ultramontanism in all its manifestations, and because, rather than promote a marriage for Elizabeth with a foreign Prince which would commit her to a perpetual peace with the oppressor of the Netherlands, and the enemy of all free institutions, he assiduously kept her in mind of the disadvantages of a foreign union, and of the advantages—if a union had to be—of an English one?

The first aid to the projects of Leicester was the murder of Darnley. That cold-blooded crime of a man insanely brutal, and of a woman outraged, desperate, and lovesick, disturbed the policies of all Europe, blasted the life and prospect of a young Queen, rich in beauty, talent, intelligence, and charm, and gave pause to the activities on behalf of Elizabeth's marriage. The events that followed in swift succession — Mary's hushing up of enquiries; her marriage with Bothwell; the battle of Carberry Hill; her incarceration in Loch Leven

Castle—destroyed for ever the popularity of the claim of the Scottish Queen upon the English succession, and prevented, for a time, even the most Catholic and the most casuistical from deeming her an acceptable heiress-presumptive.

Yet no more bewildering blow was ever struck at Elizabeth than was inflicted by the crime of her sister - sovereign. Like Mary, Elizabeth had been bred in the belief that " Kings can do no wrong," and that though Queens may sin against God, their subjects may not judge them. We have the picture of the attitude of Elizabeth when the news of Mary's arrest by her lords first reached London, in two letters of Leicester, one written to the Queen's dictation as the very hand of Her Majesty, the other, the composition of Leicester himself.

These letters were addressed to Throckmorton, who had been sent to the northern capital as a special emissary from the Queen of England on behalf of the Queen of Scots. In the official despatch, Leicester directed Throckmorton "to use all means to let the Queen of Scotland know the Queen's grief for her and how much she takes care for her relief," and "the Queen takes the doings of these lords to heart, as a precedent most perilous for any Prince." In his private communication, Leicester told Throckmorton that his " other

letter was written by the Queen's commandment," but "to be plain" with him, the Queen
was "in great mislike with these lords for this
strange manner of proceeding with their natural
Sovereign." There is no persuading the Queen,
so he averred, "to disguise or use policy, for she
breaks out to all men her affection in this matter,
and says most constantly that she will become an
utter enemy to that nation if that Queen perish."
He confessed the acts of Mary to be loathsome
and foul for any Prince, yet was her punishment
most unnatural. People had plain commandment in the Scriptures to obey and love their
Sovereigns, though they be evil. He wrote
"not to serve his Sovereign but for conscience
sake. Though the Queen [of Scots] has deserved punishment at God's hand, she has
deserved better consideration at some of her
servants' hands."

These words of Leicester were a confession of
his faith, and they formed the text of Throckmorton's official remonstrances with the Scottish
lords. They are evidences to us of how great
was the dismay of Elizabeth at the culmination
of the tragedy in the north. Yet the downfall
of Mary Stuart removed a pressing occasion for
the foreign marriage, and provided Leicester
with justification for laying before his Queen
a list of reasons against a mixed union, such

as many of Elizabeth's faithful peers and commons desired for her.

Leicester's objections were that the marriage of Queen Mary to Philip of Spain had exposed her to much trouble, and "put England in danger of the Spanish yoke; that the manners, inclination, and disposition of foreigners could not easily be discovered, which were yet very necessary to be known in a husband, who by an inseparable tie was to become one with his wife; that it was excessively disagreeable to be continually conversant with strange customs and a strange language; that the children of a foreign bed had generally an odd intermixture in their composition; that by the frequent concourse of foreigners new usages were introduced, and alterations made in a Commonwealth; that for a Princess to marry with a foreigner, was to add strength and increase to her husband's dominions, to subject herself and her people to another's command, and to lay open the secrets of her kingdom to a stranger; that it was natural for every man to love his native country, and a foreign husband could not avoid preferring his own countrymen to the English; that England had no need of foreign aid, but had strength enough to defend itself against any exterior force; that the accession of another kingdom was the new addition of greater cares, expenses, and trouble, and that empires were oft overburdened by their own weight; that it was unjustly urged in disgrace to the Nobility, that the Royal Dignity was impaired by a marriage at home, since even the Majesty of Kings, which was founded on virtue, was originally derived from Nobility and Noblemen were in a manner the roots of the royal stock; and hence the Kings of England, in their letters to Dukes, Marquesses, Earls, and Viscounts, have ever given them the titles of Cousins." Leicester further reminded Elizabeth of kingly ancestors of hers—including her own father—who had thought it no derogation of their honour to raise to the throne women of less than royal rank. Even a "new" lord like Leicester, was peer to a lady of the status of Anne Boleyn!

But not alone these reasons, which seem to indicate that the list was prepared by Leicester from purely self-interested motives, were of the kind to outweigh with Elizabeth the reasons of supposed state-interest which the approvers of the mixed marriage advanced. The suggestions of the unpleasantness of not knowing the "manners, inclination, and disposition" of one who "by an inseparable tie was to become one flesh with his wife," and that "for a Princess to marry with a foreigner" was to "subject herself and her people to another's command," were just of the intimate kind that appeals to a woman. The reminder that

" the accession of another kingdom was the new addition of greater cares, expenses, and trouble" was one bound to prevail with a housewife so diligent in cutting down expenses as Elizabeth. Yet the reminder was a very just one. The Archduke was without means, and had begun the negotiations by making excessive demands in the way of personal allowances. However selfish the ultimate design of Leicester in drawing up his reasons, it must be admitted that they had force. One cannot be sure that children born to Elizabeth and the Archduke would have had any odder "intermixture in their compositions" than the children of Elizabeth and Leicester might have had. But poetic licence may be allowed to one so thoroughly convinced, when other counsellors were in a panic, that "England had no need of foreign aid, but had strength enough to defend itself against any exterior force."

For "England," Leicester might have written "Elizabeth." He saw strengths in his Queen where other men saw only weaknesses. He alone knew all the secret forces of Elizabeth's many turns and shifts; of her practices and her affabilities; of her supposed humours; and of her assumed rages and whims. And he believed, as Elizabeth believed, that, by a continuance of policy, England could be kept strong and rendered independent of foreign supports. In the opinion of Cecil, Norfolk, Sussex, and many others, policy had had its day. Danger loomed, and only a marriage—any marriage, but preferably a royal marriage—could bestow "contentment on the English people, by its hope of issue"; give "avoidance of bloodshed in a disputed succession"; secure the advantage to the Queen of "the companionship of a virtuous prince"; and lead to a universal peace.

So high were the hopes of those who should have known that the grounds for their hopes were small, that they counted on the Prince's probable conversion, and the good effect throughout Europe that such a change of faith would produce. However, the Archduke was brought to the point of agreeing to abandon in England the open hearing of the Mass, and to have it said privately in any place the Queen might appoint. He further expressed his willingness to accompany Elizabeth to services of the Established Church. These concessions had been made with the consent of the King of Spain. It was given neither to Sussex nor to Cecil, at this stage, to perceive the slow formation of the monstrous Catholic league. And when the horrible massacre of St Bartholomew's Day took place, Leicester was as much aghast at the ruthlessness of the crime as were any of his colleagues. But he does seem to have been the first of the Ministers to perceive the working of a vicious spirit in the Catholicism of the day, and was certainly in the van of those who made it the glory of England to champion single-handed the oppressed Protestants of Holland. Leicester's vision of the future for England was a vision of peace, a peace maintained by "practices," but a peace in which all things of the soul—religion, poetry, learning, and free institutions—should flourish and grow great.

The vision of Sussex communicated to Cecil, while the seer was still in Vienna, was a vision of war and ruin. Without the marriage of Elizabeth with Archduke Charles, he foresaw "discontent, disunion, bloodshed of her people —perhaps in her own time for this cause—and the ruin of the realm in the end; which bloody time threateneth little respect of religion, but much malice and revenge for private ambition on all sides; *which many by wilful blindness for other respects will not see, and yet put on spectacles to search a scruple under colour of religion.*"

It is true that Leicester was blind to the lurid picture of the England of the near future, which Sussex painted in the colours of his fancy. Yet, whether the Favourite

required very powerful spectacles to discover
a scruple against the coming of the Austrian
bridegroom, is a question that, at this time,
hardly needs answering. There were objections of fact, of convenience, and of principle
to the marriage. That there might also be
in it some advantages of a nearer and more
practical kind than those Leicester looked for,
is also true. Some idea of the turmoil he
created by his determined opposition, now that
he believed opposition to be a "safe" policy,
is obtained from the following letter from one
designated "Sir J. S." to the Earl of Derby.

"For the news which I know you are most
anxious to hear of — which is of the Duke
Charles, and of my Lord of Sussex's proceedings
therein—there is and hath been such working
to overthrow that; as the like hath not been
—which is pitiful to hear of. The Council here
at this present are in manner divided touching
the same, and it is made a matter of religion,
and they say they do it for conscience' sake.
But God knoweth what conscience is in them
which go about to hinder it. My Lord of
Leicester, my Lord Steward (Pembroke), my
Lord Marquis (Northampton) and the Vice-
Chamberlain (Heneage) be against his coming
in. . . . My Lord Chamberlain (Howard of
Effingham), my Lord Admiral (Clinton), Mr
Secretary (Cecil) and Mr Controller (Crofts)
do wish his coming in. Whereupon Jewel
made a sermon at Paul's Cross upon Sunday
was sennight, his theme being: 'Cursed be

he that goeth about to build again the walls of Jericho'— meaning thereby the bringing in of any doctrine contrary to this."

Direct opposition of this kind was annoyance enough to those who were for the "coming in" of the Archduke. It was easily believed by sophists, even by sophists of the Protestant party, that the "reasonable" Catholicism of the Austrian Prince was no menace to religious peace. Men of tolerant views and of balanced minds, like Cecil, considered it no hard thing for moderate men of all religious parties to join forces in treading a *via media*. And Elizabeth who was so convinced of the practicability of an infinite variety of opinion co-existing with an absolute uniformity of worship, would, of herself, have found no insuperable religious objections to the "coming in" of the Archduke. It was reserved for Leicester to alarm the Government and to worry the Queen with the fear of a confederation between the Pope, the Emperor, the Kings of Spain and France, and other Catholic Princes which should have for its objective a "settlement of religion," and the bringing back of Elizabeth to submission to the Pope. It was all very well for unimaginative workers like Cecil to disbelieve in such a confederation. His genius was for dealing with things as they were, for interlocutory dialogue with suspects, for bringing criminals to justice, for providing supplies for national expenditure, for saying the apt word in a disputation, and for veiling the true thought in a negotiation. It was natural also for hot alarmists and feeble administrators like Sussex, and for those of pronouncedly Catholic sympathies like Norfolk, to see only the advantages of compromising with the Papists. And it was policy in Philip to pish and pshaw over the suggestion that the monarchs of middle Europe were likely to combine in a persuasion to the Queen of England to abandon her "singularity" in religion and, failing success to their persuasion, in a dispossession of the kingdom of the excommunicate Princess. But such a confederacy was possible, if not probable, and not far distant events were soon to prove to all men that, in the sixteenth century, a Catholic sway was inevitably a sway of tyranny. The "look-out" man of the English Government—he who was the "eyes" of Elizabeth—discerned the quarter from which storms approached more accurately than Ministers less mercurial than he. The rumblings, Cecil, Sussex, and Norfolk took to be signs of interior tempests, Leicester doubted were blasts of an alien invasion.

This divergence of men's minds, and this variance of their apprehensions, explain much of the misunderstanding of Leicester's attitude at this period. Although the Queen's "outward shows of favour had greatly toned down," it was still to be seen that Leicester had the most influence with her of any one. But the character he had earned by his own earlier "practices," and that had been bestowed upon him by the jealousy of men less handsome, less gifted, or less imaginative than himself, was certainly of a kind to lead men to doubt his disinterestedness.

In November (1567) the Duke of Norfolk wrote to Cecil:

"My good-will to the match remains as firm as ever it was, and by the reasonable demand of the Archduke is more increased." And he contended that, "If the matter may come to indifferent hearing, there will be as earnest Protestants that will maintain it, making not religion a cloke for every shower, as the other, perhaps for private practices naming one thing or minding another, will shew reason to overthrow it."

In the fashion of his day, Norfolk became more obscure as he grew more emphatic. But there is no mistaking "the other" who named one thing and minded another. It was Leicester who blocked the match which had Norfolk's good-will. And Leicester had on his side, among others, the Earl Pembroke and Sir Thomas Heneage, "Protestants," if not the most spiritually minded, at least of no mean order of intellect. But Norfolk's quarrel was wholly with Leicester. Later in the same month, he wrote again to Cecil:

"If matters being hot be so soon cooled, I pray God there grow no danger to them that you and I have much care of. I like not the practices that now so fast work. My ears have glowed to hear that I have heard within these two days concerning nuptial devices. First they mind to fight with their malicious tongues, and afterwards I warrant they will not spare weapons if they may."

But Norfolk's last anxiety was groundless. The hands of Leicester and his followers were always guiltless of weapons in the fight they waged for Protestantism. And it was the "nuptial devices" of Norfolk and the Scottish Queen, not of Leicester and the English one, that proved, in the end, a treachery to England. Sussex, too, had another word to say concerning Protestant support of the Austrian suitor.

"If Protestants be but Protestants," he wrote to Cecil from Vienna, "I mistrust not a good resolution. If some Protestants have a second interest which they cloke with religion and place be given to their Council, God defend the Queen's Majesty with His mighty hand, and dispose of us all at His pleasure."

Place was certainly given to the counsel of Leicester, and the mission of Sussex failed, as perhaps it was always meant to fail. The Queen had not abandoned her habit — complained of by Sir Henry Sidney in the earlier negotiations with Austria — of changing her mind, and letting the blame of it fall on others, in particular on the favoured Robert. But that he and his supporters were not without tolerance and judgment in their Protestantism, is proved by Leicester's opposition to the extremer Puritanical methods of Church government to which Archbishop Parker was inclining. To give one instance (which even the Ambassador of "His Most Catholic Majesty" approved), when the Archbishop desired to impose the oath of the supremacy of the Queen over the Church, on the lawyers in the Court of Arches, Lords Pembroke, Leicester, and Ormonde were among the first to render aid in preventing the molestation of those who declined to take the oath. And the moderate, yet definite, character of the Protestantism, which, as a man of culture and of calculation, Leicester had been led to champion, is well shown in an account given by the Spanish Ambassador of a conversation he had with Lord Leicester, as the two rode side by side in the train of the Queen, as she proceeded on a spring day in 1568 to her Palace of Greenwich. By the way, Leicester made a long speech to his companion, to the effect that, in the interests of the King of Spain, and for the welfare of the dominions in Flanders, it was advisable to adopt some lenient and peaceful course with regard to religion and the punishment of those who had misbehaved themselves in the States of Holland. "He pointed out," so De Silva continued, "how strong the new religion was in Germany and the States, and said that even in some parts of Spain things are not quite so assured as is thought; nor in Italy either, especially near Rome. He spoke, he said, as a servant of your Majesty, and he desired your peace and prosperity, although he knew his words would be of little avail, as he was a Protestant."

These words, both the tone and the sense of them, reveal to us a different Leicester from the one, who only a year or two before, had "feigned," "practised," and bargained with the Spaniards. He was now unequivocally in the Protestant interest. And that his being in that interest, his persuading the Queen against her marriage with the Austrian, and his constant devotion to her, had not rendered her unpopular, we have the evidence of a very pretty and a very significant mid-summer scene in "Merrie England." Again it is De Silva who paints the picture, gravely elaborating detail in the usual manner of His Spanish Majesty's envoys.

"The Queen," he wrote on 10th July 1568, "arrived in this city on the 6th in good health, and continued her progress, which, as I have said, will only be in the neighbourhood, as she is careful to keep near at hand when troubles and disturbances exist in adjacent countries. . . . She was received everywhere with great acclamations and signs of joy; as is customary in this country; whereat she was extremely pleased, and told me so, giving me to understand how beloved she was by her subjects, and how highly she esteemed this, together with the fact that they were peaceful and contented, while her neighbours on all sides are in such trouble. She attributed it all to God's miraculous goodness. She ordered her carriage to be taken sometimes where the crowd seemed thickest, and stood up and thanked the people. Amongst others there approached her a presentable - looking man who exclaimed: *Vivat Regina, Honi soit qui mal y pense*, whereupon she said to me: 'This good man is a clergyman of the old religion.' I replied I was very glad he should show so openly the good-will with which the Catholics had always served their Sovereign, and that she might be sure their fidelity was advantageous to her, in order to check the disobedient people in the country. For this reason I had several times advised her not to allow them to be molested and maltreated."

This was good advice from a representative of one who had started on a course of both molesting and maltreating the Protestants of the Netherlands, and whose hands were red with the blood of Count Montmorenci de Horne, and of Count Lamoral Egmont, who, although

Catholics, had been unwilling to fight for the re-establishment of the penal laws, and of the Inquisition. Perhaps Elizabeth deemed the council an impertinence, for she answered, with a crushing docility, that she had in the matter of showing toleration to Catholics always followed the advice of De Silva, and would continue to do so. She finished with a declaration that might be taken as a knock for De Silva's master, that "one of the things she had prayed to God for when she came to the throne was that He would give her grace to govern with clemency and without bloodshed, keeping her hands stainless."

She then remarked on the "justice" accomplished in Flanders, but, so De Silva states, was not so severe as she had been on a previous occasion, he having in the meanwhile explained the situation to her.

The explanations that had appeared to satisfy Elizabeth did not appease Leicester. He also mentioned the subject to De Silva that day. "What seems to aggrieve them most," De Silva noted, "is that the persons [Egmont and Horne] were not heard in their defence." Silva denied that this was the case to Leicester and to Sussex. But Sussex said the King's envoy spoke as a King's envoy, not as a man. He would yet think very differently.

Sussex was an Englishman. Perhaps he no

M

longer regretted the spoilt union of his Queen with the " moderate " Catholic Prince, who was cousin and vassal of the oppressor of the Netherlands. In any case, in this discussion with De Silva, he was on the side of him he deemed the union's spoiler.

CHAPTER X

AMONG the many traitorously dishonest dealings imputed to the Earl of Leicester, are his intrigues on behalf of the Scottish Queen in her captivity to the English one.

Yet a shrewd policy and a keen prevision drew Leicester into his plans and negotiations with regard to Mary. The habit in Leicester of rapid calculation—his quick-reckoning mind —prompted him constantly to acts that appeared fickle and treacherous. His mathematics—it is true—had ever a dash of imagination in them. Colleagues, who thought they walked with him, were often exasperated by finding him on ahead. "He was seldom behindhand with his gamesters . . . they always went with the loss," was the verdict on his methods of one who came under the influence of Leicester's good haters. But Leicester was not a gamester in the sense of being a votary of chance. He played his cards as the result of calculation. That he was sometimes mistaken in the values of the personages and occurences he dealt with, is to say that he was human and very often erred.

As an example of the rapidity with which he formed projects and put them into execution, we have the fact that directly it became known that Mary had married Bothwell and had married him, moreover, with severest Protestant rites, Leicester busied himself to obtain Spanish aid in getting Mary's child to England, to be brought up by his grandmother, Lady Lennox. The plan was cleverly conceived. Spain was to be drawn by the religious question — Baby James must not be educated by Calvinistic Bothwell — and by the policy of depriving France of all influence over the Scottish King to be. And Elizabeth would have the child — with the child's dangerous grandmother—in her own keeping.

A letter from Leicester to Cecil, that bears date 16th June 1567, gives a picture of the situation, of Elizabeth's dismay and hesitation, and of the close relations in policy of the Favourite and the Secretary, that is sufficiently vivid to be copied almost word by word.

" Mr Secretary, upon the receipt of your letter, I repaired to Her Majesty and shewed her the letter which came from my Lord of Bedford [in Scotland] to myself as also yours to me . . . thus much my Lord [of Bedford] writes to me that the lords have not yet agreed to deliver their Prince out of their own possession, albeit they and he shall always remain under Her Majesty's protection, if Her Majesty will any

way assist them in their lawful action which
they seem only to pretend[1] against the Lord
of Bothwell, and not at all to teach their
Sovereign, wherewithal, his lordship writeth
that the Queen there is judged for certain to
be with child which maketh their cause, as also
the Prince's, the more dangerous. And how the
ambassador there doth labour to have the lords
at the French King's devotion with large and
great offers for the obtaining of the Prince.
Her Majesty . . . seemed not to be satisfied
neither resolved well what to answer because
she hath not, she said, the lords' full resolution,
but seemed that she would have the lords to
depend upon her and still so encouraged to do,
and that in all lawful things for the surety of
their Prince she will help them. The matter
of that Queen being with child, Her Majesty
somewhat mused at it and thinks it will greatly
touch her, appearing so soon after her marriage
whereby it will be thought all was not well
before, but agreed, being so, the more the
matter is to be thought on touching the lords
and the Prince. I moved Her Majesty also
for her opinion touching my Lord of Lennox
to have him conferred withal for his advice
which way the Prince might be conveyed to
his hands. . . . I told Her Majesty as much as
I could the necessity of the matter for speed
to be used and how much it concerned her, and
desired to know when her pleasure was to
have my Lord of Lennox here. She said when
he would make suit for it. I answered that he
had already sent to me to know divers times,
then she said she would first know when the
ambassadors would come to take their leave

---

[1] The words *to pretend* are crossed through in the original.

of her, and then she would appoint my lord some day this week to come hither. This is, Mr Secretary, the effect of as much as I could have of Her Majesty at this time. If you have any other matter . . . than I have here before written to move her, I pray you send it to her and write two or three words of your mind also."

But the situation in Scotland developed more quickly than even Leicester could forecast, or Bedford and Cecil manipulate and avert it. The infant King very soon became a hostage of their liberties, too valuable for the Scottish lords to part with into any hands, or upon any terms.

When Mary came to England, without giving to Elizabeth time to prepare for her reception, the question that perplexed the Council of Elizabeth at the moment, and for many a year, was what shall we do with her? The charms and the distresses, the beauty and the ingenuities of the Queen in exile, worked on men's minds and sympathies. Her bearing was all that was winning. Politically, it was out of the question for Catholics to believe in her guilt. Lady Catherine was now dead. Her boys, in the eyes of the law, were only natural sons. Her sister, the Lady Mary Grey, besides being personally unfitted for queenly dignities, had married a gentleman of quite inferior degree, and was in her turn in dis-

Mary, Queen of Scots.

grace at Court. Lord Huntingdon had shown himself indisposed to take up his claim to the throne, though he proved a staunch gaoler for Mary Stuart. England sorely needed a legitimately descended heir.

It is not therefore to be wondered at, that when the Earl of Murray, or the Bishop of Ross, or the Duke of Norfolk himself—each of these has been named as the instigator of the scheme —suggested to Leicester that Mary should be married to the Duke, and that upon certain conditions she should re-obtain the Crown of Scotland in possession, and be awarded the Crown of England in reversion, Leicester quickly took up the idea. Before entering into the scheme, Norfolk had been thus addressed by Throckmorton: "I forewarn you if you do anything in this matter take Leicester's counsel first, for you will hardly of yourself get the Queen's assent." But even with the counsel of Leicester, Elizabeth's approval was not easy to obtain. And Mary, adept in diplomacy if her affections were not involved, when courted and flattered by Leicester, on behalf of Norfolk, replied that she could enter into no engagement without the Queen of England's sanction.

Did Mary, rare diviner, see through Leicester, as no other of those he conspired with at this time, saw through him? For there was a plot within a plot. Of the outer one no great secret was made. Leicester early discussed its objects with Elizabeth herself, though it is doubtful if he told her of his cordial letter to Mary, "assuring her of the good-will of all the nobility, and the certainty of her succeeding to the Crown of England if Queen Elizabeth should die without issue." Of the inner plot, Leicester had to make very sure he had all the threads in hand before he gave them over to Cecil to unravel. It had its origin in Spain, or at least in the Spanish Embassy. De Spes — the emissary who succeeded De Silva — was a man of commoner type than any who had preceded him. He came, as Leicester was quick to discover and to resent, more as a spy and an informer than as a Minister. His sojourn in this country had but just begun when Cecil put him under arrest for insolent intermeddling in English political affairs.

Fear was growing among the councillors, of an attack by Spain on England, and Cecil and Leicester, each in his own way, worked for the cutting off of the train of circumstance that might at any moment flare out in war. Cecil took the high-handed way, while Leicester sinuously coiled himself round the confidences of the conspirators.

A plot existed to release De Spes, to arrest

Cecil, and to restore to Spain certain cargoes of treasure recently seized, not on the high seas, but in the ports of England, by British buccaneers. Of these spoils the Queen and some of her Ministers—including Leicester—had had pickings. Concerned in the plot were the Bishop of Ross — Mary's agent at Elizabeth's Court—the Duke of Norfolk, the Earl of Arundel, and — as the others fondly believed — the Earl of Leicester. But time and again their schemes for dragging Cecil down from the head of affairs; for rendering up to Spain the money Elizabeth was considering whether she should "borrow"; and for releasing De Spes, came to nothing, because, as De Spes complained, at the crucial moment Leicester "softened," and declared he would tell the Queen. Through him, at last, the project came to the knowledge of Cecil, who quickly worked for its confounding. The "perfidies" of Leicester stood his country in good stead.

Not altogether to the harm of England either, was his opposition of Cecil's designs of forming an open league of Protestant states and interests, to invite, at this moment of internal contention, a declaration of "holy war" from Spain, France, and all adherents to the Papacy. But not all of Leicester's operations were disinterested, and some words of Norfolk to the Favourite gave hope to him that, with Norfolk's help, he might yet be King - Consort of England. In any case, the curious conversation reported by De la Mothe Fénélon—the French Ambassador—as taking place about this time, deserves a record. It serves to show that certain familiarities between Leicester and the Queen, extraordinary to modern notions, had not the significance which writers of *chroniques scandaleuses* attach to them. Other times, other manners!

The *levée* of King or Queen was once an actual ceremonial of getting out of bed and dressing. It cannot, however, be argued that, in the sixteenth century, the bounds of propriety were strictly observed when a Master of Horse arrogated the privileges of a Lady of the Bedchamber. Leicester, however, showed no confusion when Norfolk, in pursuance of a suggestion of Lord Arundel, taxed the Favourite with the circumstance that, having the *entrée* to the Queen's chamber when she was in bed, he had taken it upon himself to hand her her chemise, and that, on other occasions, he had dared to kiss her without being invited to do so. Norfolk told Leicester that if he were sure of marrying the Queen he should own it, and behave in a becoming and proper manner; in which case the Duke said he would aid him to the best of his power. Leicester thanked Norfolk for the offer of his support, and said the Queen had indeed treated him with so much encouragement that he had ventured on certain familiarities with her; but they were honourable familiarities. He expected shortly to know her final determination, and would then follow the Duke's advice either to own an intention of marriage between them, or, if it were otherwise, to put an end to their intimacy. These things were easy to promise, since Leicester knew how impossible Elizabeth found it to make a *final determination* in any matter.

That the plan for Mary's marriage was no hole-in-corner business, is proved by the vote of the Council on 27th August 1569. A good majority then agreed that the succession should be settled by the union of the Queen of Scots with an English peer. The "greatest in the land" subsequently signed a bond to support Norfolk, and, following on the Council, a private meeting of Ministers was held in the Earl of Pembroke's rooms at Greenwich Palace. At this meeting the Duke of Norfolk made the proposition that all present should wait upon Elizabeth in a body, and make known their wishes, "fearing that the fewer they were, the greater should be the burden."

Norfolk was indeed in mortal terror of his Queen. Many a time — so he subsequently stated—he would have announced his position frankly to her, but that, at sight of her, his tongue clave to the roof of his mouth, and he was struck dumb. Even at a distance, messages from the dread Elizabeth threw him into an ague. Others among the Council were as terrified as he. It was impossible for them to make up their minds to brave the "Presence," even if supported by one another. Leicester came to the rescue with the opinion that "he thought it not well to have it broken to Her Majesty by a number, because he knew Her Majesty's nature did like better to be dealt withal by one or two." He offered to speak to her himself, if Cecil would support him. Cecil was not then present. He had had no part in the vote, and it was not known if he would help the plan. That Leicester desired his aid is indication that the Favourite had already come to the opinion—expressed a little later—that Cecil "could do more with the Queen in an hour, than others in seven years."

Nothing was formally agreed upon, and Leicester did not speak at once; perhaps he did not have the opportunity. Norfolk was provided with an occasion, but one of his terrible shivering fits came on; "he was fain to get him to bed without his dinner." When he recovered from his ague, the Court had gone to Richmond. Elizabeth was on progress towards Hampshire. The Duke proceeded to

Richmond by water, and came upon Leicester near his house at Kew, fishing in the river. Leicester had dared the venture. " Some babbling women," he said, "had made Her Highness believe that they intended to go through the enterprise without making Her Majesty privy to it," but he had persuaded her that this was not so. What more was to be looked for, Leicester could not say. This is the account of the incident, given by Norfolk in the "Confession" he wrote in the Tower. It is perhaps all that one not present at the interview between the Queen and Favourite could presume to tell of its character; but Camden supplies some picturesque details of Leicester's method of divulging the project. They may or may not be true. His account is that Leicester, being asked by Norfolk to impart the scheme to Her Majesty, put off doing so from time to time, till at length, falling sick or pretending sickness at Titchfield, he was visited by the Queen. He then disclosed the whole matter to her, asking her pardon with sighs and tears. But neither a sojourn nor a sickness at Titchfield square with the fact of Leicester having told Norfolk at Kew, where he was calmly "fishing in the river," that Her Majesty, who, since the meeting in Lord Pembroke's room, had proceeded only from Greenwich to Richmond, was now fully informed of the scheme, though no one could tell what would follow. We do not know if Cecil had assisted in telling Her Majesty, but he certainly backed Leicester up in counselling the Duke — Leicester having broken the ice—to go himself to the Queen and make a clean breast of everything. And Leicester was at the further pains to open the matter again with Elizabeth at a time when Norfolk was at hand to follow up the advantage gained for him.

In the Duke's "Confession" we have the picture of a morning scene in the Queen's privy chamber he came on "unawares." A child was playing on a lute. Beyond, upon the doorstep leading out from the palace room into the August sunshine, sat Elizabeth, lowly enthroned. Leicester was at her feet. He pleaded the cause of Norfolk. Seeing who entered, the Favourite rose and went away. He told the Duke afterwards that the Queen was just at the point of yielding to his pleas. What might not the sunshine, the child's lute, and the "soft" tones of Leicester effect? Elizabeth called across the room to Norfolk, and waited for him to speak. But his "stomach failed"; and after some inconsequent words, he rushed from the Presence, almost persuaded to abandon the whole design.

The good humour to which Leicester's

methods had brought Her Majesty was not disturbed by Norfolk's gawkish fright. At dinner she gave the prospective bridegroom "a nip, bidding him take heed to his pillow." This playfulness was a little grim. It was not many months since Norfolk had disclaimed all intention of marrying "so wicked a woman" as Mary, Queen of Scots. "I love to sleep upon a safe pillow," he had said; "and if I should go about to marry with her, knowing as I do that she pretendeth a title to the present possession of your Majesty's crown, your Majesty might justly charge me with seeking your own crown from your head."

The Queen fared further on her progress to the Marquis of Winchester's house at Basingstoke. All those about her on her journey were of the advice of Leicester that the Scottish Queen should marry the English Duke. Yet Elizabeth instinctively distrusted Norfolk. The attitude of all parties is represented not inaccurately in a letter from De Spes to the Duke of Alva on September 6th:

"The Bishop of Ross has been a second time with me, bringing a letter from his mistress, in which she expresses her desire to be of use to His Majesty, and to the Catholic religion. One day, it seems as if the Queen of England would allow the marriage; the next she will not hear of it. Leicester is said to take the Duke's part, the Duke giving him hopes, that after the expected changes, he will be allowed to keep his present position, and even to marry the Queen. Last Saturday the Queen of England was in such alarm that she told Leicester emphatically that the marriage between the Duke and the Queen of Scots should not be. She said that if she consented she would be in the Tower before four months were over. Norfolk has been forbidden to leave the Court, and she means to speak to him."

Elizabeth was right in having suspicions of Norfolk. She had, however, no adviser to tell her how deeply she should suspect him. Cecil believed him to be well-intentioned, and even Leicester took him to be at heart a loyalist. It was reserved for students of the latter part of the nineteenth century to discover all the treacheries of Norfolk. The record of them was hidden away for many generations in Spanish archives. Yet, when Norfolk suddenly left the Court, giving out that he was going to London, but proceeding, as was soon discovered, to Keninghall, it became obvious that things were wrong. There had been some popular outbreaks in Norfolk and Suffolk, and the Duke's presence in those counties could only embolden the disaffected. The Queen sent after him with orders to return at once to the Court. He hesitated, but obeyed the command upon the assurance of Leicester that he had nothing to fear if he obeyed. A letter from Cecil of October 3rd describes the position of those at Court.

"The Queen's Majesty," wrote the Treasurer, "hath willed my Lord of Arundel and my Lord of Pembroke to keep their lodgings here, for that they were privy of this marriage intended, and did not reveal it to Her Majesty; but I think none of them so did with any evil meaning; and of my Lord Pembroke's intent herein, I can witness that he meant nothing but well to the Queen's Majesty, my Lord Lumley also is restrained; the Queen's Majesty hath also been grievously offended with my Lord Leicester, but considering he hath revealed all that he saith he knoweth of himself, Her Majesty spareth her displeasure the more towards him."

So much for the inner and outer plots in which Leicester was concerned with Norfolk in 1569. But a more formidable project still had been brewing for some months past. Shortly after the collapse of the Duke's marriage scheme, Lord Sussex was dispatched to York to quell the disturbances that had arisen in the northern counties where the great feudatory chiefs — of the old faith — were prepared to rise in arms at a given signal, and to make war upon Elizabeth and all conformers to the State religion. Among the belligerents were the Earls of Cumberland,

N

Westmoreland, and Northumberland. With these, Leicester certainly had correspondences. The plan was for their bands to march south, to release Mary from her English prison, and to set her upon the English throne. That Leicester had ever any intention, as has been stated, of tearing the crown from the head of his beloved Elizabeth, of sending the stoutest Protestants among the bishops over to Flanders to be subjected to the "justice" of the Duke of Alva, or of arranging a marriage for Mary Stuart with a princely nominee of Spain, is not to be believed in the light of all his earlier and later history. He was at the Queen's right hand when the rebels of the north were eventually subdued. And what faith the Spanish party had in such professions as he made, is shown by the existence, a few months later, of a design for the seizure of the Queen, the Favourite, the Treasurer, and the Earl of Bedford; and for the taking of the English fleet at Rochester, by Spanish troops and Spanish warships.

How "well-affected" Leicester really was to the "interest" of the Queen of Scots, and how traitorous (?) to the English Queen at this time, is perhaps best shown in a "long, cumbersome letter," as Leicester himself called it, that he wrote to Sussex while that nobleman was still in York, and—very ill-equipped for the purpose — under orders to quell the rising of the northern Catholics.

Leicester, as usual, wished to subdue the rebellion by management; to disarm the rebels by granting their requests upon terms. He wrote to Sussex for the reason, as he told him, that "the place you hold presently doth require all the understanding that may be, to the furtherance of Her Majesty's good estate," and reminded him that the Queen had "for the State of Scotland," to choose whether "the Queen of Scotland, by her subjects lately deprived," or "the young King, her son, crown'd and set up in her place," was "the person sufficient to hold the principal place," and which of them was the "most fit" for Elizabeth "to maintain and join in amity with."

"To be plain with your Lordship," Leicester continued, "the most in number [of the Council] do altogether conceive Her Majesty's best and surest way is to maintain and continue the young King in this his estate, and thereby to make her whole party in Scotland, which, by the settling him with the cause of religion is thought most easiest, most safest, and most probable for the perpetual quieting and benefit to her own estate, and great assurance made of such a party, and so small charges thereby. . . . The reasons against the other are these: the title that the Queen claimed to this crown; the overthrow of religion in that country; the impossibility of any assurance for the observing of any pact or agreement made between our Sovereign and her."

Despite all these good reasons for the maintenance of James, Leicester confessed himself to be on the other side. "And God is my Judge, whether it be for any other respect in this world, but that I suppose, and verily believe, it may prove best for Her Majesty's own quietness during her time." And Leicester showed himself the man of business as well the man of State, by pointing out that "though it may be granted, the former advise the better way," it layeth not in Her Majesty's power "to go thorough withal"; the reason being that "by the taking into her protection the King and the Faction, she must enter into a war for it. And as the least war being admitted cannot be maintained without great charge, so such a war may grow, *France* or *Spain* setting in foot, as may cause it to be an intolerable war. Then being a war, it must be treasure that must maintain it." With great exactness Leicester enumerated the difficulties in the way of finding "treasure," and continued:

"Besides, we are to remember what already we have done; how many ways, even now together, the Realm hath been universally burdened.

"First, for the keeping of new bands after the furnishing of armour; and therein, how continually the charge sooner hath grown, than subsidies payed.

"And lastly, the marvellous charge in most countries against the late rebellion, with this loan of money on the neck of it."

After more acute observations on the financial position of the country, the "cumbersome" letter continues :

"And now, my Lord, I will show you such reasons as move me to think as I do. In worldly causes men must be governed by worldly policies; and yet so to frame them, as God, the Author of all, be chiefly regarded. From Him we have received Laws, under which all men's policies and devices ought to be subject; and through His ordinance the Princes of the earth have authority to give Laws, by which also all Princes have the obedience of the people. And tho' in some points I shall deal like a worldly man for my Prince, yet I hope that I shall not forget that I am a Christian, nor my duty to God."

After which characteristic piece of sixteenth-century religionism, Leicester went on in more business-like strain :

"Our question is this : Whether it be meeter for our Sovereign to maintain the young King of *Scotland* and his authority; or upon composition restore the Queen of Scots into her Kingdom again? To restore her simply we are not of opinion, for so I must confess a great oversight, and doubt no better success than those that do object most perils to ensue. . . . It is granted and fear'd of all sides that the cause of any trouble or danger to Her Majesty is the title the Queen of Scotland pretends to the Crown of this Realm. . . . If it be so, Whether doth the setting up the Son in the Mother's place, from whence his title in the opinion of those Princes, or no, notwithstanding she remain a Prisoner? It appeareth plainly, No; for there is continual labour and means made from the greatest Princes, our neighbours, to the Queen's Majesty, for restoring the Queen of Scotland to her Estate and Government, otherwise they protest open relief and aid for her. Then though Her Majesty do maintain the young King in his present Estate, yet it appears that other Princes will do the contrary: And having any advantage, how far they will proceed, men may suspect. And so we must conceive, that as long as this difference shall continue, by the maintaining of these two, so long shall the same cause remain, to the trouble and danger of the Queen's Majesty. And now to avoid this while she lives, what better mean is there to take this cause away, but by her own consent to renounce and release all such Interest or Title as she claimeth, either presently or hereafter, during the life of Her Majesty and the Heirs of her body. . . .

" Then must we consider, what may be assurances, for here is the difficulty: For that

Robert Dudley, Earl of Leicester.

objections be, that Princes never hold promises longer than for their own commodity, and what security soever they put in, they may break if they will. All this may be granted; but yet that we must grant also, that Princes do daily treat and deal one with another, and of necessity are forced to trust to such bonds and assurances as they contract by. And as there is no such surety to be had in worldly matters, but all are subject to many casualities; yet we see such devices made, even among Princes, as doth tie 'em to perform that, which if they might conveniently choose, they would not. And in this matter of the Queen of *Scotland*, since she doth offer both to leave the cause of the difference that is between the Queen's Majesty and her, and also to give all surety that may be by ourselves devised to observe the same; I do not see but such means may be devised to tie her so strongly, as though she would break, yet I cannot find what advantage she shall get by it. For beside, that I would have her own simple renunciation to be made by the most substantial instrument that could be devised, the assent of some others should confirm the same also. Her own Parliaments at home should do the like with the full authority of the whole estates. They should deliver her son and such other principal Noblemen of her Realm for Hostages, as the Queen's Majesty should name. She should also put into Her Majesty's hands some one piece or two of her Realm, and for such time as should be thought meet by Her Majesty, except *Edinburgh*. The Queen's Majesty might also by ratifying this by a Parliament here, make a forfeiture if the Queen of *Scotland*, should anyway, directly or indirectly go about to infringe this agreement of all such Titles and Claims that did remain in the Queen of *Scotland*, after Her Majesty never to be capable of any authority or sovereignty within this Realm. These I would think to be sufficient bonds to bind any Prince, specially no mightier than she is. And this much more would I have, that even as she shall be thus bound, for the relief of her Title, to the Queen's Majesty and her issue ; so shall she suffer the Religion received and establish'd in *Scotland* already, to be confirmed, and not altered. In like sort, the amity between these two Realms to be such and so frankly united, as no other league with any foreign Prince should stand in force to break it. For I think verily, as the first is chiefest touching Her Majesty's own person, so do I judge the latter, I mean, the confirmation of the Religion already there received, to be one of the assuredst and likeliest means to hold Her Majesty a strong and continual party in *Scotland*. The trial hereof hath been already sufficient, when Her Majesty had none other interest at all, but only the maintenance of the true Religion, the same cause remaining still, the same affection in the same persons that do profess it, I trust, and it is like, will not change. And though the *Scots* Queen should now be settled in her Kingdom again, yet is she not like to be greater or better esteemed now than heretofore, when both her authority was greater, and her good-will ready to alter this Religion, but could not bring it to pass. No more is it like, these further provisions being taken, she shall do it now. And the last cause also is not without great hope of some good success. For as the oppression of strangers heretofore had utterly wearied them of that yoke, so hath this peaceable time between them and us made known the liberty of their own, and the commodity of us their neighbours."

The worst fault that can be found with the policies of this letter is that Leicester left out of his calculations the pride of the Scots. That they, whatever the promises of their Queen, would have humbled themselves to deliver up to Elizabeth such valuable hostages of persons and places, as Leicester reckoned on, is not likely. Some substantial pledges they might have given. The letter as a whole bears admirable testimony to Leicester's capacity for business, to his genuine concern for the security of Elizabeth and for the maintenance of her state, to his sensible views on financial questions, and to his economical methods of administration. "Some noblemen will be men." Leicester was also a statesman and an Englishman.

CHAPTER XI

To maintain his place of adviser and confidant to the consortless Queen, and to keep alive in her, her early ambition for a maiden sovereignty, Leicester deprived himself, in part, of his manhood. He forfeited independence of mind and denied himself personal indulgences in order to create a medium, in which the chief characteristics of Elizabeth should be preserved unaffected by the disillusions of an ordinary experience, or by the consciousness of a peculiar loneliness.

The atmosphere of flattery and adulation Leicester breathed about her, became the vital air of Elizabeth's being. Yet so great were the intellectual ability and the power of detachment in both, that the two — philanderers, triflers, sinners, call them as one will—emerged from the gaseous element of their own generating when they sat down to letters of business, or took their places at the Council Board. They returned to an atmosphere, high charged with compliments, conceits, and fantastic familiarities, when they re-entered the Privy Chamber.

It had come to be the chief pleasure of Elizabeth to hold in the toils of her fascination, some troubadour, gallant, lover, other than Leicester, on whom, in a sense, the mantle of Leicester fell. We have seen how she entered into coquetries with Sir Thomas Heneage, who was a respectably married man with a wife, who came to Court with him, though remembering the usual attitude of Elizabeth towards her favourite's spouses, one doubts if she came often. A charmer of a little later period than Heneage, was Sir Christopher Hatton. He had been appointed a Gentleman - Pensioner about 1564, but it was not until 1568 that Elizabeth took special notice of him. Then his graceful dancing suddenly evoked enthusiasm. The story goes that Leicester instantly grew jealous, and told the Queen that, since she was so delighted with Hatton's accomplishment, he would engage a dancing-master to amuse her. "Pish! I will not see your man, it is his *trade*!" was the rejoinder.

There appears to be no authority for this story, though Agnes Strickland tells it. But it echoes the truth of Elizabeth's liking for people who did things out of their trades. Leicester was Master of the Horse; yet the least part of his occupations and industries related to the stable. He rode finely and cared well for his charges. But more absorbing than his duties in the royal mews, were those to which he was so constantly called in the Council Room and Presence Chamber. And more grateful still to Elizabeth than the counsels and the flatteries of Leicester, were his manners, his accomplishments, and the art of his bearing and attire.

Leicester's jealousy, if he ever had jealousy for Hatton, was not of long duration. Both Hatton and Heneage were early considered of Leicester's party at Court. Their friendship strengthened as the years went on. Elizabeth's *engoûement* for the delightful Hatton was neither gradual nor restrained. He was a man of ability beneath the peculiar fantasies of his speech and behaviour. But not his ability so much as his ecstatic admiration of herself, Elizabeth found charming. Very soon Hatton's name was joined with Leicester's in scandals circulated by the ignorant and the envious.

Archbishop Parker, writing to Cecil, told of a man, examined by the Mayor of Dover, who had uttered " most shameful words " against the Queen, " namely that the Earl of Leicester and Mr Hatton should be such towards her as the matter is so horrible, that they would not write it down."

It was inevitable that men of the " common herd " should not think otherwise of Elizabeth's relations with her favourites than is "too horrible" to write down. The fantasies and the familiarities of self-conscious "souls" are stuff and nonsense, if not rank immorality to materialists. And the majority of men and women are materialists in their judgments of one another. Elizabeth and her "lovers" undoubtedly knew that, at times, they skated on thin ice. The peril of their sport gave edge to its enjoyment; but their pastimes may be more properly considered as play of intellect than as indulgence of sense. They substituted for real emotions, artificial conceits. They toyed with sentiment and revelled in imagery.

Hatton came upon the scene of Elizabeth's personal life at an opportune time for Leicester. He who was the Queen's "eyes," as well as her "Sweet Robin," could leave her to the diversion of coquetting with her "lidds"—one of the Queen's pet names for Hatton — while he, for on him despised Nature was taking a sure revenge, passed passionate hours in the company of Lady Sheffield.

Besides being her "lidds," Hatton was also for Elizabeth her "sheep" or "mutton," her "*peccora campi*," and her "bell-wether." The biographer of Hatton (Sir H. Nicholas) has supposed the term "bell-wether" to indicate his position as Captain of the Queen's Guard.

He offers no explanation of the other names. The designation "lidds" seems to him specially obscure. It is only a surmise that the "sheep" or "mutton" was destined thus early in the thoughts of Elizabeth for the woolsack on which he subsequently took his seat. But the name "lidds" may more surely be interpreted. Leicester being the "eyes" of the Argus of her people's needs, Hatton, by a natural sequence, became the "lids" of those "eyes." In the entrancing presence of Hatton, Elizabeth could "steep her senses in forgetfulness" of every anxious care.

The lines of Ovid's *Metamorphoses*, rendered subsequently by Dryden,

"The head of Argus (as with stars the skies)
Was compassed round and wore a hundred eyes;
But two by turns their lids in slumber steep,"

must have been familiar to such students of the classics as were Elizabeth and her favourites.

The language of rapture in which Hatton invariably addressed the Queen, was hyperbolic enough to lull even Elizabeth's active mentality to repose. He was indeed the master of extravagance. Only one highly skilled in the verbal art of expressing more than it is possible for any man to feel, could have supplied the lack of Leicester to Elizabeth. And Hatton certainly did prove a substitute for, if not a supplanter of, Leicester in the favours of the Queen. As an example of the heights of ecstasy touched by his language, we may take his letter of 5th June 1573, when he was two days on his journey to Spa, whither he had been ordered for his health. With him, by Her Majesty's express command, travelled Dr Julio, an Italian physician to the Queen and Leicester:

"The time of two days hath drawn me further from you than ten, when I return, can lead me towards you. Madam, I find the greatest lack that ever poor wretch sustained. No death, no, nor hell, no fear of death shall ever win of me my consent so far to wrong myself again as to be absent from you one day. . . . The great wisdom I find in your letters, with your Country counsels, are very notable, but the last word is worth the bible. Truth, truth, truth. Ever may it dwell in you. I will ever deserve it. My spirit and soul (I feel) agreeth with my body and life, that to serve you is a heaven, but to lack you is more than hell's torment unto me. My heart is full of woe. Pardon (for God's sake) my tedious writing. It doth much diminish (for the time) my great grief. I will wash away the faults of these letters with the drops from your poor Lydds, and so enclose them. Would God I were with you but for one hour. My wits are overwrought with thoughts. I find myself amazed. Bear with me, my most dear sweet Lady. Passion overcometh me. I can write no more. Love me ; for I love you. God, I beseech thee, witness the same on behalf of thy poor servant. Live for ever. Shall I utter this familiar term (farewell)? Yea, ten thousand, thousand farewells. He speaketh it that most dearly loveth you. I hold you too long. Once again I crave pardon, and so bid your own poor Lidds farewell.

"Your bondman everlastingly tied,

"CH. HATTON."

June 1573.

And again, after the Queen had sent him a token of a little branch of gold, Hatton wrote:

"The branch of the sweetest bush I will wear and bear to my life's end. God doth witness I feign not. It is a gracious favour, most dear and welcome unto me. Reserve it to the sheep, he hath no tooth to bite, whereas the Boar's tusk may both rase and tear. . . . Humbly on the knees of my soul I pray God bless you for ever. Your slave and EveR your own."

Though Leicester was without jealousy of Hatton, it is evident that Hatton was not free from the fierce passion in regard to the Earl of Oxford, who is signified by the Boar. The cypher of Hatton's signature as of his usual address

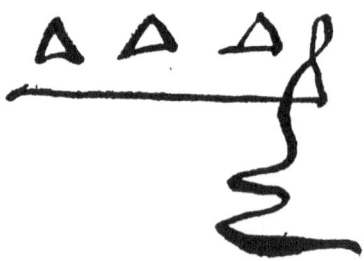

in his letters to the Queen, we may leave to experts in occultism to interpret. The symbol in " EveR your own " is not difficult to understand.

Yet filled as his letters are with what resembles the very rhapsody of passion, we have proof that, though Hatton and Elizabeth went very far in emotional indulgences and in mutual understanding, the keystone of their relations was that frenzy of homage from subjects to their Queen, which Elizabeth knew so well how to kindle, and which is memorialised in the many eulogies of the professed poets and men of letters of her day.

Read Spenser's praise of " Fair Eliza."

> " Tell me have ye seen her angelike face,
>   Like Phœbe fayre ?
> Her heavenly haveour, her princely grace,
>   Can you well compare ?
> The redde rose medled with the white yfere,
> In either checke depeincten lively chere :
>   Her modest eye,
>   Her majestie,
> Where have you seen the like but there ?

> " I sawe Phœbus thrust out his golden hede,
>   Upon her to gaze ;
> But when he saw howe broad her beams did sprede,
>   It did him amaze.
> Hee blusht to see another sunne belowe,
> Ne durst again his firie face outshowe.
>   Let him, if hee dare,
>   His brightnesse compare
> With hers to have the overthrowe."

"Her words were like a stream of honny fleeting,
The which doth softly trickle from the hive :
Hable to melt the hearer's heart unweeting,
And eke to make the dead againe alive.
Her deeds were like great clusters of ripe grapes,
And fill the same with store of timely wine.
Her looks were like beames of the Morning Sun,
Forth looking through the windows of the east,
When first the fleecie cattell have begun
Upon the perled grasse to make their feast.
Her thoughts are like the fume of frankincense,
Which from a golden censer forth doth rise,
And throwing foth sweet odours mounts fro thence
In rolling globes up to the vauted skies.
There she beholds with high aspiring thought,
The cradle of her owne creation,
Emongst the seats of angels heavenly wrought,
Much like an angell in all forme and fashion."

Read also the verses made by Sir Philip
Sidney, and presented by him to the Queen
on his bended knee.

"Her inward worth all outward show transcends,
Envy her Merits with Regret Commends,
Like sparkling gems her Vertues draw the Sight
And in her Conduct She is alwaies Bright ;
When She imparts her thoughts, her words have force,
And Sence and Wisdom flow in Sweet Discourse."

Shakespeare's eulogy must also be quoted.

"She shall be . . .

.   .   .   .   .

A pattern to all princes living with her,
And all that shall succeed : Saba was never
More covetous of wisdom and fair virtue,
Then this pure soul shall be : all princely graces,
That mould up such a mighty piece as this is,
With all the virtues that attend the good,
Shall still be doubled on her : truth shall murse her

Holy and heavenly thoughts still counsel her;
She shall be loved, and fear'd : her own shall bless her ;
Her foes shake like a field of beaten corn,
And hang their heads with sorrow : good grows with her :
. . . . . . and those about her
From her shall read the perfect ways of honour."

Language cannot more highly extol charms and virtues in a Sovereign, or graces and kindnesses in a woman. Yet no one is scurrilous enough to see impropriety in the poet's praises. Hatton's eulogies, though they go unrhymed, and though he had undoubtedly free access to his mistress's presence, need not be maliciously construed.

In another letter of the same period, the Favourite, on his travels, concluded a passage of more than usual fervour with the words: " Live for ever most excellent creature, *and love some man* to show yourself thankful for God's high labour in you. I am too far off to hear your answer to this salutation."

The answer hoped for was probably that Elizabeth had determined either to wed in England, and take Leicester, or to conclude a French marriage then in negotiation. Two fragments of letters of the Queen discovered by the biographer of Hatton at the Record Office, that bear internal evidence of having been written to Hatton at this time, serve to show how Elizabeth regarded the passionate pleadings of her " sheep," her " boars "

or her "Sweet Robins," when they over-
stepped the mark of the accepted courtliness
of the day.

"A question once was asked me thus: Must
aught be denied a friend's request? Answer
me yea or nay. It was said—Nothing. And
first it is best to scan what a friend is, which
I think nothing else but friendship's harbour.
Now it followeth what friendship is, which I
deem to be one uniform consent of two minds,
such as virtue links, and nought but death
can break . . . for friend leaves he to be, that
doth demand more than the giver's grant with
reason's leave may yield. And if so, then my
friend no more; my foe. God send thee mend.
And if needly thou must will, yet at the least,
no power be thine to achieve thy desire. For
where minds differ and opinions swerve, there
is scant a friend in that company. But if my
hap have fallen in so happy a soil, as one such
be found that wills but that beseems, and I
be pleased with that he so allows, I bid myself
farewell,—and then I am but his."

The "one such" who could make Elizabeth
bid herself farewell, was never found. And
the apostrophes of her "lovers" become less
significant when we read—not in questionable
poets' rhapsodies, but in ordinary social letters
from irreproachable men of State—phrases in
which it was the habit of her servants not only
to address, but to refer to their mistress. Sober
Burghley, writing to Hatton in 1582, in reply
to a letter of condolence for family bereave-

ment, declared that he besought God to be his comfort, " as in some part I feel thereof, by the comfortable messages sent to me and mine by His principle Minister, my Sovereign sweet Lady, the Queen's Majesty, whom I pray God to preserve from all grief of mind and body, whereby her poor people may long enjoy her, as a mother and a nurse of general peace."

And Bishop Aylmer addressed Leicester in 1583 in these terms : " I fear not, therefore, my good Lord, in this strait that I am in " [he had offended Leicester in some way] " to appeal from this Lord of Leicester . . . unto my old Lord of Leicester, who in his virtue of mildness and of softness [which the apostle so commendeth] hath carried away the praise from all men. . . . Our Gracious Queen, when she was highly displeased with me for Mr Rich, yet the beams of her grace, soon upon my humble writing to Her Majesty, as it were dispersed the clouds of her indignation. Oh, my Lord ! will God forgive and Her Majesty forget, and my Lord of Leicester retain, and keep that which is not worth the keeping, I mean the remembrance of offences ? . . ."

Friendship between man and man was also expressed in words that to modern ears sound more than necessarily sentimental and adulatory.

Heneage wrote to Hatton : " I find your most honourable and kind remembrance of your poor friend, that, when he seeth you not, desireth nothing more than to hear from you . . . the whilst and ever I will love and honour you, as I have cause."

And at another time the favourite Heneage addressed the favourite Hatton in affectionate manner, and went on to tell him of Her Majesty's kindly reception of a token of a bucket—a tiny charm of gold—sent for the purpose of bailing out "water." Whether from his love of nautical adventure, or as a play upon his name, Sir Walter Raleigh had the *soubriquet* of "water."

"Sir," wrote Heneage, "your knowledge of my love shall suffice, I trust, to satisfy you of my best endeavour to do that which may best content you. I received your letter with your token to Her Majesty . . . and presented her withal . . . which she took in her hand smiling, and said 'there was never such another' . . . that which I was willed to write unto you is this: that . . . if Princes were like Gods (as they should be) they would suffer no element so to abound as to breed confusion."

Heneage was also enjoined to recall to Hatton the fact that his Queen was a "Shepherd," therefore her "sheep" must remain dear to her.

The dear "Prince" who sent the message, undoubtedly thought herself a greater than Canute, and able to say to engulphing elements: Thus far and no farther!

Her presentation of herself in the character of Shepherd is a reminder of the prevailing literary conceit, so wonderfully elaborated by Spenser. In *The Faerie Queene*, all personages of innocent intentions and lively fancy are designated "Shepherds." And the pretty games of love and jealousy, hope and despair, joined in by the sophisticated Elizabeth and her far from ingenuous courtiers, by a quaint conceit, were believed to be the untrammelled sportings of simple children of Nature.

"Shepherds," in the sixteenth century, "souls" in the nineteenth, are creatures of kindred breed. And while even so harshly misjudged, are even as fatuously self-deceived.

So much has been written of the relations of Elizabeth and of Hatton, both because Leicester's story is directly connected with them, and because, by implication, the final innocency of Hatton's association with the Queen is added proof that the "*privautés*," between Leicester and Elizabeth, were always, as he declared, "*honnêtes privautés*." None of the love - making between Elizabeth and Leicester bore so close a resemblance to illicit intercourse as the flirtations of the Queen and Hatton sometimes assumed. And yet, from the facts presented to us, it would be an absurdity to think that Hatton was for Elizabeth an accepted lover.

Of very different character from that of the relations of Elizabeth and her Favourite of favourites, was the nature of the association of that Favourite with Lady Sheffield. Shakespeare's

"little western flower,—
Before, milk-white, now purple with love's wound,"

springing in the path of the "Imperial Votaress," who moved on "fancy-free," has been held to be that Douglass, daughter of the first Lord Howard of Effingham, who became the wife, and was left the widow, of John, Lord Sheffield. It is reasonable to suppose that the incidents of "A Midsummer Night's Dream," were suggested to Shakespeare by his sight, as a boy, of the pageant of marvels wherewith Leicester greeted his Queen at Kenilworth in 1575. But it is doubtful if the flower, — "before milk-white" on which the bolt of Cupid, who took certain aim

"At a fair vestal, thronèd by the west;"

fell at last, was Lady Sheffield. At the time of the midsummer masque, this lady had been contracted twice over to Lord Leicester, and was then the mother, by him, of a boy two years old. Yet the blossom

"purple with love's wound,—
And maidens call it love-in-idleness."

might very fitly typify the Lady Sheffield.

Douglass, Lady Sheffield.

The story of her passion for Leicester is the old, old story of the pretty wife, languishing in country boredom, divesting herself of self-respect and modesty, at the sight of a gallant of the town. A legend in the Holles family (Lord Sheffield's sister was married to a Holles) tells how Queen Elizabeth being on progress through Lincolnshire, was entertained by the Earl of Rutland at Belvoir Castle, where the fair, frail Douglass and her husband were summoned, with the rest of the county, to greet the Queen. It tells also how, after the Court had moved on from Lincolnshire, letters came from the Favourite to Lord Sheffield's wife. Douglass, inadvertently, dropped one of these. The inquisitorial Holles sister - in - law picked it up and read it. In it, Leicester considered the removing of an " obstacle . . . which hindered full fruition of their contentments."

When Lord Sheffield, after denouncing his wife's conduct, died, it was said Leicester had bribed an Italian doctor—supposedly Julio— to poison him. Lady Douglass then expected Leicester would (as he had promised) marry her. But after cohabiting with her for some time, and having his " base son " by her, he married the Lady Essex. It is evident from this account that the Holles ancestors had no knowledge of any ceremonial of marriage having been celebrated between Lady Sheffield and Leicester. The poisoning episode is undoubtedly fictitious. Not one of the many charges of poisoning, preferred against the much libelled Earl, was proved at the time. And all the evidence now to be produced contradicts the charges.

Lord Sheffield died in 1568, leaving behind him a two-year son. The "little western flower" was no longer in the bud when she met Leicester. In 1573, the Favourite and Lady Douglass joined hands under some religious form in the presence of Sir Edward Horsey, Robert Sheffield, Esq. and his lady, Dr Julio, and six other persons.

When Leicester's boy, Robert, was born, so the boy's mother subsequently stated, the Earl wrote to Lady Douglass a letter, in which he "thank'd God for the birth of his said son, who might be the comfort and staff of their old age," and he subscribed himself "Your loving husband, Rob. Leicester." After this, she was served in her chamber as a Countess, until fearing noise of it should get to the Queen's ears, the Earl forbade it.

All these statements were accepted by a Court of Charles I., reversing the decision of a Court of James I., and Letters Patent were granted by Charles for "creating Alice Lady Dudley" (the wife of baby Robert, grown a man) "a Duchess of England." But by that time the crown of England had become loaded with responsibilities towards the Dudley estates in general, and the manor of Kenilworth in particular, and some satisfaction was due from the King to a family—well or base born—that had been so deprived.

It was never discovered by Elizabeth that her Favourite and the beautiful Douglass had exchanged vows, though she made efforts to ascertain the truth about their relations. On 11th May 1573, Lord Gilbert Talbot at Court wrote to his father, the Earl of Shrewsbury:

"My Lord Treasurer,[1] even after the old manner, dealeth with matters of the State only, and beareth himself very uprightly. My Lord of Leicester is very much with Her Majesty, and she sheweth the same great good affection to him that she was wont; of late, he hath endeavoured to please her more than heretofore.

"There are two sisters now in the Court that are very far in love with him, as they have been long, my Lady Sheffield and Frances Howard: they of like striving who shall love him better are at great wars together, and the Queen thinketh not well of them, and not the better of him; by this means there is spies over him. . . . My Lord of Oxford is lately grown into great credit; for the Queen's Majesty delighteth more in his personage, and his dancing and valiantness, than any other. I think Sussex doth back him all that he can; if it were not for his fickle head, he would sure pass any of

[1] Cecil was created Baron Burghley, February 1571, and became Treasurer about the same time.

them shortly. My Lady Burghly unwisely has declared herself (as it were) jealous,[1] which is come to the Queen's ear; whereat she hath been not a little offended with her, but now she is reconciled again. At all these love matters my Lord Treasurer winketh, and will not meddle any way. Hatton is sick still . . . . the Queen goeth almost every day to see how he doth. Now is there devices, chiefly by Leicester (as I suppose), and not without Burghly's knowledge, how to make Mr Edward Dyer as great as ever was Hatton; for now, in this time of Hatton's sickness, the time is convenient. It is brought thus to pass. Dyer lately was sick of a consumption, in great danger; and, as your Lordship knoweth, he hath been in displeasure these two years: it has made the Queen believe that his sickness came because of the continuance of her displeasure towards him, that, unless she would forgive him, he was like not to recover; and hereupon Her Majesty hath forgiven him, and sent unto him a very comfortable message: now he is recovered again, and this is the beginning of this device. These things I learn of such young fellows as myself."

Leicester grew weary of Lady Sheffield before long. In 1577 he tried to break altogether the connection that, because of the Queen's certain anger, should it be revealed, he had insisted on keeping secret. In an arbour of the Park at Greenwich he offered Douglass £700 a year to ignore their relations ever afterwards. The

[1] Lord Oxford was married to a daughter of the Treasurer and Lady Burghley.

sum was equivalent to £7,000 to-day. She subsequently made a great virtue of her refusal to sell her boy's legitimacy. One does not know all the truth of the story. But within a year of this refusal, and upon the marriage of Leicester to Lady Essex, Douglass married Sir Edward Stafford.

It has been said that the circumstances that the validity of the union of Lady Sheffield with Stafford, and the legality of Leicester's subsequent marriage, were never questioned, are no disproof that Leicester and Lady Sheffield had not been ceremonially wedded. It is proof, however, that something was wanting in the solemnisation of their union, and that it had been contrived so as to be easily ignored. Here, again, the libellers have dragged in the poisoning tendencies of Leicester. Lady Sheffield, forsooth, married Sir Edward Stafford because Leicester had begun to administer doses of poison to her. The accusation is preposterous. Yet by constant throwing, some mud sticks, and in view of Leicester's real sophistries and cruelties, and of the reckless assertions and re-assertions of his murderous proclivities by his enemies, one is not surprised at the stigma of the author of "Fragmenta Regalia": "He was too well seen in the aphorisms and principles of Nicholas, the Florentine, and in the reaches of Cæsar Borgia."

CHAPTER XII

BENEATH all the dishonest methods of Elizabeth's policy, one honest intent persisted. It was her true wish to be at peace with all parties within, and with all nations without, her realm. "I'll have no war, no war," she thundered at the Council Board, and by withholding to the last pinch the wherewithal for the purchase of armaments and the payment of men, she gave even more forcible expression to her fixed desire. Leicester, too, was a child of civilisation. He abhorred carnage, and was a lover of peace.

In view, therefore, of the Queen's unchanging design, and of his own strong inclination, it cannot be accounted his disloyalty that, though aware of the treasonable correspondences with Spain, of Norfolk, Arundel, Lumley, and other friends of theirs, he yet, while Norfolk still lay in the Tower, brought back to the Council Board nobles implicated with him, and subsequently urged the Queen to deliver Norfolk himself. He believed that friendly treatment of unfriendly people rendered them less inimical.

In any case, he meant to manage all parties in the Queen's interests and, while strengthening the defences of the country in the royal dockyards, as well as at his own castle of Kenilworth, he resisted to the uttermost all proposals of fellow-councillors that he conceived might widen the divisions of home-parties, or cause ruptures with foreign nations. Yet war with France was now supposed to be imminent.

England had already given a hospitable reception to Huguenot refugees, and Elizabeth had replied to the reiterated applications of the French Court for the relief of Mary, that "she would not be herself the author to hazard her own person, her estate and honour, the quietness of her realm and people, without further consideration how, in doing it, she could maintain her crown and public peace among her subjects."

In answer to these rebuffs of Elizabeth, there had been delivered by the French Ambassador frequent threats of war. From more irresponsible sources, had come hints of a plot under the direction of the Cardinal of Lorraine —Mary's uncle—for the assassination of the Queen of England and of Cecil, and for the placing of Mary on the throne. In addition to these terrors, Elizabeth knew that a Bull of Excommunication against her had been privately fulminated in Rome. Leicester was, therefore, keener than ever for the release of Mary upon terms; thereby, as he believed, securing peace and religion in the two realms, and investing Elizabeth with the queenly grace of mercy.

In May 1570, a special council for the discussion of Scotch affairs was held, at which the Lord Keeper and the Favourite enunciated their respective views with clarity. Sir Nicholas Bacon declared that "Her Majesty was deceived and trifled with. The men whose advice she was preparing to follow were the secret servants of the Queen of Scots." Then, in commendation of the long understanding between the English Government and the Scottish Covenanters, he proceeded: "Go on as you have begun, and there will soon be no Queen's party, no French party, no Catholic party to trouble that country more. English influence will be supreme there, and religion, the Protestant religion, will be established beyond reach of error from end to end of Britain. No advice but this will be given to a Sovereign by any loyal Englishman." And, pointing to Leicester, Bacon added: "You, my lord, pretend to be loyal to your Mistress, and you are in league with the worst of her enemies. If France lands a force in England to try to take the Queen of Scots from us, with Her Majesty's permission, I would strike her head from her shoulders with my own hands."

Leicester replied with his usual dignity and

control: "In what I said, I spoke according to my honour and my conscience. I will maintain my opinion, if necessary with my life, against all who impugn it. It is my duty as a councillor to declare what I truly think. Her Majesty may do as she will; I hold to my own convictions, and I speak for others besides myself."

Elizabeth was pleased with neither speaker, but most displeased with Bacon. His counsels were like himself, she said, rash and dangerous. Her cousin's life should not be touched, not for a second realm. She would sooner die herself. At his peril, the Lord Keeper must ever again speak such words to her.

It was characteristic of the great Queen that she let fly her anger against both parties, and followed the advices of each, up to a certain point. The Queen of Scots was still kept fast in an English stronghold; but no aggressive Protestant league was formed. Nevertheless, as a counterpoise to Catholic plottings for and with Mary, friendship with the French Huguenots was maintained, and a conference of Scottish and English lords was arranged for the discussion of the terms of release of Mary on Leicester's lines.

Throughout the period of the war between the Guises and the Huguenots, Cardinal Chatillon, brother of Admiral Coligny, and

P

the Vidame de Chartres had found an asylum in England. When the Cardinal left England in September 1570 he told the Queen she could not please the Protestants of all nations better than by marrying Leicester. This was equivalent to telling her that she was unapproachable and majestic as the Sovereign of Protestant liberties, and that she—*Regina Ceolorum*, reincarnate in the Protestant cause—had brought forth in her kingdom, a true prophet of the "new" religion.

The number and diversity of the symbols, under which Elizabeth was regarded, was legion. And because he understood so well the taste of his Queen, and desired so greatly to keep her and her kingdom self-contained, Leicester, to whom an actual marriage with Elizabeth would have been merely an incident of a general plan, set himself once again to minister actively to her sense of victorious maidenhood.

On New Year's Day, 1571, the Favourite's gift to Her Majesty was "a jewel containing a painting in which the Queen was represented on a great throne, with the Queen of Scots in chains at her feet, begging for mercy; whilst Spain and France were covered by waves of the sea, and Neptune and the rest of them [presumably the gods and goddesses] were bowing to Her Majesty." "With these vanities," sneered De Spes, "they flatter her to the top of her bent."

But the objects, for which Leicester flattered his Sovereign in this way, were not all perceived of De Spes. Spy though he was, he saw only half the game at this, or at any other time. He did not know that with the view of preventing a talked-of marriage of a French Prince with the Queen of Scots, as well as for signalising that truce between Catholics and Protestants, which the Treaty of St Germains had declared, and which the general ignoring of the Excommunication of Elizabeth seemed to confirm, Leicester was assisting his Queen in angling for the Duke of Anjou, brother of the French King, as a husband for herself.

In the first days of the negotiations, so well was the secret kept that, in January 1571, De Spes informed his master that Leicester was dismayed at the sudden turn given to the English treaty with France by Cardinal Chatillon proposing a marriage between Anjou and Elizabeth. Yet this "turn" had been an integral part of the scheme from the first. At least five months before, "the negotiations for making a French - Catholic Prince, King-Consort of England under Huguenot control" had been begun. The mere proposal of the plan had "sufficed to overthrow"—Mr M. A. S.

Hume is quoted — "all international combinations, set France and Spain by the ears, turned the Guises as relatives of Mary Stuart against their principal supporter [the Duke of Anjou] in France, and reduced the Queen of Scots herself to quite a secondary element in the problem."

Since an earlier scheme of the French had been the marrying of Anjou to Mary, one is not surprised to learn that in marrying Elizabeth to the Duke, Leicester and Cecil were "for once" (?) in accord.

It had been found impossible to release the Scottish Queen, as Leicester had designed. Every month, if not every week, fresh evidence came to hand of her active plottings with the disaffected of Elizabeth's subjects, and of her persistent arrangements for the landing in England of a Spanish force, to proclaim her Queenship and Elizabeth's bastardy. Mary's life—as one politician said—was but a step to Elizabeth's death. The Duke of Norfolk continued his treasonable correspondence with, and for, her, though she had once more higher views, and was manœuvring for a marriage with the French princeling, who was so true a Guise and so confirmed a Papist, that the French King announced to the English Ambassador his resolve to separate his brother from the "superstitious friars" who nourished his "new holiness." It was the desire, equally of the Queen-Mother, and of the leaders of the Huguenot party in France, to rid their country of the fanatical Prince, round whom the extreme Catholic party rallied. Chatillon and the others, who looked to English Elizabeth, and to her Leicester, for the support of Protestantism in France, thought to draw the claws of Anjou, by making him Elizabeth's husband. Elizabeth and Leicester sought the match for the reason that there seemed at the moment no way for her to "remain long quiet and safe, without such a strong alliance as marriage must bring." In any case, it was desirable to decoy Anjou from advances to the Scottish Queen. And though Guisan-French interest was undesirable in England as in Scotland, it was better to allow that interest than to have a third power [Spain] stepping in.

It was not, however, from wholly patriotic causes, that Leicester so hardly pushed the marriage of his Sovereign at this time. It had been his policy and his patriotism to appear to favour the Austrian marriage for Elizabeth, when it was forward, while he had played the Queen's game, in raising obstacles to its celebration. But in his promotion of Elizabeth's suit of Anjou, he was single - minded enough. For his own sake, as well as for England's, he desired at the moment to see her married. Perhaps the little "western flower" was jealous of the "Imperial Votaress"! In any case, Leicester was cohabiting with Lady Sheffield, and for fear of the Queen's anger, and of the loss of his influence with her, he did not dare to transform his "love-in-idleness" into love-in-duty. But let Elizabeth give herself to a princely husband, and it might be permitted to him to take a wife of less than royal degree.

Upon the dispatch to Paris of Sir Francis Walsingham, as special Ambassador for the French alliance, Leicester had been vociferous in declaring that the Queen must be made to marry. Yet, when the French Ambassador —De la Mothe Fénélon—first approached him with the proposal of Anjou, the Favourite made a virtue of his eagerness. He said he had been always against an Austrian alliance, but as the Queen had determined not to marry a subject, he would sacrifice his own chance in favour of Monsieur. After their long recommendation of Leicester as King-Consort, the French could not do less than give the charge and credit of the new negotiations to him. He accepted the charge, and such *douceurs* as accompanied it, willingly enough. Yet he seemed to be a little doubtful if the *parti* were altogether to be commended. "I confesse our estate requireth a match, but God send us a good one, and meet for all parties," was a phrase of one of his first letters to Walsingham in Paris.

Cecil, created in February 1571 Lord Burghley, was extremely anxious for the alliance. Now, as always, Elizabeth was for him only a figure - head of State. His chief concerns in arranging the match were to settle the form of religion to be allowed to Anjou in England, and to gain assistance in driving the Spaniards out of Flanders. Leicester, more careful for the woman in Elizabeth, was anxious to know how the person of Monsieur was likely to please her whom an envoy of Monsieur had aptly designated "Madame l'Isle." The Island Queen had had those about her for many a long year, who were calculated, for grace, manliness, and beauty, to give her a delicate and a distinguishing eye. One cannot therefore be sure that the description of the Prince that Walsingham sent to Leicester on January the 28th was encouraging. Anjou was three inches taller than Walsingham—one does not know how high that was—"his body very good shape, his legs long and thin, but reasonably well - proportioned." What help he had to supply the defects of Nature, Walsingham did not know. But the Ambassador found the Prince not "so well coloured as when I was last here." A picture of him done by a French courtier for Walsingham, and doubt-less remitted by him to Leicester, gave greater promise of attracting Elizabeth's fancy.

"It is his misfortune," wrote the insinuating Frenchman, "that his portraits do not do him justice. . . . His eyes, that gracious turn of the mouth when he speaks, that sweetness which wins over all who approach him, cannot be reproduced by pen or pencil. . . . Do not ask me whether he has inspired the passion of love! He has conquered wherever he has cast his eyes."

Leicester seems to have felt no jealousy of such a charmer, though we may be sure the attributes described commended their owner to Elizabeth. In April, we find Walsingham— who had come to be regarded politically as Leicester's *alter ego* — assuring Cecil that his Lordship "findeth well to allow of any marriage which Her Majesty liketh, though otherwise wrongfully doubted, so especially of this that is now in Treaty." Leicester's own letters confirm the statement of Walsingham.

Agreement to the marriage conditions of Elizabeth, not being obtained by Walsingham as quickly as was hoped, Leicester wrote in March (1571):

"We perceive they deal very daintily, and doubt much Her Majesty's intention to marriage, at least that she had rather hear of it than perform it. But, assuredly, I do verily believe Her Majesty's mind therein is otherwise than it hath been, and more resolutely determined than ever. . . . The person of Monsieur is very well liked of, his conversation is hardest known. I see Her Majesty misliketh not of his estate; for she is of mind to marry with the greatest; and he is left almost alone, the greatest to be had. The conditions will be all: wherein I am right glad, and we are bound to thank God to see Her Majesty so well to stand to the maintenance of Religion. For as there will be no great difficulty in respect of his person and estate to cause a marriage between them, so yet I perceive with the impeachment any way of the true Religion here now established, she will for no cause deal with him, as you may perceive by Her Majesty's own letters to you. Albeit, she doth not mean in respect of his policy to drive him in open shew, in the meantime, to renounce his own profession, but conditionally, that if they should match, then wholly to maintain this, as well privately as publicly. God send Her Majesty always during her life, so to stand to the defence of so just a cause, and withal His blessings upon her for us all, that we may live and see her bring forth of her own body, as may hereafter succeed her as well in that happiness as in the enjoining of her kingdom."

It will be seen from this letter, which, since it was to Walsingham, there is no cause to consider deliberately deceptive, that Leicester had persuaded himself, since the Queen was persuaded, that Anjou's person was not to be misliked. About his "conversation"—his bearing, manners, and mode of thought—opinion was suspended. Elizabeth had now quite convinced her favourite that she meant to marry only with the "greatest," and, as Leicester admitted, Anjou, although seventeen years younger than Elizabeth, was "alone the greatest to be had." Yet already Leicester showed himself anxious about "conditions," and opposed to any "impeachment" of "the true Religion here now established." He supported the Queen's policy of not driving the Duke "in open shew, in the meantime, to renounce his own profession," but, "if they should match," to require her bridegroom to observe the Anglican practices "as well privately as publicly."

Lord Burghley, although stoutly Protestant, was more upon the side of law, order, and the prelates, than was Leicester. He had no Puritan prejudices. One cannot believe that in his heart Leicester had any either; but he had given pledges for their advancement. It was more important for him than for Burghley to prevent any restoration of the Catholic offices. Undoubtedly, he believed with one of the Spanish Ambassadors that the first openly celebrated Mass in London would be the signal of a bloody revolution. But at first the assurances of the French King had persuaded

both statesmen that Anjou was as likely as not
to be converted to Protestantism. Leicester
was the first of the two to harbour doubts of
such an outcome of the negotiations. He was
suspected by Burghley of persuading the Queen
to make her conditions impossibly stringent.

"It was strange," the Lord Secretary wrote
to Walsingham, "that any one man should
give comfort to the Ambassador in the cause,
and yet the same man to persuade the Queen's
Majesty that she should persist. Both these
things are done, but I dare not affirm by any
one."

As in March, Leicester had informed Walsingham that "Her Majesty hath only broken
of this matter with my Lord Burghley and me,"
one may not doubt that the adviser referred
to, but not named by Burghley in May, was
Leicester. De la Mothe Fénélon certainly
thought Leicester to be in the French interest.
"Unless he is entirely *sans foy*, he is with
us." In his dealings with foreign emissaries,
the Favourite, like his mistress, was only too
often *sans foy*. Yet it is possible that in the
course of months Leicester's opinions had
modified. Burghley had made up his mind
to a course of policy, and was determined to
go through with it; breaking on the wheel
of State the butterfly of Elizabeth's tastes
and whims. But Leicester, from the first,
had given some consideration to the human

side of the question. He had desired from Walsingham particular account of Anjou's appearance and health. We have heard what the gentleman looked like. Particulars of his physical condition were not so easy to obtain. The report sent by Walsingham, who certainly did not do much to advance the marriage, was not the pleasantest kind of report to receive of a prospective bridegroom. "Touching the health of his person, I find the opinions diverse, and I know not what to credit, but, for my part, I forbear to be over curious in the search thereof, for divers respects."

These ambiguous phrases did not satisfy Leicester. He made other enquiries, and received the information that Anjou had some unpleasant complaint — a "leprosy" it was called. Diseases were not very well defined in those days. Mr Froude, in his splendidly detailed history of Elizabeth's reign, makes a pathetic picture of "the poor Huguenots" in France, "telling Walsingham, in tears, that an affront from England would bring back the Guises, and end in a massacre of themselves," while Leicester worked privately upon the Queen, feeding her, through her Ladies of the Bedchamber, with stories of Anjou's infectious disorder, "assisting his Penelope to unravel at night the web which she had woven under Cecil's direction in the day."

Queen Elizabeth, with Lord Burghley and
Sir Francis Walsingham.

That Leicester could consider nastiness and indecency in a marital relation a deterrent to a stroke of good policy, was considered by Mr Froude, and has perhaps been considered by some later historians, a crime in the Favourite, while Burghley's complete disregard of Elizabeth's ultimate pleasure and satisfaction in her marriage was accounted as a virtue. Leicester was, in some respects, too civilised for the age he lived in; he was also in some respects in advance of the mean of sentiment of the age we live in.

By September, it was plainly seen that Leicester was doubting the Queen's intention to proceed in the matter. He had come to doubt also the wisdom and the expediency of urging her on. Burghley also had been brought to the view that the affair was dead. Leicester wrote:

"There is no new accident of the marriage matter to write of, and I suppose my Lord of Burleigh hath written plainly to you his opinion how little hope there is that ever it will take place, for surely I am now persuaded that Her Majesty's heart is nothing inclined to marry at all, for the matter was ever brought to as many points as we could devise, and always she was bent to hold with the difficultest. For my part, it grieveth my heart to think of it seeing no way, so far as I can think, serveth, how she can remain long quiet and safe, without such a strong alliance as marriage must bring, for other amities may serve for a time, but there is no account to be made of them longer than to serve the turn of each party, and Her Majesty's years running away so fast causeth me almost to despair of long quietness. . . ."

Oh, traitor Leicester, who must ever remember Elizabeth was mortal, though he, himself, had raised her by his glorifications to a heaven of self - satisfaction, in which she fancied herself immortal!

Leicester further described the attitude of Elizabeth in the words:

"Her Majesty is still persuaded they will yield in the matter of Religion for Monsieur, and so doing, she seemeth that she will, according to her word, proceed; but to say my conscience, I think she had rather be stood fast to it; and rather increased some hard point than yielded in it: well, I commit them to Almighty God, with my continual prayer for her long preservation."

At the moment, Catherine de Medici and her son the King had been disposed to "yield in the matter of religion," but by the beginning of the year 1572, Anjou's adherence to "High Mass . . . with priest, sub-deacon, chalice, altar, bells, candlesticks, paten, singing-men, the four mendicant orders, and all the thousand devils," was found to be absolute. So Leicester set to work on an offensive and defensive alliance with France that would stand without the sacrifice of a woman in the prime of her health, intelligence, and beauty, to a diseased youth, "dominated by voluptuousness."

And Leicester had come now to see, with Burghley, a way out of difficulty and danger for Elizabeth, if she could but be induced to take it. This way was the punishment of Mary of Scotland, and of the Duke of Norfolk, and the joining with France in a declaration of war against Philip in the Netherlands. But Elizabeth shrank ever from decisive action, and hated to pass final condemnation on any one connected with her by ties of blood or bonds of friendship. In particular, on her cousin, consecrated to the queenly destiny and her own next heir, she detested to give judgment. By the laws of all nations, and of common human practice in her day, Mary now merited the sentence of death. Yet Elizabeth would not sign the warrant the estates of her realm demanded of her. She would, however, have given Mary up to the Scottish people on the condition of their delivering the death-thrust. This could not be done. It was the same with regard to sending an army into Flanders. Horrible atrocities were being perpetrated there in the name of religion, and for the exaction of taxes. Moreover, the Pope's Bull of Excommunication and Deposition had been nailed to the door of the Bishop of London's palace, and the conspiracies of Spain with Mary were getting thicker every day.

But Elizabeth would not put to death the Scottish arch-conspirator and she would not declare war. She consented only to the long deferred execution of Norfolk.

It was becoming a mania with Elizabeth not to disturb the *status quo* of European politics. Her madness, however, was not without a method. Yet the method congenial to her feminine temperament — the method of suspense, of coquetry, and of a thousand pretences—was not a method, in the extremes to which Elizabeth was now carrying it, to be followed by a masculine mind, even by a mind so sinuous and dissembling as Leicester's. It is defiance to some of the most literary of our English historians to say so, yet it is perhaps permissible for an anxious student of motives, feelings, and facts, to believe, that Leicester's association with the Puritan party was beginning to have an effect upon him that was, in some sort, morally beneficial.

He had joined himself to the party upon an intellectual conviction that liberty of thought and belief had to come into the world. He had shown his determination in favour of the severest Protestant school, by his preferment of the men and methods of that school in the University of which he was Chancellor, and in dioceses and livings of which he had the disposition. He was now to display it more

conspicuously by his championship of the dis-
tressed States of Holland, and by his understanding with William of Orange. Of words in
the matter he spoke directly as few as his great
taciturn ally; but he worked for England's inter-
ference in the Netherlands, and for her final
defiance of a Papal and a Spanish overrule.

The treaty now being drafted with France
was the beginning of this business. Had
Elizabeth been other than she was, it had
been perhaps possible, even with Catherine
de Medici a party to it, to leave "love-
matters" out of it altogether. But not alone
the Queen of England's delight in being
sought for her own self, but the fear among
her councillors as well as among French
diplomats that she would never, if left to
herself, hold to her word, made Catherine
desire, and Leicester and the rest acquiesce
in, the plan of putting a marriage between
Elizabeth and Catherine's third son, D'Alençon,
in the place of the marriage broken off, of
Anjou and Elizabeth.

So, when in May 1572, the Duke of
Montmorenci and one De Foix were sent
to obtain the Queen of England's ratifica-
tion of the treaty, the end of which was "to
bridle the greatness of the King of Spain,"
these special envoys were instructed to offer the
hand of the youngest brother of the French

King to Queen Elizabeth, and to say that "marriage was the surest bond of treaties."

The envoys were royally welcomed to England, and most sumptuously entertained by the Queen at Windsor, and by Leicester and Burghley in their respective houses. To make the Court gorgeous enough to dazzle nobles accustomed to the splendours of a royal *entourage*, glorious from far longer time than that of England's Queen, Leicester sent an order into Flanders for much cloth of gold and other rich stuffs for princely apparel. In addition to the proposals for the Queen's hand, Montmorenci brought with him the offer of a Bourbon Princess for the Favourite. But, as at the time when a Princess of Cleves had been proposed to him as a bride by Austria, Leicester paid no regard to the offer. These were not honours that allured him. His patriotism was firm; his ambition not all self-seeking. It was partly because he thought he had in himself the power to make England great that he desired greatness. A Princess as a mate was no incitement to one for whom a Queen had been a comrade.

At the same time that Montmorenci and De Foix were being welcomed to England, Admiral Lord Clinton and the Earl of Lincoln, with the counterpart treaty for the signature of the French King, were magnificently fêted in

Paris. And in June, Leicester gave to Lord Lincoln the encouraging news that "it seems Her Majesty meaneth to give good ear" to the suit of the Duc d'Alençon, if—of course there was a saving clause—"if his person be in any way to content." And he instructed Lincoln that he would do well to observe the Duke thoroughly, and "to enquire diligently of his disposition." Leicester added: "I would be glad to receive a word or two from you what ye think of him, I mean his person." No one could think any more of him, it seemed, than that he was swarthy and pock-marked; not so tall as his brother, and very thick-set. His legs, in the portrait of him that is most familiar, are excessively thin. The doubt whether Art had been used to supply Nature's defects in his nether limbs, which had disturbed Walsingham in regard to Anjou's calves, could not have exercised the mind of Lincoln when describing Alençon. The pock-marks were the greatest obstacle to the free course of Elizabeth's affections, if we are to believe Elizabeth's own account of her hesitations. Lord Burghley, ever concise and ready to take an advantage, suggested that France should compensate for her Princeling's pock-marks by throwing Calais into the bargain with him.

Loaded with presents of gold and silver plate, but with no conclusions of arrangements for the marriage, the Ambassadors of both nations returned to their own countries. The next step was the sending to England of La Mole, a youthful spark from whom the fancy of Elizabeth quickly took flame. Leicester introduced La Mole to the Queen's presence at a private interview, at which only the friend of Anjou, Leicester himself, Sir Thomas Smith, and La Mothe Fénélon were present. The next day, the French lad had a formal audience. His messages were to the effect that the King of France could not fully carry out the treaty between himself and England, in regard to hampering the power of Spain. The Catholic powers were already alarmed, and the King was being menaced by Philip, by the Guises, and by Rome. The Huguenot faction was no longer to be tolerated, though of the doom so speedily to fall, La Mole gave no hint. Indeed he had received none.

Meanwhile, the English Court was all blandishment and gaiety. Elizabeth was on progress, and carried with her to Kenilworth the ingratiating French boy. There she presided at a supper, drank his health, languished, and chattered, played on the spinet, deprecated, invited, and deferred the marriage business. Leicester stood sponsor to the Queen's talkativeness, the substance and wording of which had been carefully drafted beforehand by Burghley. So craftily could Elizabeth disguise business beneath frivolity (!).

La Mole remained for twenty-one days with the Court, and then left Windsor for London on his way to Paris. But he was not to quit England as easily as he had come. While the Queen was out hunting on the day following La Mole's departure, a despatch was handed to her. In the saddle, in Windsor Great Park, Elizabeth read the first account that came to England of the massacre of St Bartholomew. Word went after La Mole and La Mothe Fénélon that they were to be detained in their own rooms, until Her Majesty knew if Sir Francis Walsingham, Leicester's nephew Sir Philip Sidney, and others of her servants in Paris, were safe. It fell to Leicester to write to France the official letter declaring the horror of the Queen's majesty, of himself, and of all England, at the terrible crime that had been perpetrated.

" The lamentable tragedy," wrote the Earl to Walsingham, " that hath been there used of late, doth make all Christians look for a just revenge again at God's hands, as it hath pleased him to fear us, and so pinch us in the meantime with the scourge of correction, by the sufferance of his people thus to be murdered, but our sins deserve this and more ; but I trust he will hold his holy hand over us, not to reward us altogether as we deserve. . . ."

Thus far, the natural outburst of indignation,

with an infusion of the Puritan's consciousness of sin! But Leicester had also to consider the necessary moral attitude of his Government.

"If that King be author and doer of this act, shame and confusion light upon him," was his denunciation of the authority in whose name the dark crime had been committed. But, fortunately for the peace of two realms, Leicester was able to add: "The Ambassador [Fénélon] hath inwardly dealt of late with me, and would have me believe that we shall shortly see that this matter is not the King's, and that he doth detest it so much as he will make revenge of it. God grant it may be so, but you may easily understand it, and surely you shall do well, inwardly, as Her Majesty hath written unto you (but warily) to discover it, even with himself; and if it may appear he stands in any fear of his person, or doubts his force to assist him, I know Her Majesty will venture twenty thousand of her best subjects for him and with him, in so good a quarrel."

Elizabeth did not put her "twenty thousand" in the field. It was more politic to believe — as was doubtless true of the young King — that the rulers of France had not personally desired a butchery so universal. The negotiations for the marriage of Anjou were resumed; but the people of England reserved their opinion of the guilt of the royal youth and his unscrupulous mother, and, for a time, the responses of Elizabeth to the re-advances of the French, were kept secret. Leicester was still for the treaty, and still antagonistic to Spain. The Queen had reverted to all her old insincerity. The "pock-marks" were just the kind of pretext she had the knack of using to her own advantage. Leicester was satisfied that the popular cause was served by the insincerity of the negotiations.

CHAPTER XIII

IT is a rare, if not an impossible, thing for man or woman to play with fire day by day, for years in succession, and never to burn a finger. There came the time in the life of Elizabeth when her valiant attitude towards men and matrimony, inflicted a real injury on her womanhood, and when Leicester, like Frankenstein, found himself responsible for the existence of a human being whose conduct and conversation were too appalling and embarrassing to be tolerated.

The wooing of Elizabeth by the Duc d'Alençon — by the death of Charles XII. and the succession to the throne of the Duc d'Anjou as Henry III., become, in his turn, Duc d'Anjou—makes a story of passion and politics that has no counterpart in the published history of the world. For the credit of human nature, one hopes it has few replicas in the private experiences of mankind. It had its instance in statecraft and in policy— in the particular form of statecraft and in

248

the particular kind of policy practised by Elizabeth of England, and Elizabeth's Favourite, Leicester.

Emboldened by her past successes — it is perhaps more exact to call them her past immunities—Elizabeth coquetted, procrastinated, and prevaricated with the second Anjou to an extent that even she, the *Intriguante par excellence* of the nations, had not previously dared with any one. Leicester, though declining from the policy of gaining French help in destroying Spanish dominion in the Netherlands, was so satisfied that his Queen's aversion from marriage was fixed, that he gave complacent assistance to Elizabeth in her flattering reception of the advances of the young Prince, while he opposed, with his Sovereign, Anjou's design of being the sole aid of the "oppressed people" of the Netherlands, and the single-handed humiliator of "the pride of Spain."

Leicester had backed his belief in the future independence and greatness of the States of Holland under an Orange rule, by advancing considerable sums of money to the Netherlanders; others of the English had done the same. Was there ever a war, for the most righteous cause, that was not, in some sense, a war of shareholders? Yet Britain, true to her higher mission, gave also for the defence of Liberty her chivalrous young sons. England was ready herself to be the One Deliverer of the Low Countries from the yoke of the oppressor; and Leicester was ready to represent the One Deliverer in his own person. But the Queen desired no heroics; she wanted to keep Anjou out of Holland. If a French Prince got the credit of rescuing the Netherlands from slavery, English *prestige* and English trade would suffer. So all her cajolery was exerted to draw Anjou from his design.

The Duke professed undying affection for the goddess on England's throne. He was determined, so it was said, to marry " either the Queen or the Netherlands." It was his truer determination to gain possession of both. He attempted the matter in earnest when, in July 1578, he sent an agent to England to tell the Queen " he would be directed by her in all his actions in the Low Countries." The intimation had previously been conveyed that if Elizabeth did not smile upon his projects, he would go over to Don John, Philip's recently appointed pacificator of the provinces, who had succeeded ill enough in pacifying anything or anybody. Elizabeth had provided in her own way for the prevention of Don John's success in the fulfilment of his set task, by secretly aiding Hans Casimir (a German Princeling) to enter Flanders with a strong force of mercenaries. Leicester was a firm friend to the enterprises of the Protestant Casimir.

In the meantime, emissaries of Anjou were entertained as only one who never forgets that angels, unawares, may be at her board, can entertain. The Queen was on progress in the Eastern Countries and the Earl of Sussex, as acting Lord Steward, had seen to it that a plentiful supply of plate should be on her sideboard at each stopping-place. As usual, at political junctures of the kind being celebrated, Sussex was gushingly eager for Elizabeth to marry. But Elizabeth was less eager for a wedding than for a show of her wealth, and for a display of the subserviency of her nobles. At table with the envoys she found great fault that so little plate had been brought to adorn the stages of her progress. Sussex protested that more plate was being carried than had ever been taken by English Sovereigns on their progresses. The Queen shouted at him to hold his tongue for a rogue, and said the more she did for people like him, the worse they became. Lord North, on being appealed to, said there was very little silver, and agreed it was the fault of Sussex. The baited peer waited for North outside the banqueting room, called him a knave, and threatened to give him a thrashing. Leicester, the suave, intervened, and told Sussex " Knave " was not a name to apply to a gentleman of Lord North's quality.

The Spanish Ambassador related this episode

to prove how quickly Elizabeth's councillors were "brought to discord." But these Court flarings, to which the Queen herself so often set match, were only ignitions of wills and tempers of the members of one household, and, moreover, of a household less divided than outsiders hoped and thought. It is not easy to determine the true quality and real meaning of quarrels in the homes of our neighbours. Very often the foreign representatives at England's Court had to learn the lesson that it is as unwise to interfere between two quarrelling Englishmen, or to calculate on their permanent disunion, as it is to attempt to adjust the differences, or to depend upon the finality of the divisions between a bickering husband and wife. Between Sussex and Leicester there was certainly a strong antipathy. Yet even they agreed, at times, to sink their differences and to unite in a policy or a plan.

On this occasion, it is not easy to determine how much they were united, or how much opposed. Sussex was for the French marriage, and Leicester still for the French treaty, although he urged upon Elizabeth that her strength and safety were the better sustained by continued emphasis of her insularity. But as to the measure of the consideration to be paid to the French emissaries, there was an interesting difference of opinion. North had helped to make a fool of Sussex who, since he was then as always, anxious to get Elizabeth married, must be supposed to have wished to do honour to the guests; and North was Leicester's *protégé*. Then the young Earl of Oxford— Burghley's son-in-law, and a most distinguished libertine and coxcomb, whom Sussex had recommended to the honour of a favourite— chose further to mar the pleasantness of the occasion by refusing the command of the Queen to dance before the Ambassadors. He professed to be readier to serve Don John in the Netherlands than to be the sport of Frenchmen. Sussex, his sponsor for Elizabeth's favour, was in the pay of Spain.

It will be seen, therefore, that the motives that led Leicester and Sussex to give the envoys from France welcome, were of a different nature. Those of Sussex domestic, sentimental, and of the type of impulse that leads the "heavy father" of comedy to say "Bless you, my che-ildren," while Leicester but kept the French in play as cover and support of the deeper, sterner intentions with which he was now animated. These intentions were to constitute England a harbour of refuge for the free spirit of dissent, enquiry, and better principle that had riven asunder the Rome - enslaved Church; to make Elizabeth the Guardian Angel of Protestantism throughout the world; and to add to the English crown the fair jewel of the dominion of the States of Holland, Flanders, and Brabant—Leicester, be it added, to be the Lord-Lieutenant of those States. We shall see how Elizabeth coquetted with and kept in play those intentions, even as she philandered with Anjou, and alternately encouraged and rebuffed the Governments of Spain and France.

In January 1579, there came to England a Gentleman of the Household of the Duc d'Anjou, whose persistence and ingenuity, though not his impish spirit and indecent talk, were worthy of a higher cause than that he had undertaken, partly, as it would seem, of his own volition. The genius of this conscious sprite of mischief, named by Elizabeth her "monkey," was for insinuating and suggestive chatter that kept a perpetual blush on women's countenances, and was provocative of emotions, he was content, with a chuckle, to leave to others to respond to. Yet the gibbering trifler could rage downright, and be downright vindictive too. His name, Jean de Simier, was deemed by Elizabeth to be a play upon his simian nature. Monkeys can be angry and spiteful in good earnest. But, before he lost temper, Simier languished and laughed, coaxed, teased, and simulated the transports of a passion he sought vicariously to stimulate in Elizabeth herself. And the little ape succeeded; succeeded, at least, to a point. He brought the Queen of England to a state of personal consciousness and excitement no other lover of hers had ventured to provoke in her.

Simier wasted no time in adorations; he made love. He did not celebrate the Queen's immortal parts or quail before the goddess in her. He spoke not of her mental excellencies, or of the beauties of her spirit. He talked—and it was talk Elizabeth liked to hear—of her personal graces, and continually asserted his own and his master's impatience to gaze upon the Isis of Anjou's destiny unveiled. The ingenious Frenchmen, the "Monkey," and the "Frog" —for "Frog," Elizabeth designated the princely oddity himself when he arrived—had doubtless planned this new method of attack on the integral princeliness of Elizabeth. Against other kinds of assaults, the Queen of England had defended the castle of her maidenhood, with preliminary batteries of archness certainly, but, in the end, with flinty walls of unimpressionability and watery moats of discursiveness.

There was no beating about the bush with De Simier. To English courtiers might be left the practice of those modish "amorosities," which, so a cotemporary historian declared, only conjecture can say whether they were "natural, or merely poetical and personated."

Simier meant to invoke in Elizabeth a clamorous appetite—all the fiercer because wakened so late in life. He assailed such modesty and such delicacy as dwelt in her, with the thousand rhapsodies, paroxysms and professions, experience, and his Gallican temperament informed him, must work like poison in the blood of any Princess so vain and so self-conscious as Elizabeth. The indecent assault upon the sensuality of the child of Henry VIII. and Anne Boleyn, had its result.

"This discourse rejuvenates the Queen; she has become more beautiful and blooming than she was fifteen years ago," was the pronouncement of the French Ambassador.

When matters came to this point, Leicester forgot policy, and remembered that his Sovereign was a woman—one, whom by many vows and declarations, he had promised to love and to honour; to protect even against herself. He remembered also that he was an Englishman, and Simier a dirty little foreigner. Even the vaporous blood of Hatton boiled as he saw Elizabeth stooping from her estate of majesty, and her attitude of jolly, good fellowship, which, however gawkish at times, was, in its inner impulse, a proud attitude, and yielding her ear, and her company to one whose mother-wit and glib patter could not disguise the lechery of his nature, and the criminality of his antecedents.

Any feelings of rivalry there might have been between Elizabeth's favourites were swallowed on the instant that a change of tone in their Queen's love-converse was heard. They had all winked at, even smiled upon her follies and vanities, while those follies and those vanities were the expression only of an exuberant mentality, an indomitable conceit and strong affections in which there was no shame. But when the Queen giggled, bridled, and ogled like a wench of the town; when her audacities in the *décolletage* required of single women became strangely marked; when she took to spending hours with Simier in *déshabillé*, and, not content with asking those who took her messages to the Prince if they had thought to mention to him the beauty of her hand and foot, became possessed to give Anjou's deputy, ocular proof of her general shapeliness, Leicester and her other stalwarts were goaded to an indignation that, for all the fortunes to be won, and the peace to be purchased by their silence, had to be expressed.

But before that hour came, Leicester, according to his wont, played the Queen's game assiduously. On the evening of Simier's first audience, he made a great supper for the envoy; the supper was followed by a ball, given by the Queen. So amiable was Leicester's treatment of Simier during the early weeks of his stay in this country, that,

R

in February, Mendoza — the lately - appointed
Ambassador of Philip — was making deter-
mined endeavours, by suavity, to win over the
Favourite from his friendliness with France.

Don Bernardino de Mendoza, one of an
aristocratic family of statesmen, was the
wisely - appointed successor of the underbred
"spy," De Spes. Between the going of De
Spes, and the coming of Mendoza, there had
been an interval of years; so great had been
the danger for England of the residence in
London of the accredited agent of a Government plotting actively for the release of Mary
Stuart.

Mendoza was an adept in methods that had
their acceptable features. Yet, for all the
acceptability of his ways, he did not find the
Earl of Leicester as easy to bribe and to cajole
as had been Lord Robert Dudley, in the days
of Mendoza's predecessors. "I . . . find it very
difficult to bring him round or hold him for
any great length of time, however much we
may give in, unless he is forced by circumstances. In the meanwhile, I will entertain
him with trifles." The "trifles" had to become
substantials before long, so opposed to Spain
became all the councillors, even Sussex. In
May, the advices of Mendoza to his Sovereign
included the information: "Hatton, although
attached to your Majesty's service, has joined

Leicester in the French affair, so that if your Majesty thinks fit, a jewel worth £1,500 may be sent, and he may be entertained until we see how he goes on. . . . If your Majesty thinks well, it would be desirable to give something handsome to Leicester, just to make him think we have not found him out."

Within a few months from Mendoza's coming, all the English councillors were in receipt of "presents" from both French and Spanish Governments. Simier had come to England laden with jewels for the adornment of the courted bride and the bedazzlement of her favourites. The councillors put the presents in their pockets, pinned them on their breasts, or stuck them in their caps, and went the way their British inclinations prompted them.

In March, the French Ambassador, jealous of Simier and pushing to have his own finger rather than the "monkey's" in the pie of the *entente cordiale* of the hour, was treating with Leicester for the granting of Elizabeth's re-iterated request that before matters proceeded further, Alençon should pay her a visit. The French urged that it was not becoming the dignity of their Prince to proceed to England in person until the marriage-contract was signed and sealed. Leicester replied for the Council that this course was most undesirable, and pressed for the Duke to come in May, when the English Parliament would be sitting. Then he and his friends would ask the estates of the realm to back the French suit, and thus all the country could unite in requesting the Queen to marry Anjou. This project seemed not undesirable to the French. To Leicester it was most desirable, since nothing was surer than that Parliament would oppose the union. And it was the first intention of the Queen and of Leicester so to contrive matters that, when the negotiations for the marriage had to be broken off, the blame of the severance should lie on Religion and on the Parliament. But the French demanded stouter pledges of the Queen's good faith.

Matters approached a crisis. Whatever their private opinions and wishes, the English councillors knew that the English people had not forgotten "St Bartholomew." The bloody pageant that celebrated the wedding - day of Protestant Henry of Navarre and Margaret of Valois—Anjou's sister—might be repeated to signalise the union of Anjou himself and Protestant Elizabeth. In any case, Anjou could not be acquitted, even by less panicy politicians than the Puritan representatives of the boroughs and shires of England, of a secondary intention of setting at liberty the Scottish Queen, and, in the event of the death of his first wife (Elizabeth) without a child, of marrying Mary (of course under papal dispensation), and thus securing his own and his sister-in-law's succession.

Besides these objections to a treaty once deemed by Elizabeth's Ministers so desirable, there were those of its precipitation of war with Spain, and of its introduction into the Netherlands of a rival influence to that of England. It was not to be supposed that France, any more than Spain, would allow Anjou and Elizabeth to enjoy calmly the honours and the profits of the suzerainty of the Netherlands. And for a dominion of some kind for Elizabeth in the Low Countries, Leicester was now working. Burghley alone, of the Council, showed inclination to temporise with Spain. He thought the Queen had gone too far in aiding the refugees from the Spanish wrath in Holland, and in supporting with money grants the administration of William the Silent. Not that he had not a desire, as anxious as that of Leicester and his following, to see Protestantism established in all countries, but he believed that Elizabeth weakened her position as a foe to Spanish oppression by underhand helping of the oppressed. War with Spain on just grounds, and for a righteous excuse, was what Burghley, even now that his coadjutor Sir Nicholas Bacon had been taken from his side by death, still wanted. But until the opportunity for open conflict came, he wished to temporise. Leicester also was not averse from certain conciliations. Elizabeth was always ready for understandings.

In view of all these interests and considerations, as well as of others it were tedious to enumerate, the treaty Anjou's envoy and France's resident Ambassador pressed for, could not be agreed offhand. Elizabeth, who had found the hardy blandishments of her "monkey" so seductive, and who was revelling in a correspondence with a Prince, the weakness of whose orthography was atoned for by the ardour of his sentiments, was undoubtedly reluctant to bring the affair to issue. She apprehended the opposition of her people, and the fascinations of Anjou's novel method of love-making had not yet turned to *ennui*.

So when Simier threatened to leave England in two days unless a reply to his demands for the coronation of Anjou immediately after marriage, for the Duke's association with the Queen in the Government and in the distribution of offices, and for the bestowal on him of an annual stipend of £60,000, were given, Elizabeth carried the "monkey" and Castlenau de Mauvissière —the new resident French Ambassador—to Wanstead with her, summoning at the same time Burghley, Leicester, Sussex, and Walsingham. Wanstead was Leicester's seat near

Greenwich. In the Favourite's house, discussion could be more free than in the Royal Palace. Elizabeth wished this discussion to be final, but she intended its outcome to be a further postponement of the treaty's confirmation, on the ground that as her Ministers were opposed to the concessions demanded, though she herself desired the union, further time would have to be allowed to bring the country round to her view of the matter.

At Wanstead, the four councillors remained all day and far into the night in conference, but the Queen's disinclination to dismiss Simier or to rebuff Anjou prevented them from coming to a decision. On the return to town of Leicester's business-like house-party, a full meeting of the Council was held at Whitehall, to which Simier was bidden. He was told at once that his request for the association of Anjou with the Queen in the management of her country's affairs and in the appointment to offices could not be acceded to, and was asked to wait in an adjoining room while the points of the coronation and the annual grant came under discussion. This he did, and the questions were debated, the vote of the Englishmen going in the end for the views of the newly-appointed Lord Chancellor Bromley, who had been raised to his post on the recommendations of Leicester and Hatton, these two, as it was believed, having assisted his preferment with the express design of gaining the support of his high office for the defeat of the match with France. Frenchmen, the uncompromising Bromley urged, were the traditional enemies of England, and were dangerous guests to harbour. The marriage was unpopular; there was little likelihood of any issue. Sussex was the one dissentient. The sands were running out, and it was now or never for the realisation of his dream of seeing the wedding of his maiden-Queen. Poor Sussex! His *Nunc Dimittis* was never to be sung.

When Simier had information of the decision of the Council, his anger knew no bounds, and he performed all the antics of the enraged of the Simian race. He rushed from the Council Chamber, banged the door in the face of Sussex who had made to console him, and flew to the Queen, who waited in the garden for results. She flamed at her "monkey's" heat, swore she would marry and defy them all, affected a deep melancholy of disappointment, and, by nighttime, dispatched a letter to Anjou full of protests of unchangeable affection.

Elizabeth now probably congratulated herself on being in a position to blot out the marriage clauses of the treaty, and to preserve only the bonds of friendship it insured. But matters were not to settle themselves so easily, and the dangerous employments of her hours of leisure

were to continue. Before her letter reached
Anjou a new envoy had been started off with
splendid presents for Leicester and others of the
lords. Anjou further upset the calculations of
the Queen by declaring that he would marry
her on her own terms, if his attendance, in
private, at the mass might be allowed; and he
announced his determination to come himself
to England in the middle of August. The
visit was to be *incognito*, so perhaps the
gorgeous clothes for the courtiers, and other
adornments for the Court that had been
prepared for the State coming anticipated in
May, were not required to be displayed.
And Leicester, if ever in his life he had a
grudging thought concerning money, must
have grudged the 4,000 crowns' worth of
crimson, black and coloured velvet, satin and
silk, and the £400 worth of gold and silver
tissue he had ordered from Flanders in the
previous April.

In any case, the waiting interval for the
coming of the Prince was a period hard to
be borne with. In anticipation of her suitor's
appearance, Elizabeth indulged in all the loverlike impatiences and preoccupations proper
enough between a young affianced pair, but
odious in a schemer of forty-six, who, in spite
of all avowals, had no intention of entering
the married state, and who played at love

with her suitor's deputy and not with her
would-be husband himself. For hours she
would be closeted with Simier, while Leicester
was detailed to keep Castlenau amused with
hunting, and the like. When she invited
Simier to dine at her table, Leicester was
bidden to invite Castlenau to his. Not a day
passed but the Queen sent for her "monkey"
from the French Embassy, and once, in her
impatience, she came in her barge to the
river-gate of Castlenau's residence so early in
the day that the ape was not fully dressed,
and had to go out to greet her with only his
doublet on. The people said their Queen had
drunk of a love-philtre. Where was Doctor
Dee with his "godly and artificial" methods to
deliver her from the ungodly spell? Leicester
does not appear to have employed his arts on
this occasion. On the contrary, the supple
Favourite went to work in a dogged, downright, natural manner. He believed Elizabeth
to be beside herself. She was reaching the
climacteric of her years, and fierce Dame
Nature was revenging herself upon her daughter
for many curious avoidances of her power. In
her reckless humour, and under the influence of
an adept in provocation, the Queen might give
herself irrevocably to the young wooer who
had, with her, the hereditary title to call such
men as Leicester, servants.

Great as was the moral danger of Simier's society, the political danger of the companionship of Anjou would be greater. Leicester implored his Queen not to sign the passport that should frank the French Prince to her kingdom.

But the fascination of Simier prevailed, and the Favourite took the bold step of retiring from Court, and shutting himself up at Wanstead, feigning an illness engendered by his Queen's perversity. Elizabeth was alarmed. She wanted her Leicester's aid in all her machinations. With some secrecy, she followed him to Wanstead, and stayed for two whole days in his house, striving, in all probability, to gain him over to her view of the situation, which was, undoubtedly, that she only played with Anjou, as she had played before with suitors, for a politic end, and that she was still mistress of herself, and in no danger of overstepping bounds. But Leicester could not be persuaded that all that she had said and done was " play - acting." He would not at once recover from his illness of desperation. And since the Queen would not abandon her flirtations with the offensive Frenchman, an attempt was made—it has been said at the instigation of Leicester and of Hatton—to assassinate him. But neither the Frenchman nor the Queen was a coward, and both were furious.

The grounds for believing Leicester and Hatton to have resorted to this desperate method to deliver Elizabeth from the thraldom of Simier's insinuations, are that the attempt was made by one of the Queen's guard, of which Hatton was the captain, and that the suspicion of Simier himself fell immediately upon Leicester. Desperate ills require desperate remedies. The sinfulness of attempting the life of a fellow-creature was not regarded then as it is now. Yet such an attempt—if Leicester made the attempt—cannot be justified, except upon the principle that attacks upon the honour of a woman honourably beloved, justify retaliations on the life of the attacker by the one animated by the nobler affection. In any case, the lynch‑law that to this day holds a sway over sexual relationships had been applied not long before by Simier himself. For Simier had come to Elizabeth's side fresh from a tragedy in which he had played the part of Malatesta, and his brother and his wife had been a true Paolo and a true Francesca. But a man's own revenges are things apart from those of other men. Simier flew at the noble lord he presumed to have aimed at his life. And more hurtful than any physical blow it had been in his power to inflict, was the arrow of accusation the "monkey" let fly.

For some months Leicester had been married.

The fact of the duly-solemnised union of the widow of Walter, Earl of Essex, with Robert, Earl of Leicester, was an open secret in the Court, the Queen alone not sharing it. Now she was informed of the true state of affairs, and her rage at the murderous affront to Simier was mild in comparison to that she hurled at the Favourite who had deceived her, and at the "she-wolf" who had devoured her pride and her darling.

Leicester was denounced before all the Court, and not only dismissed the presence of his Sovereign, but imprisoned in a fort in Greenwich Park; the while, to further humiliate and insult him, Simier was carried ostentatiously to the Palace, and assigned a lodging near the Queen. One may picture the delight of the trickster. All his schemes had worked. He was the intimate of Elizabeth, the recipient of her confessions of impatience to behold her Prince, the ouster of the Favourite whose influence protected England from French inroads.

In August, Anjou came on his secret visit. Elizabeth's satisfaction was immense. Her pock-marked lover became her *grenouille*—the froggie Frenchman that he was! Embraces were indulged in, tokens exchanged, a diamond engagement ring of fabulous worth placed upon the Queen's finger. And Anjou saw his lady dance; as "high and disposedly," we may be sure, as nearly twenty years before she had danced before the Ambassador of the Queen of Scots. Then, after two days of delirium, the Prince and his mischief-making henchman dropped quietly down the Thames with the tide, and sailed out upon the channel satisfied, and more than satisfied, with the entertainment they had received, and confident that the pledges Elizabeth had given them were guarantees of a devotion that must inevitably endure.

CHAPTER XIV

THE sailing of the Frenchmen left the coast
clear for Leicester. Yet he was still in disgrace.
The account of his retirement provided by the
family history of the Dudleys and Sidneys, is
that his withdrawal from Court was voluntary,
a sturdy protest against the projected marriage
he deemed so ill-advised. But apart from the
informations of foreign recounters of events left
undescribed by those of his own household, the
distresses of Leicester at this time, and for four
or five years afterwards, have been too decidedly
chronicled by his own pen to have been all
assumed. Some design, however, may have
mingled with the grief of a letter to Hatton
that was almost certainly written about this
time. Leicester had been summoned to a
Council, but "forebore to go," being "troubled
and grieved both in heart and mind. I am not
unwilling, God knows, to serve Her Majesty,
wherein I may, to the uttermost of my life, but
most unfit at this time to make repair to that
place, where so many eyes are witnesses of my

open and great disgrace, delivered from Her Majesty's mouth."

Yet as soon as Anjou departed, Leicester emerged. The Queen received him in private audience. When he came out from the interview, his emotion was remarked. And so far was Leicester emboldened by the understanding then established, that a little later, when the marriage question came again before the Council and, under the persuasions of the presents so liberally distributed by Simier, some of the more venal (or was it more sensible of obligation?) voted for a neighbourly *rapprochement*, Leicester headed the group of nobles who threw themselves on their knees before the Queen and besought her, as she loved England and the English, not to marry a French Prince. Not satisfied to take arms of entreaty alone against Elizabeth's vanity, Elizabeth's madness, and Elizabeth's ingenuities, Leicester provided himself and the popular party with a collection of elaborately reasoned arguments and stirring sentiments of patriotism, brought together by his accomplished young nephew, Philip Sidney, in his *Letter to Queen Elizabeth, touching her marriage to Monsieur*.

In this epistle Her Majesty was besought to consider the "goods or evils" that would come to her in her "estate or person" by the marriage. "To your estate, what can be added

to the being an absolute born, and accordingly
respected Princess? But, as they say, the
Irishmen are wont to call over them that die,
they are rich, they are fair, what needed they
to die so cruelly? Not unfitly of you, endow'd
with felicity above all others, a man might well
ask, what makes you in such a calm to change
course? to so healthful a body to apply so
unsavoury a medicine? What can recompense
so hazardous an adventure?"

And Sidney told the Queen that her "inward
force"—apart from the treasures which are the
sinews of her crown—consisted in her subjects.
These subjects, "generally inexpert in warlike
defence," were divided into two mighty factions
"bound upon the never-dying knot of religion."
To one of these factions Elizabeth's "happy
government" had "granted the free exercise of
eternal truth," and by her own "dealings both
at home and abroad against the adverse party,"
her state was "so entrapped," that it would be
impossible for her without excessive trouble to
pull herself out of "the party so long maintained." This party, therefore, was her chief,
if not her sole strength, but it would be
"galled, if not aliened," by the Queen taking
for a husband "a *Frenchman* and a Papist, in
whom (howsoever fine wits may find further
dealings or painted excuses) the very common
people know this, that he is a son of a *Jezebel*

S

of our age; that his brother made oblation of
his own sister's marriage, the easier to make
massacres of our brethren in belief; that he
himself, contrary to his promise and all grate-
fulness, having had his principal estate by the
Huguenots' means, did sack *Lacharists*, and
utterly spoil them by fire and sword." It is
to be remembered that Sidney was in Paris at
the time of the horrible massacre, and that the
impression then received was still vivid.

After instancing the dangers and charges of
housing a foreign and Catholic prince in
England, and reminding the Queen that the
"unspeakable comfort" of children appertains
no more to Monsieur than "to any other to
whom the height of good haps were allotted"
to be her husband, young Philip told her
further that "the honourablest thing that can
be to a well-establish'd monarchy is 'standing
alone, with good foresight of government . . .
those buildings being ever most strongly durable
which lean to none other, but remain from their
own foundation.'" His peroration was divided
into a tirade and an apostrophe. The tirade
came first.

"As for this man, as long as he is but
Monsieur in might and a Papist in profession,
he neither can nor will greatly shield you;
and if he grow to be King, his defence will be
like *Ajax's* shield, which rather weighed them
down than defended those that bore it." The

apostrophe followed: — "Against contempt, if there be any, which I will never believe, let your excellent virtues of piety, justice, and liberality, daily, if it be possible, more and more shine: Let such particular actions be found out (which be easy, as I think, to be done), by which you may gratifye all the hearts of the people; *let those in whom you find trust, and to whom you have committed trust in your weighty affairs, be held up in the eyes of your subjects;* lastly, doing as you do, you shall be as you be, the example of Princes, the ornament of this age, the comfort of the afflicted, the delight of your people, and the most excellent fruit of your progenitors, and the perfect mirror of your posterity."

The passage in italics—not underlined by Sidney—is a plea for Leicester which, under the circumstances, must be regarded as a very moderate and quite justifiable demand. But though Elizabeth read the letter and took no exception to its arguments, she included thereafter in her displeasure against the uncle, a dissatisfaction with the nephew. A quarrel with the Earl of Oxford added to the young man's offences. Sidney retired from Court to Wilton, the place of his sister, Mary, married to the Earl of Pembroke — he who had been the first husband of the ill-fated Catherine Grey, and who was to be, by "Sidney's sister," the father of the Lord Pembroke celebrated as the friend of Shakespeare. In his retirement, Sir Philip wrote his master-piece, "'The Countess of Pembroke's Arcadia," and devoted himself to purely literary pursuits.

Leicester could not attain to the serenity that came by nature to his nephew, though even that paragon of virtue and gentle singer of Arcadian joys made, in his time, the cynical admission — "Need obeys no law and forgets blushing."

With Leicester, the need to maintain the habits of his princeliness and the mental freedom only to be purchased by absence of material anxieties, made him ever quick to divert channels of wealth. For some time after the revenge of Simier, the influence of Leicester was at a discount, and his income reduced. In 1850, he reminded the French Ambassador that the Government of *Henri Trois* had failed of late to make him any presents; and this, although he had had to sell his plate to recoup himself for his outlays on behalf of France. He also displayed towards the Spanish dolers of bribes some of that gratitude which is the lively sense of favours to come, by hints of an anxiety to bring about a new secret treaty between Spain and England. Indeed some treaty with Spain had come to be a necessity, unless Elizabeth could be persuaded either to marry the still willing Anjou, or to pay the "charges" of an occupation of the Netherlands. And the two actions most repugnant to her nature were marrying and paying. In the following year it was noted that Sussex, Burghley, and Crofts were favouring the once again revived French marriage scheme, in order to oppose Leicester. So the whirligig of politics spun round!

But Leicester was now withdrawing his opposition. Elizabeth's tenacity had outlasted his. When he was once more seen in his old place at Court, he was in favour of the French alliance.

And Elizabeth, having had her way with him, having put him in a corner for a naughty boy for daring to remark upon his betters and having punished him for the *lèse-majesté* of lighting a little fire of love upon his domestic hearth, when outside the skies were all ablaze with the glory of England's sun!—Elizabeth having done these things, was somewhat appeased, and began to miss the long-enjoyed understandings. Yet she, of all women, was not likely to bestow whole-hearted pardon. Reminders of his misdoings were not lacking in the revived intercourse of Queen and Favourite; neither did she fail to celebrate to others of her councillors, her wonderful grace and mercy in receiving Leicester back.

In April 1581, there arrived in England a wonderful embassy from France, headed by a prince of the blood, and composed of a glittering suite of nobles, to treat anew for the marriage of Anjou and Elizabeth, or, at least, to form a league of open war against Spain.

The French King now agreed to be at the charges of a war if the Queen of England would marry his brother. If she would not marry, France would share with England the expense of the inevitable campaign. Leicester, remembering the lengths to which Elizabeth had gone in promises two years before, went to her on the eve of the coming of the plenipotentiaries, and pointed out the danger she was in by carrying the matter so far. He was more certain now than the Queen was herself, that she would never marry. He knew also her marvellous disinclination to pay a fair price for even the most substantial advantages to her kingdom. But Elizabeth had anticipated this encounter with Leicester's cautions, and was armed for it. If the Embassy became too pressing, she would send for the Duke himself and buy him off with a money grant. So it had come to that. Rather than marry, Elizabeth would pay. There was hope, in such a case, that matters could be advanced.

Once more the Queen and her Favourite were colleagues in an intricate policy. They played into each other's hands right royally. At a supper given by the Earl of Sussex, Elizabeth expressed her approval of the overtures of the French to Leicester, and assured the envoys that her Favourite had done his best to forward their views. This was in May.

But in August the Queen was still coquetting, and Walsingham, again her Ambassador in Paris, wrote to her a stern letter. His distance from her probably emboldened him, although he did not lack the ordinary courage of a man. In this letter, he said that to give the French

"occasion to think that your Majesty dallies with them both in marriage and in league, cannot but greatly exasperate them against you ; and how your Majesty shall be able to bear alone the malice of Spain, France, and Scotland—for such a concurrence against you is to be looked for—I do not see. You have to consider whether you had not better join with France against Spain, than have them both, with Scotland, to assail you. . . . The solution is very easy. The only difficulty rests upon charges. It were hard your treasure should be preferred before safety. For the love of God, Madam, look to your own estate, and think there can grow no peril so great to you as to have war break out in your own realm, considering what a number of evil subjects you have. Your Majesty cannot redeem the peril at too dear a price. Bear with my boldness, and interpret the same to the care I have of your Majesty's preservation."

An honest letter, characteristic of Sir Francis. "Leicester, whose spirit is Walsingham," had been a description of the Favourite upon one occasion by an Ambassador of Spain whose interests were being disregarded of the spirit and body alike. It is certain the character of Leicester grew sturdier, and his plans developed, as his association with Walsingham became closer. During the blank interval, when Leicester had been little about the Court, a marriage had taken place between Sir Philip Sidney and Walsingham's daughter. Leicester now supported the arguments contained in the letter from Walsingham, in Paris. This letter reached the Queen at a moment when her mind was most chaotic, and her feelings most contradictory in regard to the French affair. The acid in its composition served as a precipitant. Elizabeth raved and stormed, dissolved into hysterics, and sobbed like a little child. It was all the fault of Leicester. She had sacrificed herself, her reputation, and her better judgment for Leicester. He had persuaded her to her ruin. On Walsingham, too, blame was poured. He had done his message ill—had betrayed her.

Monsieur wanted her money. The King of France wanted money. She would keep her money, and they should have none of it. Even Burghley did not have a very happy time that day. He told her "if she would not marry, she must spend."

She replied, if she must have war, she would

have the marriage, too. But all her councillors knew that she meant to have neither, if she could help it. Burghley and some of the more practical ones were of opinion that the only way out of the blind alley Elizabeth had led them into was to make friends with Spain, bargaining for good terms for the Netherlands, restoring the long "borrowed" Spanish treasure, and restraining the buccaneering enterprises of Drake and other founders of England's sea-power. But this was no programme for Leicester's following. Before any negotiations had been entered into between William of Orange and the Duke of Anjou, the States had asked to have Leicester sent to them with an English force, and there had been much talk of sending him. But, as usual with Elizabeth, the "charges" had prevented his going.

Leicester, however, had never ceased to work for Elizabeth's eventual response to the call of the Dutch. The Catholic states of Belgium had preferred the assistance of a Catholic prince. Now or never was the opportunity for England and her most distinguished "prince" to get foot in the business of the Netherlands.

Leicester, with Walsingham, Hatton, and his other allies, were vehement that no treasure should be restored to Spain. Rather let it be expended for the assistance of the French

Huguenots and the struggling Dutch. As for terms with Philip, it would be better to push Anjou in as a figure - head of English help; better to have the French in Flanders than that the power of Philip from the coasts of Portugal to the northern seas should be consolidated.

So Anjou came again in October, and Leicester gave him smiling welcome; entertained him; served him on bended knee. Simier, too, came about the same time, but he had lost the favour of Anjou since his first visit, and had other fish to fry than that for Monsieur's eating. His interests now were for the French King, and he was conciliatory to Spain. Elizabeth was loverlike enough with Monsieur—her "moor," her "Italian," her still hideous little "frog"! Leicester assisted the French alliance in the way the Queen required, but he found his temper hard to contain when, once more, he saw the "chaste huntress" of his English woods acting realistically her part of a beguiling French Venus.

In November, the Favourite made an effort to bustle the Prince off to Flanders with three ships and £30,000. The States were prepared to take the oath of allegiance to him. There seemed to be no cause to prevent his going; but the Earl of Sussex, still animated by the praiseworthy desire to see Elizabeth respectably married, and still under the mistaken impression that only the influence of Leicester prevented her establishment among matrons, warned Anjou not to go with pledges; they would never be redeemed. The King of France and the Queen-Mother also cooled off a little about this time, and their change of face made Elizabeth only more satisfied that she could follow her plan with impunity. She went so far that on the morning of 22nd November, in the gallery at Whitehall, she declared, in the presence of Leicester, Walsingham, and the French Ambassador, that the Duke of Anjou should be her husband, and turning to the long-cajoled creature, she kissed him on the mouth. Drawing a ring from her hand, she gave it to him as a pledge. Anjou placed his ring on her finger, and the Queen almost immediately summoned the ladies and gentlemen from the presence-chamber and repeated to them, in clear tones, what she had just said.

The "dodge" of Elizabeth this time was the same as that once resorted to by Leicester. She meant to put the onus of forbidding the match on Parliament and the French King. She and Anjou were united; it was only a question of the "terms" of two governments. These terms had yet to be agreed.

But Leicester was not so sure that terms would not be arranged. Were not Ministers—

and subjects, too—sick to death with the long
philandering? The cause of Holland, which
Anjou, in some sort, represented, was a popular
one. St Bartholomew's "Feast" was not
forgotten, but there had been no repeti-
tions of its crimes. And Leicester himself
was now committed to the bolder move —
the straighter course. He wanted Anjou in
Brabant as a forerunner of England's aid, not
as representing in his own insignificant person
the true emancipator of the Flemings and
the Dutch. Leicester was soon circulating his
belief that the Queen's act of betrothal was
only another subterfuge to keep the French
in play; but he joined with Hatton in making
a terrible to do about the business. By his
contrivance, ladies of the Court wailed and
lamented the terrible sacrifice Elizabeth was
to make of her beauty to French interests.
Hatton pleaded with her, with tears and sighs.
Leicester asked her sarcastically if she were a
maid or a wife. She replied a maid, since the
conditions for her union — privately discussed
with Anjou — could never be fulfilled. He
then advised her to send the Duke a message
to the effect that her attachment to him would
be greater as a friend than if he were her
husband. This put the would-be husband into
a terrible rage. He cursed the inconstancy of
women, and hinted at revenge.

Elizabeth renewed her insidious policy of kisses, blandishments, and the ordinary familiarities of the affianced, and appointed Leicester, with Burghley, Bromley, and Sussex, to meet in conference the French King's latest envoy, just arrived. The upshot of this meeting was Leicester's proposal in Council for a large money aid to Anjou or the French King, on the condition of their making war upon Spain in the Netherlands. This proposal was, of course, objectionable to Elizabeth. She was still confident of her own powers of " management." Leicester's confidence in her keeping her head under all circumstances was not as strong as it had been once, and he desired, not the butchery, but the policy and the righteousness of this war that had to be.

The abominable seed of mischief—Simier—got into a quarrel just about this time with some of Anjou's followers, and these enemies of his own nation sought the aid of Leicester in exterminating the little germ of infection. Leicester was held to be responsible for ways whereby cut-throats were hired to do the dark business. Simier again escaped, and again appealed to England's Queen. The Royal lady called the Earl of Leicester to his face a murderous poltroon, only fit for the gallows; but when asked to add injury to insult, she said he was too powerful to be disgraced all at once. And this excuse she made for him after Simier had once more tried to revenge himself upon the Favourite for his supposed assistance in attempting his life, by an attempt to revive the Queen's anger against Leicester's wife. But Leicester was playing Elizabeth's game too helpfully to be visited with any disfavour then. Anjou was persuaded that Leicester was the best friend he had in England. In the end, the aims of both Queen and Favourite were gained. Anjou left London laden with Elizabeth's "pledges." His affianced, herself, sped him on his journey as far as Canterbury. The Earl of Leicester, with the Lord Howard (Lord High Admiral), Sir Philip Sidney, and others, accompanied him to Flushing. The Duke entered the town in state. On his right hand rode William of Orange (the Silent); on his left, the Queen of England's Master of Horse.

The Master of Horse was at his side also when he took the oath of his coronation with upraised hand, and was vested in the cap and mantle of Brabant; Leicester walked afterwards in procession with Monsieur down the lily - strewn streets. The enthusiasm of the populace was "impossible to describe." But the thunders of joy that resounded through the crowd were louder for the pledge of Leicester's presence than for that of the Prince of France. The letters from his Queen that the English nobleman presented to the lords of the States and the Prince of Orange, contained her entreaties to receive and honour the Highness sent to reign over them, as long as he observed the terms he had agreed, and to reverence him as Elizabeth's affection and his own rank required. The Queen would do all that in her lay to maintain the authority of the Prince.

Before Anjou left England, Lord Sussex had urged him to keep Leicester in Flanders. But to Leicester and to Lord Howard had been entrusted the money - bags. They were the masters of the expedition. And Leicester had secret instructions to arrange with William the Silent for the long detention of Anjou. He it was, not Leicester, who was never to come back to England. The Favourite left his Sovereign's princely *fiancé* "stranded like a hulk upon a sandbank." This was just what Elizabeth desired. Yet she still played the part of a forlorn maiden, and declared she would give a million to have her "frog" swimming in the Thames again, instead of being left to croak alone in the stagnant marshes of the Low Countries.

CHAPTER XV

FAMILY devotion was a characteristic of the Dudleys, root and stem. We have seen how Lady Sidney, the gentlest and truest of them all, supported the ambitious schemes of her father and of Leicester, though she was too honest by nature not to lose patience with her brother when he doubled on his track. Yet she recognised great parts and endearing qualities in Leicester, and believed him guiltless of the grosser crimes imputed to him. Her husband was constant in the defence of his brother-in-law, and Sir Henry was a man of integrity. It was he who made rigorous enquiry into the death in Ireland of the Earl of Essex—supposed to have been poisoned by the direction of the Favourite, in order that he might marry Lady Essex. Examination of facts left it indisputable that Essex died of dysentery, brought on by drinking impure water. The Earl of Warwick too, a man of action — rough, and lacking the sweetness, as Elizabeth herself said, of Leicester, but "brave

Ambrose Dudley, Earl of Warwick.

enough and noble enough to deserve the hand of a princess "—was, for all his life, his brother's sturdy and devoted friend. Warwick had no jealousy of Leicester, but regarded his high place at Court, and in the councils of the nation, as the fitting tribute of a genius there was no gainsaying. And Leicester himself, whatever his covert cruelties to his first wife Amy, and to his second mate Douglass, was unfailing in kindness to all members of his father's house. Affairs of State never pressed so heavily upon him, that he could not also concern himself with family affairs.

In the midst of the business of the war with Scotland he found time to correspond with the Earl of Bedford at Berwick, in regard to a match between his brother and Bedford's daughter. To his nephew Philip and his niece Mary, he was ever gracious and benevolent. He provided the dowry of Mary when he brought about her marriage with Lord Pembroke. He had also a hand in the marriage of Philip with the daughter of Sir Francis Walsingham. His desire was strong to found a family; to see grow up around him children who should be the interest and the comfort of those days when personal greatness would have lost its taste, and the excitements of political scheming have become stale. Through the dark mists of the future

T

— especially of the future he and others thought to be nearer than it was, when Elizabeth of England should be no more—a dream beckoned to him. It was the hereditary "familiar" of the Dudley nature—the dream of seeing one of his own name and line upon the throne of England. Very early, as we have seen, in his association with Elizabeth, he knew that from her he would never receive the title of King-Consort. And he had no taste for marriage with any other Princess or presumptive - heiress, not even with Mary Stuart — "Mistress of Enchantments whereby men are bewitched!" But he had the desire of marrying a son of his to a claimant for the succession. And it seems to have been this wish, rather than any inclination to regularise, for her sake, his irregular union with Lady Sheffield, that led Leicester to go through a form of marriage with the infatuated Douglass.

He desired to render his son's parentage indisputable, in order that at any time, if occasion served, he might declare him his child. Obscurity overhangs the second marital venture of the Favourite. This alone is clear; there was nothing in it that was creditable, unless it were Leicester's determination that his "base son" should be recognised as his.

On the third conjugal episode of his career,

light falls a little obliquely, but light is thrown. One of the most prejudiced historians of the Favourite's character wrote of him that he was "much given formerly to Women, and in his latter Days doating extremely upon Marriage." Whatever this may mean, it is certain that in the beauty and in the understanding of Lettice, Countess of Essex, the Earl of Leicester found contentment. Original, opulent, and affectionate creature that she was, she managed him, while she loved him. Their union was twice celebrated; once in some private manner at Kenilworth, and again by solemnisation in accordance with the rites and ceremonies of the Church of England, at Wanstead.

It is said that the lady's father, Sir Francis Knollys, insisted upon the second ceremonial, knowing Leicester's propensity for illegal forms of marriage. This looks as if old Knollys, a particularly well-balanced and worthy person, much concerned for the respectability of himself and his family, was quite convinced that the second marriage of Leicester had been no marriage, and that his lordship was perfectly free to enter into a new contract. The fact of the Wanstead wedding was known throughout the Court. Only Elizabeth was left in ignorance of it.

It was understood among Elizabeth's courtiers that favourites of the Queen had no wives.

More and more the Queen was being worshipped by statesmen, by poets, by discoverers, and by all the learned and the noble of the land, as the Divine Agent of Regality for England, a creation rather than a creature, a being half-goddess and half-woman, concerning whom the ordinary laws that govern the relationships of men and women could not be observed. It was understood that by the maintenance of certain imaginations and delusions, Elizabeth preserved the self-confidence and the sense of infallibility that were essential to her in her combat with the great temporalities and greater spiritualities arrayed against her.

She had been angry enough with her Favourite for his marriage, and for his apparent instigation of attempts upon the life of Simier. She had been annoyed also at his participation in the kingly honours paid to the Duc d'Anjou at Flushing. Yet in 1583, she once more extended favour to him. On St George's Day, in that year, he held for Her Majesty an Institution of the Order of the Garter, and in January 1584 he was one of the five councillors — Walsingham being spokesman— who gave Mendoza his *congé* on the grounds that he had corresponded with the Queen of Scots, encouraged her to rely for support on Spain, formed plans for her escape, joined with traitorous English Catholics in projects for bringing in the Duke of Guise to conquer England, and constituted his house a *rendez-vous* for conspiring Jesuits and other disaffected subjects of the Queen of England.

But the sunshine of that face, on which men declared they could not gaze for its blinding brightness, was again to be darkened. Faint rumblings of a storm had been heard for some ten years past, but only at this moment did it burst on Leicester. Elizabeth, who never went on Progress without a retinue of traitors, and who persistently ignored disaffection for its confusion, had seasons when she exploded in invective against treacheries of quite a minor kind, if she did not discern treason in words and deeds that only just failed of owning her the highest concern, political and personal, of the one accounted treasonable. In this case it was that one disloyalty of Leicester — his consciousness that his Queen was mortal, and that after her some one else must reign in England—that led to all the trouble.

As far back as 1577, the Queen had been aware of certain intelligences existing between her Favourite and that "shrew" of many households, Elizabeth, Countess of Shrewsbury. In 1574, following on to a "political" reconciliation between Margaret, Countess of Lennox, and the murderers of Margaret's son Darnley, a "political" wedding had taken place between

Margaret's younger son, Charles Stuart—by the death of his father in 1571 become Earl of Lennox—and Elizabeth Cavendish, daughter of Lady Shrewsbury in her previous marriage with Sir William Cavendish. The chief contrivers of this marriage were undoubtedly the two mothers, though the affair had many promoters among Spanish spies and Catholic agents. It was accounted a means of strengthening the position of Mary Queen of Scots in the event of the decease of Elizabeth.

Lennox, after Mary and James, was next heir in blood to the Queen of England. Both he and his young wife were absolutely pliable to the wills of their respective mothers; both domineering and intriguing women, prepared at the instant Elizabeth should, by any means, be carried out of the world, to do homage to Mary. But the life of Mary also was one that demanded to be heavily insured. The young King of Scots was likewise in precarious case. England might never allow an alien Prince to become master of her realm. The Earl of Lennox was no unlikely successor to Elizabeth. His marriage at Rufford Abbey brought about the result for which all parties were undoubtedly prepared. The bride and bridegroom and their two mothers were summoned to the capital, and temporarily imprisoned in the Tower. Her ability to act a

part stood the Countess of Shrewsbury in good
stead. During her detainment, she made friends
with the Queen's most powerful favourite. Of
Leicester, Gilbert Talbot wrote to his father,
Lord Shrewsbury, after the release and return
to Chatsworth of Lady Shrewsbury:

"I never knew man in my lyfe more joyfull
for their frende than he at my Lady's noble and
wyse governm't of her sealfe at her late leaving
here, saynge that he hartely thanked God of so
good a frende & kynseman of yor L. and that
you are matched wth so noble & good a wyfe."

But in addition to the "wise government of
her self" which made her inevitably admirable
to a long practiser of the art of control, Lady
Shrewsbury had other helps to her deliverance.
The Earl of Shrewsbury pledged to the Queen
his good faith that his wife had not "any
other intent or respect than wyth reverent
dutie towards your Matie she ought." Lady
Shrewsbury ill repaid her husband for his
championship of her in this affair.

But before she dealt the blow at her husband
and his Royal charge that is the disgrace of
her womanhood, other developments of the
Shrewsbury-Lennox scheme had taken place.
The union of Lennox and Elizabeth Cavendish
resulted in a daughter—the Lady Arabella Stuart
—whose luckless birth preceded the deaths of
both her unfortunate young parents by only a

few short months. This precious sprig of Royalty
was nurtured by Lady Shrewsbury with the
utmost care and solicitude. The promises of her
descent apart, she seems to have nestled to a
place in her grandmother's heart that no other
babe of the many stern Bess had reared had
ever reached to. And we may be sure the
busy, forward mind of her grandmother's friend,
the Earl of Leicester, would be quickly filled
with some scheme for the child's future which
should include an advantage to his own house,
as well as to the Protestant cause in England.
Indeed it may almost be said that Leicester
participated from the first in the arrangement,
whereof one looked-for result was the production of offspring, negotiable in the interests of
the succession. For it is a curious fact that
at the time the Rufford Abbey marriage was
celebrated, the rumour was about in London
that Leicester and others had the design of
seizing the baby-King of Scotland, killing him
and his mother, and marrying a son of the
deceased Lady Catherine Grey and Lord
Hertford to *a daughter of the Queen and
Leicester*, who was *kept hidden*, although a
small battalion of bishops was ready to come
forward at the critical moment and swear to
the child's legitimacy. This statement was a
riot of imagination, but it serves to show the
belief of the moment that Leicester was con-

cerned in some provision for the succession, and the only actual provision then being taken was this marriage of the parents of Lady Arabella Stuart.

When Arabella was a two-year child, Leicester visited Chatsworth and Buxton, being regally entertained in both places by Lord and Lady Shrewsbury. The Favourite appears to have approved, at the time, the Shrewsburys' treatment of the Scottish Queen, who was still being served as a Royal visitor, and not "straitly kept" as a State prisoner. And he probably endorsed to his Queen some of the frequent applications for money grants made to her by the Earl for the charges of his ward, and by the Countess for a certain "portion" promised by Elizabeth to that "jewel" of her grandmother, Arabella.

In any case, some apprehensions of too great friendliness between the Favourite and the Shrewsburys were aroused. But it was Elizabeth's policy just then not to ascertain too particularly the designs among her courtiers and others, of which the still most innocent babe, Arabella, was the centre. She betrayed her uneasiness at the situation of affairs at Chatsworth only by a letter of sarcastic thanks for the entertainment of Leicester, the cost of which had evidently been insisted upon by the Shrewsburys.

" Right trusty," wrote Elizabeth to the Earl and Countess on the 4th of June 1577, " Being given to understand from our cousin, the Earl of Leicester, how honourably he was lately received and used by you and our cousin the Countess at Chatsworth, and how his diet is by you both discharged at Buxton, we should do him great wrong holding him in that place in our favour in which we do, in case we should not let you understand in how thankful sort we accept the same at your hands—which we do not acknowledge to be done unto him but to our own self; and therefore do mean to take upon us the debt, and to acknowledge you both as our creditors so as you can be content to accept us for debtor, wherein is the danger unless you cut off some part of the large allowance of diet you give him, lest otherwise the debt thereby may grow to be so great as we shall not be able to discharge the same, and so become bankrupt. And therefore we think it for the saving of our credit meet to prescribe unto you a proportion of diet which we mean in no case you shall exceed, and that is to allow him by the day, for his meat, two ounces of flesh, referring the quality to yourselves, so as you exceed not the quantity, and for his drink the twentieth part of a pint of wine to comfort his stomach, and as much of St Anne's sacred water as he listeth to drink. On festival days, as is meet for a man of his quality, we can be content you shall enlarge his diet by allowing unto him for his dinner the shoulder of a wren, and for his supper a leg of the same, besides his ordinary ounces. The like proportion we mean you shall allow to our brother of Warwick, saving that we think it meet, that in respect that his body is more replete than his brother's, that the wren's leg allowed at supper on festival days be abated, for that light supper agreeth best with rules of physic. This order our meaning is you shall inviolably observe, and so may you right well assure yourselves of a most thankful debtor to so well-deserving a creditor."

This letter had a further point than that of informing the hosts of Leicester that the Queen considered hints of theirs concerning the charges of his entertainment to be in exceedingly bad taste. It was a playful twitting of Lord Leicester, Lord Warwick, and other "curers" at the baths, with the abstemious diet they prided themselves upon.

From Buxton, at this time, Leicester wrote to Burghley:

" We observe our physician's orders diligently, and find great pleasure both in drinking and bathing in the water. I think it would be good for your Lordship, but not if you do as we hear your Lordship did last time; taking great journeys abroad ten or twelve miles a day, and using liberal diet, with company dinners and suppers. We take another way, dining two or three together, having but one dish of meat at most, and taking the air afoot or on horseback, moderately."

In 1577, Leicester contemplated the marriage of his son by Douglass Sheffield with the Lady Arabella, but the birth of his child by Lady

Essex altered his first design. The "noble Imp, Robert of Dudley, Baron of Denbigh," whose little remains rest beside those of father and mother in the Lady Chapel of the Parish Church of St Mary, Warwick, is described upon his tombstone as "a Childe of greate Parentage, but of farre greater Hope and Towardness." We may not now know if in truth the child of Robert and Lettice Leicester was more "toward" than is common with those of his "tender age." He must have been about five when "taken from this transitory unto Everlastinge Life." It is likely that a son of such parents would be of a grace and of an intelligence beyond the mean of his years. He was certainly of a hope "farre greater" even than his parentage, for by marriage with Arabella, his parents intended him to become one day that which his father had missed being—King-Consort of England.

Yet even upon a hope so high, Leicester could not rest. The bow of his ambitions had a second string. In March 1583, we hear of a proposal made to the King of Scotland, on behalf of Leicester and Walsingham, that he should marry Dorothy, second daughter of Leicester's wife by her first husband, Lord Essex. And with the proposal it was attempted to pledge the young Monarch not to change his religion if acknowledged by the English

Catholics. The reward of such a pledge was to be a declaration by the English judges that James was heir to the Crown of England.

Mary of Scotland earnestly entreated the French Ambassador to make known to Elizabeth Leicester's design for her son's marriage, being certain that the plan "would rouse her womanly jealousy, and make her very indignant." It is supposed that Mauvissière did not at once take the tale to the Queen, but contrived that a hint of it should reach her. The result, as crafty Mary had anticipated, was the emptying of phials of wrath upon the Favourite.

It was being officially arranged by Leicester, Bedford, and Walsingham, that Elizabeth should have the marrying of James to a lady of her own choice, in exchange for certain pensions and subsidies to be granted to the Scottish Government. The envoy who came to England for the purpose of these negotiations was surprised by the point-blank question from the English Queen, if it were true Lord Leicester had proposed the King's marriage with his wife's daughter, the Lady Dorothy Devereux. The envoy denied all knowledge of such proposal, but the Queen became excited, and flung out that she would rather the King took her crown away than see him married to the daughter of such a "she-wolf," and if she could find no other way to repress her ambition and that of the traitor

Leicester, she would proclaim her all over Christendom for the bad woman she was, and prove that she deceived her husband. When the news of this outburst reached Leicester's ears he immediately set about marrying the girl to a private gentleman. But the Queen was not soon mollified. She instinctively distrusted the joined interests of so haughty and pushing a couple as the Lord and Lady Leicester. But the repression of their ambition was in higher hands than hers. A year from the time of this renewal of Elizabeth's disfavour, there fell on Leicester and his wife the blow of the loss of the child for whose future they had reserved the supreme efforts of their contrivances.

The letter written by Sir Christopher Hatton from the Court to the Earl of Leicester in his hour of grief, and Leicester's reply, need little comment. The one is infinitely curious and more or less informing. The other, together with its curiosities and its informations, is infinitely pathetic. The first one is from Hatton.

" My singular good Lord,—Your excellent wisdom, made perfect in the school of an eternal God, will, in the rule of Christian reason, I trust, subdue these kind and natural affections which now oppress your own loving heart. What God hath given you, that hath He chosen and taken to Himself, whereat I hope you will not grudge; as well for that

it is the executor of His divine will, as also
for that He hath made him co-heir of His
heavenly Kingdom. When in the meditation
of your religious conceits it shall please you to
weigh the singular blessings and benefits which
God hath conferred on you in this world, I
nothing doubt you will be joyfully thankful;
and accept this cross as the sign of His holy
love, whereby you shall become happy and
blessed for ever. Unto the Gospel of Christ
His poor flock do find you a most faithful and
mighty supporter; in the State and Government of this Realm, a grave and faithful
Counsellor; a pillar of our long-continued
peace; a happy nourisher of our most happy
Commonwealth; flourishing in the strip of
true Nobility abundantly in all virtuous actions
towards God and men; all which are the high
gifts of the High God. Leave not yourself,
therefore, my dear Lord, for God's sake and
ours. Go on in your high and noble labours
in the comfort of Christ, which no man can
diminish nor take from you; cherish yourself
while it shall please God to let you dwell on
earth; call joy to dwell in your heart, and
know for certain, that if the love of a child be
dear, which is now taken from you, the love
of God is ten thousand times more dear, which
you can never lack nor lose. Of men's hearts
you enjoy more than millions, which, on my
soul, do love you no less than children or
brethren. Leave sorrow, therefore, my good
Lord, and be glad in us which much rejoice
in you. I have told her Majesty of this
unfortunate and untimely cause which con-
strained your sudden journey to London,
whereof I assure your Lordship I find her

very sorry, and wisheth your comfort, even from the bottom of her heart. It pleased her to tell me that she would write to you, and send to visit you according to her wonted goodness; and therefore she held no longer speech with me of the matter. Thus remaining humbly at your Lordship's commandment, I forbear any longer to trouble you; beseeching God to comfort you in your lamentation and grief, with the remembrance of His gracious goodness. From the Court at Nonsuch, the 21st of July 1584. Your good Lordship's humbly to command.

"CHR. HATTON."

The Earl of Leicester to Sir Christopher Hatton

"MR VICE-CHAMBERLAIN,—I do most heartily thank you for your careful and most godly advice at this time. Your good friendship never wanteth. I must confess I have received many afflictions within these few years, but not a greater, next to her Majesty's displeasure: and, if it pleased God, I would the sacrifice of this poor innocent might satisfy; I mean not towards God (for all are sinful and most wretched in His sight, and therefore He sent a most innocent lamb to help us all that are faithful), but for the world. The afflictions I have suffered may satisfy such as are offended, at least appease their long hard conceits: if not, yet I know there is a blessing for such as suffer; and so is there for those that be merciful. Princes (who feel not the heavy estate of the poor afflicted that only are to receive relief from themselves) seldom do pity according to the

Robert Dudley, Earl of Leicester.

true rules of charity, and therefore men fly to the mighty God in time of distress for comfort; for we are sure, though He doth chastise, yet He forsaketh not, neither will He see them unrewarded with the highest blessing. I beseech the same God to grant me patience in all these worldly things, and to forgive me the negligences of my former time, that have not been more careful to please Him, but have run the race of the world. In the same sort I commend you, and pray for His grace for you as for myself; and, before all this world, to preserve her Majesty for ever, whom on my knees I most humbly thank for her gracious visitation by Killigrew. She shall never comfort a more true and faithful man to her, for I have lived and so will die only hers. 23rd July 1584. Your poor but assured friend,

"ROBT. LEICESTER."

In this letter one hears the echo of that pride in humility that characterised the last testament of Leicester's mother. Both had "run the race of the world"; both thought themselves cured by affliction of all taste for worldly things; both held the faith of the power to comfort of an earthly Sovereign. Leicester alone seems to have compassed the idea that when princes failed to pity, men might "fly to the mighty God" for consolation.

And the story of the marriage negotiations for Leicester's son had yet another sequel. Quarrels were now frequent between the Earl and Countess of Shrewsbury, and though

U

Leicester at Court urged Gilbert Talbot to keep all knowledge of the disagreements from the Queen's ears, writing: " I thinke rerely she wolde never slepe quyettly after, as longe as that Q. (of Scots) remayned wth them," the anger of the noble pair did not subside. To put herself in the right and Lord Shrewsbury in the wrong, Bess, the redoubtable, went to Court, and when the Queen enquired how her prisoner did, replied: " Madam, she cannot do ill while she is with my husband." She followed up the implication of this speech by more direct accusations of an improper intimacy between Mary Stuart and her most conscientious and impeccable jailor. A rigid enquiry was instituted. In the end, Lady Shrewsbury acknowledged her imputation false. Nevertheless, Mary was transferred to a sterner guardianship. Terrible was the Scottish Queen's anger at the scandalous reports, and more than passionate was her desire to revenge herself upon the false Countess and, incidentally, to stab the Queen of England with accusations of follies in her as gross as any her " sister " of Scotland had been guilty of. In the first impulse of her not unnatural wrath, Mary wrote to the French Ambassador in London —Mauvissière:

" I entreat that you will more distinctly show to Queen Elizabeth the treachery of my *honour-*

able hostess, the Countess of Shrewsbury. I would wish you to mention privately to the Queen that nothing has alienated the Countess from me but the vain hope she has conceived of setting the crown of England on the head of her little girl, Arabella; and this by means of marrying her to a son of the Earl of Leicester. These children have been also educated in this idea, and their portraits have been sent to each other. But for the notion of raising one of her descendants to the rank of Queen, she would never have so turned away from me ; for she was so entirely bound to me, and, regardless of any other duty or regard, that if God himself had been her Queen she could not have shown more devotion than to me."

And this letter was followed by that other missive from Mary to Elizabeth which, found among the papers at Hatfield, is supposed never to have reached its destination—oh, sagacious Burghley !—and which, under show of revealing to the Queen of England the duplicity and the treachery of those high-placed ladies, the Countesses of Lennox and Shrewsbury, makes accusations of scandalous conduct against Elizabeth herself. We need not repeat the details of the accusations which refer to the Queen's association with Leicester, with Hatton, with Simier, and with Anjou, but it should be noted that at the highest reach of the imputations of Elizabeth's immorality, Mary checks herself, to assure the Queen that

the last verdict on her conduct of both Lady
Lennox and Lady Shrewsbury was that she
was *not as other women*. The pen of Mary
Stuart was dipped in gall. She was herself
under persecution. It could not be otherwise. But, certainly, excessive credence need
not be given to the mockeries and virulences
of the lady of many marriages, who did not
hesitate, when spite urged her, to bring
against her own husband and the Queen to
whom she had been "bound," a disgraceful
accusation that she subsequently confessed
was wholly false.

CHAPTER XVI

ONE of the several writers who have delivered to themselves briefs for the prosecution of Leicester as a common murderer and low scoundrel, has urged as a satisfactory reason for the acceptation of the preposterously libellous statements contained in the tirade "Leycester's Commonwealth," that, although the book was widely circulated in his lifetime, no friend of his came forward to refute its accusations. This assertion is untrue.

Yet the circumstances that the book was recognised in the days of its publication for a Jesuit tract, that it was authoritatively suppressed by Elizabeth's Government, and denounced by Elizabeth herself, might have been regarded as sufficient cause for Leicester's friends to leave the libel unanswered. But that was not the case.

In his "Discourse in Defence of the Earle of Leycester," Sir Philip Sidney defended the family honour of the Dudleys and his uncle's personal fame. Both had been heavily assailed by the author of "A Dialogue between a Scholar, a Gentleman, and a Lawyer," more commonly known as "Leycester's Commonwealth," which Sidney described as "printed 1584 in Foreign Parts and transmitted by the English Jesuits into this Nation."

This publication, which remains anonymous, although attributed, and not without reason, to Father Parsons, who was the Captain of the Jesuit attack on the integrity of England begun about the year 1580, professed to disclose the hideous character and vile machinations of the one who was the "*Dominus fac Totum*" of the nation; "whose Excellence is above all others infinite, whose Authority is absolute, whose Commandment is dreadful, whose Dislike is dangerous, and whose Favour is Omnipotent, and for his Will, though it be seldom Law, yet always is his Power above Law."

The style of the supposed disclosure is well shown in the following passage of the " Defence."

"If the Author had fained new Names, as he doth new Matters, a Man might well have thought his only Meaning had been to have gyven a lyvely Picture of the uttermost Degree of Railing." And Sidney further characterised the "Dialogue" as "such a bundle of Railings, as if it came from the Mouth of some half-drunk Skold in a Tavern."

In regard to the charges of low blackguardism

and gross profligacy in his uncle, Sir Philip seemed to think particular refutations super-fluous, the accusations in the mass being so horrible and wide of the truth as to provoke only a general discredit : " Dissimula-tion, Hipocrosi, Adultery, Falshood, Trecheri, Poison, Rebellion, Treason, Cowardis, Atheism, and what not ; and all still so upon the Superlative ! " cried Sir Philip. How is one to beat off from an honoured relative such an extravagant array of charges ? And yet their very extravagance, as well as the virulence with which they were pressed, imply a compliment to him against whom they were brought. " But to the Earl himself, in the Eyes of any Men, who with clear judgments can value Things, a true and sound Honour grows out of these dis-honourable Falsehoods." Lord Leicester, Sir Philip conceived, "may justly say, as a worthy Senator of Rome once in like case did, that no man these twenty years hath borne a hateful Hart to this estate, but that at the same Tyme, he hath shewed his Enmity to this Earl; testefying it hereby that his Faith is so linked to her Majestie's Service, that who goes about to undermine the one, resolves with-all to overthrow the other." And the doughty Sidney, in possession of some of those terrible secrets of conspiracy against the throne and the life of Elizabeth which his father-in-law,

Sir Francis Walsingham, had such ability to bring to light, did not hesitate to attribute the design of the pamphlet to an association of Catholic desperadoes with whom it "is their Plott of late, by Name first to publish something against the Earl of Lester, and after, when Tyme served, against the Queen's Majesty." This plot by "their own intercepted Discourses, is made to manifest."

The contempt with which the abounding libels on Leicester were regarded by those closest to him in natural kin and political fellowship, was well expressed in the penultimate outburst of the "Defence." "But hard it wear if every Goos Quill could any Waj blott the Honour of an Earl of Lester, written in the Hartes of so many Men thorow Europe." And Sir Philip gave the anonymous mud-thrower the lie in his throat, and announced himself ready any time within three months to meet and justify himself to his uncle's traducer, face to face.

The "Defence" is valuable not only as evidence of Leicester's power of inspiring devotion in the chivalrous young England growing up around him, but also as testimony to the source whence the defamation of Leicester sprang.

One of the exercises of Elizabeth's famous visit to Oxford in 1564 had been a discourse from a young Oxford graduate, who complimented the Queen and her Favourite on their mild disposition towards Religion. The same orator had previously preached a funeral sermon for Lady Robert Dudley, in which a glowing eulogy of Oxford's Chancellor revealed the hopes that were entertained of him by "sound Catholics," who utterly condemned the "new religion" of Queen and Council. In his government of Oxford, the Earl of Leicester belied those hopes. The flatteries of this Oxford speechifier, at a moment when the Queen and her Favourite yet believed themselves destined to construct a middle way in religion, had rung in their ears for many and many a day. The sound of those eulogies, and of others like them, entranced them in the idea that liberty of opinion might coexist with servitude to observances. They would have dreamed their dream a good time longer, if it had not been that these very Catholics, whose private observances of their rites and ceremonies were studiously ignored, and whose volunteered services to the Court or State were cordially received, joined themselves in insolent leagues against the peace of England, surreptitiously sought the overthrow of Protestantism, and viciously designed the death of the Favourite and of the Queen.

But when the infinite industry of Cecil and

the deft handlings of Walsingham yielded at
last the sinister harvest of discovery of plot
upon plot against the religion, the government,
and the sovereignty of the country, Leicester
became convinced that only by the strenuous
side-path of a Puritan Protestantism could the
high-road of complete freedom from an alien
despotism be reached. When he acted on this
conviction by reforming the organisation of
Oxford University; by supporting Archbishop
Grindal's appeal to the Queen against her
objections to the "prophesyings"—the proto-
types of our Church Congresses—though he
suggested the compromise, "the malapertness
of brainless men considered," of excluding lay-
men from the conferences; and, above all, when
he came to side openly with William of Orange
and the oppressed Netherlanders, the fury of the
Jesuits fell upon him. And Leicester, for all
the subtlety of his nature, was not the man
to be struck at and not to strike back. Yet
the freedom of his political antagonisms from
personal hatreds is evidenced by his treatment
of the eloquent flatterer of Oxford, turned Jesuit
and intriguer against the State.

Edmund Campian, though an ordained
deacon of the Church of England, left Oxford
in 1567, because he could not undergo an
examination by Leicester's commissioners for
imposing the oath of allegiance and the sub-

scription to the thirty-nine articles of religion, without revealing the Romanism of his secret faith. In 1580, he received in Rome his commission to convert England without entering into political matters, but, nevertheless, to tell the Catholics of his native land that the Pope's Bull against Elizabeth, releasing subjects from their obedience to her, was to be enforced when circumstances should permit. Under cover of his spiritual office, he was to prepare the way for the great invasion by Spanish, French, and Scottish troops, designed for the restoration of Roman Catholicism and for the setting up of Mary in Elizabeth's place.

This traitor to his country and to his Queen, was arrested near Oxford by one of Leicester's agents for the detection of seminary priests and others engaged, in disguise, upon the work of undermining the English Constitution. He was brought to the Tower, with a placard on his head bearing the words, "Campian, the seditious Jesuit." No individual responsibility can be thrown on Leicester for the mental torture of derision or for the material pains of "Little Ease" to which Campian was subjected. Such contumelies and pains were after the custom, if not according to the law, of the time in the treatment of political offenders. Leicester's personal concern with the affair was his joining with the Queen in an endeavour to extricate Campian from the miserable predicament into which his hotheadedness, to say nothing of his ingratitude and treachery, had led him. The Earl had him brought from the Tower to the Palace, and there, in a private room, Elizabeth and her Favourite questioned the still unracked offender as to his interpretation of the Bishop of Rome's Bull of Excommunication. But the utmost loyalty the two could wring from him was that he must render to Her Majesty what was Her Majesty's, and to God the things that were God's. The Jesuit believed unquestioning obedience to the Pope to be the supreme appurtenance of God. Yet Leicester, acting for and with his Queen, gave orders that the misguided man should be kindly treated. It was by Burghley's determination that Campian at last went to the rack and to the gallows, because he would not renounce the Pope. And this Pope of Campian's allegiance was none other than he who had sung a *Te Deum* for the massacre of St Bartholomew's Day, and who explicitly approved the intention of two young English priests, who went to him for sanction of their enterprise, to murder the Queen of England. " As touching the taking away of that impious Jezebel," said Gregory XIII. of Elizabeth, " I would be loath you should attempt anything unto your own destruction, and we know not how our censure on that point amongst her subjects which profess themselves our children would be taken; but if you can wisely give such counsel as may be without scandal to the party or to us, *know you we do not only approve the act, but think the doer, if he suffer death simply for that, to be worthy of canonisation.*"

The hanging and quartering of Campian and his kind as treasonable conspirators could but provoke reprisals from the Jesuits, and from all those persons whose fortunes were linked with any of the numerous plans for the reduction of England from the rank of a sovereign kingdom to that of a fief of the Papacy. Libels of all kinds having the common purpose of destroying the free principles and vilifying the free persons of England's Commonwealth of Protestants were poured into England, and amongst them, more subvertive and more vicious than them all, was "Leycester's Commonwealth." In the majority of its particulars it can be proved to be false. We have no cause to assume that the minority of its accusations were ever more verifiable. Yet upon this outrageous document nearly all extant lives and characters of Leicester have been founded. The most odious of all the delinquencies therein charged upon him is, undoubtedly, that of murdering Amy Robsart.

And to the commission of this crime facts do not point. Next in hideousness are the accusations of poisoning, with the professional help of Dr Julio, Sir Nicholas Throckmorton, Lord Sheffield, the Earl of Essex, the King of Sweden, and many others supposed to have crossed his path or thwarted his wishes. In regard to Throckmorton, who died in Leicester's house, he had become a staunch partisan and a keen assistant of the Favourite, and of Throckmorton's loss Leicester wrote to Walsingham at the time in a strain of genuine regret.

Enquiry cannot now be made into some of the accusations. Those investigated at the time were proved to be false. Others, even enemies of his, provided they were persons of any judgment, believed, when they were made, that they had been trumped up. Julio probably aided Leicester in some more or less questionable political proceedings; but he was physician to other members of the Court, concerning whom no tradition of dark practices exists, and it was inevitable in sixteenth-century England that an Italian, cunning in the use of drugs, should seem to the popular mind made only for the uses of a Borgia.

Yet Leicester cannot be exculpated from all guilt in respect of designs on human life. He certainly suggested, if he did not attempt, some political murders, and it was more by good fortune than by good intention that they did not take place. When he rode after Queen Mary, in the hour of her accession, it is doubtful if he personally contemplated any harsher dealing than her capture, and her conduct to the Tower for detention. In regard to Simier, his application of lynch-law cannot be made to seem altogether abhorrent. As to the Queen of Scots, Leicester originally favoured her release. It was only after the revelation of her conspiracies against his Queen's life and his own that he was persuaded to the judgment that for the peace of England and the safety of Elizabeth, Mary must die. The reasons were political, not personal, for his suggestion of a *secret* execution.

When the libels of Jesuits and seminary priests multiplied against him, he certainly became more emphatic for the removal of her who was the inspiration and the strength of every assault on Elizabeth, or on Elizabeth's councillors, and in 1584 he was keenest of all the Ministers for the formation of the loyal and patriotic Association of nobility and gentry, who bound themselves by mutual vows to pursue unto death whosoever should plot anything against Elizabeth. Mary was chief of those who designed the Queen of England's death. The Association was a necessity of public order. No one knew better than Leicester how averse Elizabeth would be from putting her graceful and decorative signature to a warrant for the execution of her cousin. It was dreadful to her to sentence any one to death. The sin of Leicester was the sin of Elizabeth. Neither of them could be easily persuaded to strike a direct blow. They could not meet great causes greatly. But that the advices of Leicester concerning Mary were prompted by a commonly murderous or a personally vindictive intent is not to be believed for a moment. Lust of cruelty and gluttony of blood were not sins for which either the Favourite or his Queen had any predilection. It was rather the calculating faculty in Leicester that was responsible for his remorseless designs upon the Scottish Siren. He reckoned out the forces and counterforces of Mary's passionate persistences, and of Elizabeth's hesitations and tolerances; of the loyalty of Catholics to Rome, and of the devotion of Protestants to England. It was his genius to forestall events, and to anticipate processes of law.

The Jesuit censure on him was that his Will was seldom Law. It cannot be denied that he often argued and acted as if his Power were above Law, and this, although his Queen rarely missed an opportunity of proving

to him what were the limits of his authority,
and what the extent of hers.

Yet so long as Leicester remained in any sort
the Queen's favourite, he possessed an influence
impossible to overthrow. In 1581, the Earl
of Oxford—on whose counter-attractions Lord
Sussex had relied for the destruction of much
of Leicester's authority — got into difficulties
through his drunken and horribly dissolute
habits, and was proceeded against by his wife,
a daughter of Lord Burghley. At the same
time a quarrel flared up between Sussex and
Leicester. The Queen ordered all three earls
under arrest. A letter from Burghley to Sir
Christopher Hatton, thanking him for his "good
and honourable dealing with her Majesty in
the case of my daughter of Oxford," commented upon the collision of the two elder
peers. " I am sorry to hear of the disaster
fallen out yesterday betwixt two great Planets;
but I hear they know their Jupiter, and will
obey Her Majesty, rather to content her than
to follow their own humours."

Whatever their motives for making up, the
antagonistic peers became, as on a former occasion, outwardly reconciled, and were set free.
Oxford was detained to be "dealt with for
his wife " and " confronted with his accusers."
Sussex may have had some hope that the revelations of his *protegé's* articles of defence might do

x

for the Favourite what his own attacks had never succeeded in accomplishing. But Sussex had never been blessed with real perspicuity, and in his judgments of Leicester and Oxford, he mistook both men. Oxford was a thoroughly vicious person. Elizabeth and Hatton, even as Lord and Lady Burghley and their unfortunate daughter, recognised this fact. It was unavailing for the destruction of the "baneful" authority of Leicester, that Oxford accused the Favourite of fortifying Kenilworth under pretence of making fireworks for the Queen, and of boasting of his greatness and influence with Elizabeth, saying *he was able to make the proudest subject sweat that would oppose him.* If the Queen believed the yarn of Oxford's spinning, she was perhaps not all displeased that the noble of her own creation could make any other of her proudest subjects "sweat." The Earl of Sussex certainly must often have perspired from the heat of his rage against Leicester. But this quarrel of 1581 was the last of many famous conflicts between the "old" peer and the "new." Thomas Ratcliffe, Earl of Sussex, died in 1583.

In the following year, the light of two other "great planets" was eclipsed by the shadow of mortality. The Duc d'Anjou ended a career of failure on the 31st of May. On 10th July William the Silent, Prince of Orange, was murdered. Four previous attempts had been made upon the life of this broad - minded, peace - loving, yet heroic deliverer of Holland. The policy advocated of Pope Gregory XIII. towards Elizabeth had succeeded in the case of William of Orange. Philip of Spain was the instigator of the deed. The Pope had assisted in the crime by his excommunication of the great patriot. The actual assassinator of William was certainly as deserving of canonisation as the possible murderer of Elizabeth.

And certainly the poisoned pistol-shots that killed the hero set up a rancour in the heart of the Queen. Elizabeth, at last, realised her own and her country's danger. She knew now that the plots against her life and Leicester's, and the designs on the succession of her kingdom, did not belong altogether to the region of ideas.

In 1585, Elizabeth consented—consented after her own procrastinating and hard - bargaining fashion—to send to the Low Countries, for the defence of the liberty of the States, 4,000 foot and 400 horse under the command of the most distinguished of her nobles.

The expedition had perhaps been delayed even longer than it was, had not the terrible catastrophe of the loss of Antwerp befallen the Hollanders. Alexander Farnese, Duke of Parma, and the hosts of Spain, were in possession of this most important port and city,

when the Earl of Leicester at last set sail
with a fleet of fifty ships. Among his retinue
were Lords Sheffield, Willoughby, and North,
Sir William Russell and Sir Robert Sidney.
Secretary Davison and Sir Philip Sidney—as
special envoy and governor of the cautionary
town of Flushing respectively — had preceded
him.

Some idea of the high intentions and mixed
feelings of the Favourite, and of the contradictory policies of the Queen that assisted at
his send-off, may be gathered from some passages
of letters of Leicester written in the natural
style of outpouring of which he was a master.
In August 1585, a "shrewd wrench" of his
foot, caused by his horse falling, kept Leicester
inactive for a time in Warwickshire; but his
mind was busy, and he wrote to Burghley:

" I perceive by your letters and Mr Secretary's
that her Majesty is now in good inclination
to help the Low Countries, and you both think
her Majesty will employ me. Surely, my lord,
for my own part, I am most ready to serve
her, specially in any service where I may set
my life in hazard for her safety. My only wish
is, not only for myself but for the whole, as
well those who go to serve as they that remain,
that her Majesty will take this matter (if she
will deal withal) even to the heart, as a cause
that doth concern both her life and the State.
For if her Majesty be not persuaded and fully
resolved that the cause is of other importance

than, as it were, to make a show and become
only a scarecrow, it were better never to enter
into it. And men abroad begin to doubt her
persuasion in this case, albeit every man doth
see the necessity thereof, as well as her
counsellors."

And when at last Elizabeth seemed to be
persuaded that the great enterprise against
Spain had higher uses than those of a "show"
and a "scarecrow," and Leicester was on the
point of sailing from Harwich, there was
despatched to Sir Francis Walsingham, from
the embarking general, a succession of letters
of which the following phrases are pregnant:

"I am sorry that her Majesty hath so hard
a conceit of me, that I should go about to
cozen her, as though I had got a fee simple
from her. . . ." [Leicester had mortgaged
some of his lands to the Queen for the
expenses of the fray he led.] "I thank God
I have a clear conscience for deceiving her,
and for money matters. I think I may
justly say I have been the only cause of
more gain to her coffers than all her chequer-
men have been. But so is the hap of some,
that all they do is nothing, and others that
do nothing, do all, and have all the thanks.
But I would this were all the grief I carry with
me; but God is my comfort, and on Him I
cast all, for there is no surety in this world
beside. What hope of help can I have, finding
her Majesty so strait with myself as she is?
I did trust that—this cause being hers, and

this Realm's—if I could have gotten no money of her merchants, she would not have refused to have lent money on so easy prized land as mine, to have been gainer and no loser by it. Her Majesty, I see, will make trial of me how I love her, and what will discourage me from her service. But resolved am I that no worldly respect shall draw me back from my faithful discharge of my duty towards her, though she shall show to hate me, as it goeth very near; for I find no love or favour at all. And I pray you to remember that I have not had one penny of her Majesty towards all these charges of mine—not one penny—and by all truth I have already laid out above five thousand pounds. . . . Well, let all this go; it is like I shall be the last shall bear this, and some must suffer for the people. Good Mr Secretary, let her Majesty know this, for I deserve God-a-mercy, at the least."

And further on the same day, the Earl wrote:

" I pray God open her eyes, that they may behold her present estate indeed, and the wonderful means that God doth offer unto her. If she lose these opportunities, who can look for other but dishonour and destruction? My Lord Treasurer [Burghley] hath also written me a most hearty and comfortable letter touching this voyage, not only in showing the importance of it, both for her Majesty's own safety and the Realm's, but that the whole state of religion doth depend thereon, and therefore doth faithfully promise his whole and best assistance for the supply of all wants. I was not a little glad to receive such a letter from him at this time."

CHAPTER XVII

THE *Leycester Correspondence*, edited by John Bruce, F.S.A., consists only of transcripts of actual letters, written by and to Leicester during the space of two years, with a few more directly relating to his conduct of the Netherlands expedition. This correspondence in print covers nearly five hundred octavo pages. The analysis of Leicester's character and the record of Leicester's actions in Motley's " History of the United Netherlands " run also into some five hundred pages, in all of which there is not one superfluous word. It is difficult, therefore, to condense into the space proper to the story of two years in the history of a lifetime, all informations concerning the intentions, the doings, and the achievements of Leicester in the Low Countries. The exactions and the trials of his command there, were a fierce test of character. The attitude of his Queen did not make it the easier for him to display nobility of soul or to manifest patience and good temper. His welcome to the Netherlands was auspicious. He was hailed as a Messiah. In him an afflicted people saw their deliverer from a hated tyrant. He arrived at Flushing, equipped in the arms and accoutrements proper to his condition as Lieutenant-General of the Forces of Her Majesty, but arrayed also in all the vices and the virtues, in all the talents, capacities, and deficiencies, incident to his personality and past career.

The need of the Low Countries at this climax in the drama of their development, was for an actor to play the Prince, who knew his part. No one could have been better up in his "lines" and "business" than Leicester. Later on, when his absence from the Netherlands was greatly embarrassing the Government, a Holland patriot declared that some head was necessary for the States, if it were only an onion-head. But at the time of Leicester's going to them, the Dutch had high hopes of the sagacity, benevolence, and authority of the "Prince" they welcomed with a joy expressed vociferously and in figure. Never were such pageants, masques, decorations, fireworks and devices—poetical, mythological and scriptural! A master himself in the arrangement of mummeries, the host of Kenilworth found symbolic ingenuities of the kind he himself had often perpetrated, outdone by his hosts of Flushing, Utrecht, the Hague, Leyden, and Amsterdam.

For a time entertainers and entertained gave

themselves up to banquets, processions, and ceremonials, civil, ecclesiastical and regal. But Leicester was no "onion-head," and neither in Holland, nor elsewhere, could he vegetate.

Things required doing. Leicester set about doing them. The way he did them displayed his powers and betrayed his weaknesses. There was no lack of energy and industry in his methods. The sin of sloth was not among his failings. His application to business was incessant. And, though his generalship was far from equalling that of his opponent in the field, Alexander Farnese, Duke of Parma, he was keen to fight, and not one of the young "gallants of England," who were his lieutenants in the campaign, displayed more dash and courage than he. Yet among these gallants were his stepson, the Earl of Essex, and his nephew Sir Philip Sidney.

No Prince of blood Royal ever rode statelier at the head of his troops. No genius among military commanders ever strove more assiduously to outwit the enemy by tactics, nor concerned himself more devotedly for the victualling, clothing, pay, and general fitness of his soldiers. By day or by night, as need required, he went afoot among his men, climbed in and out of trenches, and superintended the making of boat-bridges and other means of communication and assault. And no

Minister of State or ruler of a kingdom ever spent more time over negotiations, conferences, despatches, public processions, and receptions of State. It is true that in generalship, as in Government, he made blunders, and chose paths of risk when he might have walked in ways of safety. But that was because a man of many talents, industries, and designs, cannot attain to infallibility in any given direction.

Yet failure is written large across the history of Leicester's command in the Low Countries, and little credit or honour to England was the outcome of the expedition. The discredit and the dishonour, however, were not wholly brought about by the Earl. An impartial and rigorous examination of the events of the campaign, and of the conditions of the occupation, lead to the view that Elizabeth at Greenwich and at Windsor, was responsible for more of the disaster and failure than Leicester at the Hague or at Grave, Venloo, or Zutphen.

In the laboratory of Time, no harder or more exhaustive test of the individual characters of Elizabeth and of Leicester, and of the nature of their relations to one another, could have been applied than that of this war in the Netherlands into which Elizabeth, against her will, and Leicester, with eager response, were drawn. Here was the call to Elizabeth to spend men and money in defence of righteousness, honour, freedom, and — what England's careful housewife valued more — safety. She gave the flower of her generals and of her sea-captains, of the youth and of the chivalry of England; she sent even that "creature of her own," described by her to the States as a "man of such quality as all the world knows, and one whom I love as if he were my own brother," to oppose the power of Spain. But having made this armed demonstration of her right and her might, she took care, by withholding supplies, and by entering into underhand negotiations with the enemy, to prevent her army from accomplishing the purpose for which it was sent. And Leicester, who was always urging, and urging justly, that the way to peace was through a "good, sharp war," and who was able, as none other, to represent the majesty of Elizabeth and the virility of England, while possessing an undeniable courage and some capacity for the conduct of a campaign, made at the outset of his enterprise a grave and irremediable mistake. It was a mistake Elizabeth's wrath over his countenancing the assumption by the *Duc d' Anjou* of a sovereignty over the States, should have taught him not to make. But Leicester was Leicester, even as Elizabeth was Elizabeth.

It was inevitable that Robert Dudley should dream of being a king.

Leicester's "Instructions" from his Queen on his going to the Low Countries contained the order

"To let the States understand, that, whereby their commissioners they made offer unto her Majesty, first, of the sovereignty of those countries, which for sundry respects she did not accept, secondly, unto her protection, offering to be absolutely governed by such as her Majesty would appoint and send over to be her lieutenant. That her Majesty, although she would not take so much upon her as to command them in such absolute sort, yet, unless they should show themselves forward to use the advice of her Majesty to be delivered unto them by her lieutenant, to work amongst them a fair unity and concurrence for their one defence in liberal taxations and good husbanding of their contributions, for the same speedy obtaining of a place, her Majesty would think her favours unworthily bestowed upon them."

This rather indefinite instruction, Elizabeth afterwards construed into an emphatic prohibition of Leicester consenting to be invested with any further authority than that he wielded as the Lieutenant-General of the English troops. Yet she had in it enjoined the Hollanders to "use the advice" of her lieutenant, who was to work "for their one defence in liberal taxations and good husbanding."

Queen Elizabeth as "aiding friend" of the
Netherlands.

Taking into consideration these "Instructions" alone, it is not surprising that Her Majesty's Lieutenant-General, when he entered upon his duties, acceded to the pressing demand of the States to take the name and place of Governor-General of all their forces and soldiers, with the disposition of their whole revenues and taxes, the appointment of all officials, and the power of summoning the States-General of the United Provinces of Gelderland, Zutphen, Flanders, Holland, Zealand, Utrecht, and Friesland. There was a real need for the centralisation of the executive power of the numerous States, and for the establishment of a single control over all forces, civil, religious, military, and financial, English, Flemish, and Dutch, that were arrayed against Spain.

The carrying out of Elizabeth's ideal of the place and power of Leicester in the Netherlands was bound to render his position anomalous and inoperative. She nominated him only Commander-in-Chief of her army. Leicester's objection that "for him to be merely commander over five thousand English troops, when an abler soldier than himself, Sir John Norris, was at their head, was hardly worthy Her Majesty's service or himself," was a sensible objection. The dual, even quadruple, office of general and councillor for her, and general and councillor for the Provinces, was impossible to exercise without some further authority than the Queen's commission. And the Favourite maintained that Elizabeth had privately given him to understand that she would approve his acceptance of the post of Governor-General, provided the proposition of it came from the States, and not from her.

It was so much the custom of Elizabeth to advise privately what she not only did not urge, but even absolutely forbade officially, that it is quite believable that the Earl may have wrung from her, at an interview, an assent to the idea of his assuming in the Provinces an office more generally authoritative than that of Captain-General of a small body of auxiliary troops. But though persuaded against herself before the event by the honey-tongued Earl, it was impossible, when the news of his installation as " Governor-General of the United States of the Netherlands" reached her, for her to approve his appointment. She had already receded from the position she had been hardly brought to, of denouncing "the cruelty and tyranny of the Spaniards," of proclaiming the ancient friendship of England and the Netherlands, and of declaring her intention to suppress the Spanish plot for the invasion of England. And the Earl's acceptance of a more absolute government than had been agreed on between herself and the commissioners of the States, was made the more an abomination, because the news of it was communicated to her by other pens than his own.

" Your honour's forbearing to write to her Majesty all this while, notwithstanding so many messengers as cometh from thence, doth greatly offend her, more and more, and in very truth maketh all your friends here at their wits' end, what to answer or say in your behalf,"

wrote his agent, Thomas Dudley, to him.

The failure of Leicester at this momentous crisis to fling himself upon the mercy and the tenderness of the woman whose mercy and whose tenderness, hard to be evoked, his arts could rouse to pardon many insolences, constitutes a problem of his history difficult to solve. Yet when one considers the effect upon his bearing and conversation of the tremendous demonstrations of joy excited by the institution of his rule in the Provinces, a clue to the enigma of this omission of his is suggested.

Right up to this stage of his career, and throughout all the season of his influence, power, and grandeur, Leicester had never for one moment been allowed to forget that he was a creature of another—a " raised up " and " extraordinarily favoured " creature, certainly, nevertheless, a dependent minion, so completely behoven for position, sustenance, lands, wealth, liberty, and life, to his Queen, that, in sorrow or adversity, he had no thought to look even

to his God for succour, until he was quite
convinced that no help would be forthcoming
from Elizabeth. And all the while that he
had played the part of Favourite—with some
relish since Elizabeth Tudor was the Queen
he flattered, and with some cunning, for he
served also personal ends — he had been
conscious of powers in himself beyond those
of a parasite. In youth, he had selected as
his device a sprig of oak. In manhood, the
crawling, climbing ivy had been a fitter symbol
had he not chosen the emblem of the "eyes"
of Elizabeth. Yet he aspired to be an oak.
"Until the twig becomes the tree," was the
motto of the son of William the Silent—
young Maurice of Nassau — who, during the
period of his upgrowth, was serving Leicester
in Holland. Leicester's sapling days were far
behind him. Not the sprig, but the spreading
tree was the device of his present choice. He
thought the marshlands of the Provinces his
appointed rooting soil. Planted there, not
only of Elizabeth's disposition, but by the
invitation of a free people—for it was always
the conceit of Leicester to fancy himself
Governor by acclamation of the populace,
rather than by appointment of the constituted
States—Leicester trusted that the very independence of his authority would commend it
to Elizabeth's grace.

ROBERTVS DVDLEVS LEICESTRIÆ COMES REGINÆ ANGLIÆ
MISSV BELGARVM PRÆFECTVS.

Leicester in the Netherlands.

Removed from her corrective society, and relieved from her disciplinary conversation, Leicester developed an "exaggerated Ego." His pride and self-esteem stopped short only of the point of insanity. But the orations of the crowds, the compliments of the city fathers, and the deferences of the States, sufficiently turned his head for him to declare, in the course of a conversation at Delft, that the harsh punishments meted out to the Lady Jane, to Lord Guilford Dudley, and to his father, had unjustly deprived his family of their lawful inheritance—*the crown of England!*

The success of his appearance among the Netherlanders brought about a *bouleversement* of his ordinary estimates and understandings. His exaltation of mind over his attainment of a practical sovereignty, lasted sufficiently long for him to cheat himself with a vision of Elizabeth on her knees before him worshipping that wonderful thing, a Governor - General created by a power extraneous to her own.

But the Queen of England threw herself into a very different attitude from an adoring one when the portentous news from the Hague reached her. Her oaths and vituperations were frequent, choice, and most embarrassing to listen to. Her fury was increased by the information that the hated Lettice was about to join her husband with a train of servants,

Y

carriages, side-saddles, and other *impedimenta* of a travelling Household of State. "She would have no more courts under her obeisance but her own," was the Queen's avowed determination. Lady Leicester had already provoked the Queen's ire by proceeding through the city of London in a coach drawn by four milk-white steeds, and attracting all the attention that belongs to a Royal *cortège*.

The Ministers and favourites about Elizabeth who desired no impediment to the enterprise against Spain, as well as members of Leicester's household anxious to ward off from his Countess the anger of the Queen, tried with many representations and assurances to "pacify her stomach." But their efforts were unavailing. The Queen appointed Sir Thomas Heneage her Special Commissioner to inform the States that she "held it strange" that "this creature of her own" should have been pressed by them to "commit so notorious a contempt" as to accept a government more absolute than she had agreed to, "as though her long experience in government had not taught her to discover what was fit to do in matters of state." In consideration of the said contempt, the Earl was to be commanded to make a public and open resignation of the government in the place where he had accepted the same.

The Royal wrath boiled over on to pages of instructions for Heneage, in every line of which she scouted the "contempt" with which she had been treated, and on to a letter to the States, in which she announced that she had decided to recall the Earl very soon. But the last bubblings of her rage were the fiercest, and these were contained in a missive — it were perhaps better called a *missile*—to Leicester himself.

" *To my Lord of Leicester, from the Queen, by Sir Thomas Heneage.*"

"How contemptuously we conceive ourselves to have been used by you, you shall by this bearer understand, whom we have expressly sent unto you to charge you withal. We could never have imagined, had we not seen it fall out in experience, that a man raised up by ourself, and extraordinarily favoured by us above any other subject of this land, would have, in so contemptible a sort, broken our commandment in a cause that so greatly toucheth us in honour; whereof, although you have shewed yourself to make but little account, in most undutiful a sort, you may not therefore think that we have so little care of the reparation thereof as we mind to pass so great a wrong in silence unredressed. And therefore our express pleasure and commandment is, that — all delays and excuses laid apart—you do presently, upon the duty of your allegiance, obey and fulfil whatsoever the bearer hereof shall direct you to do in our name. Whereof fail not, as you will answer the contrary at your uttermost peril."

Before Heneage could depart with these letters, there arrived a messenger from Leicester to the Queen in the person of Davison, who, with Sir Philip Sidney, had been the chief adviser of the Earl in the matter of his acceptance of the supreme authority. This conscientious and painstaking man of state, though greeted with terrifying accounts of the Queen's temper, lost no time in representing to Elizabeth how strong were the causes that had led her Favourite to the step he had taken. Davison pleaded that the "corruption, partiality, and confusion" of the States' Government had made it necessary that "some one person of wisdom and authority should take the helm." Had Leicester refused, there was no one else. Besides, "Her Majesty's found favour," in which the States "reposed hope," would have been "utterly despaired of by his refusal."

But all Davison's arguments could not alter the burden of her frenzied complaint: "How dared he come to such a decision without at least imparting it to me?" She would not break the seal, in Davison's presence, of a letter from the Earl he had brought with him. If she read the communication in private, its official tone failed to touch her heart.

Leicester's second ambassador, Sir Thomas Shirley, had little more success. He urged "the necessity of the case was imminent," and

he besought Her Majesty to remember that
to the King of Spain "the government of his
lordship is no greater matter than if he were
your Lieutenant-General there; but the voyage
of Sir Francis Drake is of much greater offence
than all."

The trim little fleet, under the command of
the famous corsair, was indeed regarded by
Spain as a greater menace of her wealth and
her dignity than the more unwieldy expedition
of Leicester in the Low Countries. The reply
of Elizabeth was characteristic. "I can very
well answer for Sir Francis. Moreover, if need
be, the gentleman careth not if I should disavow him."

The Queen had subscribed a large share of
the cost of Drake's enterprise, but her contri-
bution was agreed to be private, and Drake
and his captains had laid out much money
of their own. If the expedition should be
a success — the might of Spain considerably
infringed and much treasure brought from the
Indies—England (or Elizabeth) might own the
success a national one. But if trouble ensued
therefrom, and Spain should talk of retaliation,
then England (or Elizabeth) would disown
Drake for an impudent pirate. The adventurer
was aware of the nature of his commission.

The response of Sir Thomas Shirley to the
Queen's significant utterance was apt and

instant: "Even so standeth my Lord, if your disavowing of him may also stand with your Highness's favour towards him."

In this reply we have a suggestion of another explanation of Leicester's omission to write with his own hand, or to send a token to his Queen at the moment of his venturing to exceed her written instructions, and to follow a course of which—so he maintained—he had had her approval by word of mouth. He may have purposely refrained from the direct communication in order to leave her free to disavow his action, and to state, without risk of contradiction, that he had "most contemptuously" neglected to acquaint her with his step.

However that may be, Elizabeth was now caught in a trap of her own setting. She had for so long been in the habit of waiting the issue of events before taking action, and of coquetting with every side of a question and all possible developments of a case before making cause with any one, that Leicester, who knew all her moods and all the many variabilities of her opinion, may have felt quite assured that odds were even as to her ultimate approval of any step he might take. She had undoubtedly considered the idea of the States conferring on him a greater authority than she equipped him with, and since Leicester took the course he did, we may believe that she at first considered the idea with no special disfavour. It was perhaps no great disloyalty for him to think that some of the glory and greatness he had so lavishly helped to pay for, and which he desired to appropriate to his native land for ever, he might enjoy himself for a time; especially did he seem to be entitled to an office he meant to use to the best of his ability for the suppression of the Spanish and Papal plots that were now aimed more directly than ever at the invasion of England, at his own and at Elizabeth's assassination, and at the placing of Mary Stuart (married, perhaps, to the Duke of Parma) on the throne of England.

But Elizabeth was again blinding her eyes to the dangers that threatened, and working more actively than when Leicester had left her, to effect a peace that would restore the Provinces to Spanish dominion, with or without certain safeguards of their religious liberties, but decidedly with compensation to Elizabeth for the expense she had been at in assisting the States to rebel against their head! Even in the age so justly called Elizabethan, only Elizabeth could have imagined a peace so monstrous. But the defiance of Leicester's attitude was the click of the lock to the trap her own diplomacies had made. And her rage continued. Yet not all of the fury was for thwarted policies. Sir Thomas Shirley, at the conclusion of a long and succinct argument with the Queen, made bold to suggest that other causes than the public one fed her anger.

"His Lordship's giving up of the government," Sir Thomas pleaded, "may leave them [the Netherlanders] altogether without government, and in worse case than they were ever in before. For now the authority of the States is dissolved, and his Lordship's government is the only thing that holdeth them together. I do beseech your Highness, then, to consider well of it, and if there be any private cause for which you take grief against his Lordship, nevertheless to have regard unto the public cause, and to have a care of your own safety, which, in many wise men's opinions, standeth much upon the good maintenance and upholding of this matter."

"I believe nothing of what you say concerning the dissolving of the States," said the Queen curtly. What a woman she was! "I know well enough that the States do remain states still. I mean not to do harm to the cause, but only to reform that which his Lordship hath done beyond his warrant from me."

Shirley made one more appeal to the woman in her. On the following day, he told the Queen the Earl was "again attacked by the disease of which Dr Goodrowse did once cure him," and he asked Her Majesty to give the

said Goodrowse leave to go to the Netherlands
to attend on his Lordship. "Certainly—with
all my heart, with all my heart he shall have
him," said the Queen, "and sorry I am that
his Lordship hath that need of him."

But when Shirley tried to press his advantage
with "Your Highness is a very gracious prince,
who are pleased not to suffer his Lordship to
perish in health, though otherwise you remain
deeply offended with him," Elizabeth replied
sharply: "You know my mind. I may not
endure that my man should alter my commission and the authority that I gave him
upon his own fancies and without me."

Sir Thomas Shirley sent to Leicester a full
account of his interviews with the Queen,
making this comment: "Your Lordship now
sees things just as they stand. Your Lordship
is exceeding wise. *You know the Queen and
her nature best of any man.*"

Who should have known them better? Yet,
in the opinion of his best friends at Court,
Leicester had behaved as if he had never made
any study of her character. We know that
this was not the case. Yet he miscalculated
the effect of his personal silence. The Queen
neither disavowed his enterprise while favouring him, nor adopted his policy as her own.
Before the arrival of Sir Thomas Heneage
in the Netherlands, Leicester had noted that

"the Prince of Parma feels himself in great jollity that her Majesty doth rather mislike than allow of our doings here, which, if it be true, let her be sure her own sweet self shall first smart." And a few days later, Lord Warwick in England wrote to his brother:

"Well, our mistress's extreme rage doth increase rather than diminish, and she giveth out great threatening words against you. Therefore make the best assurance you can for yourself, and trust not her oath, for that her malice is great and unquenchable is the wisest of their opinions here, and as for other friendships, as far as I can learn, it is as doubtful as the other. Wherefore, my good brother, repose your whole trust in God, and He will defend you in despite of all your enemies. And let this be a great comfort to you, and so it is likewise to myself and all your assured friends, and that is, that you were never so honoured and loved in your life amongst all good people as you are at this day, only for dealing so nobly and wisely in this action, as you have done; so that whatsoever cometh of it, you have done your part. I praise God from my heart for it. Once again have great care for yourself, (I mean for your safety), and if she will needs revoke you to the overthrowing of the cause, if I were as you, if I could not be assured *there*, (*i.e.* in the Provinces), I would go to the farthest part of Christendom, rather than ever come into England again. Take heed whom you trust, for that *you have some false boys about you.*"

This letter, besides containing a direct incitement to Leicester to hold to the control of

the Low Countries, no matter what political
friendships Elizabeth might enter into, reflects
very truly the opinion of "all good people"
—the Protestants and Patriots of England, to
which party the Earl of Warwick was staunch
—on Leicester's dealings in the Low Countries.
And truly the intention of Leicester's enterprise was admirable. Fearlessly—for, besides
the risks of battle, the pistol that had slain
William of Orange was pointed at the
Governor - General of the Low Countries
wherever he went — Leicester made himself a
target to divert attacks on England. Liberally
he poured out money, fittingly to represent
the majesty of his Queen. Laboriously he
worked to make his hold upon the Government of the Provinces firm for his native
country, and secure against Spain.

The following account of himself to Lord
Burghley is confirmative of the sincerity and
nobility of his intentions.

"I know not how her Majesty doth mean
to dispose of me. It hath grieved me more
than I can express, that for faithful and good
service she should so deeply conceive against
me. God knows with what mind I have
served her Highness, and perhaps some others
might have failed. Yet she is neither tied one
jot by covenant or promise by me in any way,
nor at one groat the more charges, but myself
two or three thousand pounds sterling more
than now is like to be well spent. I will

desire no partial speech in my favour. If my doings be ill for her Majesty and the Realm, let me feel the smart of it. The cause is now well forward; let not her Majesty suffer it to quail."

But for too long had Leicester crept round about, and clung like ivy to the throne from which upsprang the oak-like form of Elizabeth Tudor, for him to stand aloof now, a sturdy, independent tree. One pities him in that when he had the mind to play the man, the habits, the associations, and the practices of his past life rose up and mastered him. The lightning of Elizabeth's jealous wrath blasted the rearing crest of the spreading oak beside her. She could not be propitiated by reasoning, and no greatness in States or men could overawe her.

With dignity Leicester bowed to the will of the Queen: "I speak from my soul for her Majesty's service. I am for myself upon an hour's warning to obey her good pleasure," was the conclusion of his letter to Burghley. It was not in him to do as his brother Warwick had advised, and, since he could not be assured in his governorship of the Netherlands, "go to the farthest part of Christendom rather than ever come into England again." To the feet of Elizabeth, the woman, he crawled at last with a letter too tender and too intimate to survive either in draft or in original among the State-papers of a nation.

CHAPTER XVIII

BUT if there never has been, never will be found the letter that made peace again between Elizabeth and her favourite, we have the record of Lord Burghley of its effect upon her.

"She read your letter, and, in very truth, I found her princely heart touched with favourable interpretation of your actions; affirming them to be only offensive to her in that she was not made privy to them; not now misliking that you had authority."

And Elizabeth signalised the return of " Sweet Robin " to her favour by writing to him a letter wherein her flattered womanhood struggled hard for expression with the only half-mollified anger of the Queen.

"It is always thought," wrote Elizabeth, "in the opinion of the world, a hard bargain when both parties are losers, and so doth fall out in the case between us two. You, as we hear, are greatly grieved in respect of the great displeasure you find we have conceived against you. We are no less grieved that a subject of ours, of that quality that you are, a creature of our own, and one that hath always received

349

an extraordinary portion of our favour above all our subjects, even from the beginning of our reign, should deal so carelessly, not to say contemptuously, as to give the world just cause to think that we are had in contempt by him that ought most to respect and reverence us, which, we do assure you, hath wrought as great grief in us as any one thing that ever happened unto us.

" We are persuaded that you, that have so long known us, cannot think that ever we could have been drawn to have taken so hard a course therein had we not been provoked by an extraordinary cause. But for that your grieved and wounded mind hath more need of comfort than reproof, who, we are persuaded, though the act of contempt can no ways be excused, had no other meaning and intent than to advance our service, we think meet to forbear to dwell upon a matter wherein we ourselves do find so little comfort, assuring you that whosoever professeth to love you best taketh not more comfort of your well-doing, or discomfort of your evil-doing, than ourself."

This expression of a qualified affection, formed the preamble to instructions to the Earl to retain the authority of absolute governor while —if the arrangement could be made—dispensing with the title. And the variability of the womanly moods of the great Elizabeth was responsible for the Queen very shortly picking a quarrel with the States, because — on the second thoughts excited by the Queen's anger over their first performance — they were not disposed to allow Leicester absolutely to play the autocrat.

The character of the Favourite's letter of rejoinder to Her Majesty's epistle, undoubtedly indicates the nature of the communication that made the peace between them.

"Most dear and gracious lady," he wrote on the 2nd of June, "my care and service here do breed me nothing but grief and unhappiness. I have never had your Majesty's good favour since I came into this charge—a matter that from my first beholding your eyes hath been most dear unto me above all earthly treasures. Never shall I love that place or like that soil which shall cause the lack of it. Most gracious Lady, consider my long, true and faithful heart toward you. Let not this unfortunate place here bereave me of that which, above all the world, I esteem there, which is your favour and your presence. I see my service is not acceptable, but rather more and more disliketh you. Here I can do your Majesty no service; there I can do you some, at the least rub your horse's heels —a service which shall be much more welcome to me than this, with all that these men may give me."

One cannot but applaud the cleverness of the contemptuous "these men," whose commission to defend the liberties of two nations was but a poor thing in comparison to rubbing the heels of a jennet of Elizabeth's riding. And the conclusion of Leicester's letter is still more strongly in the vein that was the only offering to Elizabeth's benignity.

"I do, humbly and from my heart, prostrate at your feet, beg this grace at your sacred hands, that you will be pleased to let me return to my home-service, with your favour, let the revocation be used in what sort shall please and like you. But if ever spark of favour was in your Majesty toward your old servant, let me obtain this my humble suit; protesting before the Majesty of all Majesties, that there was no cause under Heaven but his and yours, even for your own special and particular cause, I say, could have made me take this absent journey from you in hand. If your Majesty shall refuse me this, I shall think all grace clean gone from me, and I know my days will not be long."

And on June 6th Leicester still burned fires of propitiation before the altar of his divinity.

"But that my fear is such, most dear and gracious Lady, as my unfortunate destiny will hardly permit, whilst I remain here, any good acceptation of so simple a service as mine, I should greatly rejoice and comfort myself with the hope of your Majesty's most prayed-for favour. But of late, being by your own sacred hand lifted even up into Heaven with joy of your favour, I was bye and bye, without any new desert or offence at all, cast down and down again into the depth of all grief. God doth know, my dear and dread Sovereign, that after I first received your resolute pleasure by

Sir Thomas Heneage, I made neither stop nor stay, nor any excuse to be rid of this place and to satisfy your command. . . . So much I mislike this place and fortune of mine, as I desire nothing in the world so much as to be delivered, with your favour, from all charge here, fearing still some new cross of your displeasure to fall upon me, trembling continually with the fear thereof, in such sort as till I may be fully confirmed in my new regeneration of your wonted favour, I cannot receive that true comfort which doth appertain to so great a hope. Yet I will not only acknowledge with all humbleness and dutiful thanks the exceeding joy those last blessed lines brought to my long-wearied heart, but will, with all true loyal affection, attend that further joy from your sweet self which may utterly extinguish all consuming fear away."

Thus was Elizabeth won! The method of Leicester's conquest was not admirable, yet one is tempted to regret that he did not apply it earlier. The long wait for the signification of the Queen's approval of his acceptance of the governorship gave scope to the industry of the "false boys," of whom Lord Warwick had warned his brother. "Bruits" of the "mislike" into which Leicester had fallen and of the Queen's intention of making peace with Spain, marred any possible success Leicester might have had. Another letter addressed to the Queen by Leicester on the 27th of June, shows the depth of the fall of the "terrestrial Lucifer" from his

z

ideals. It shows also that for all his abject professions, his manhood and its ambitions died hard within him.

"As the cause is now followed," he wrote, "it is not worth the cost or the danger. Your Majesty was invited to be Sovereign, protector or aiding friend. You chose the third, and if your aid had been indeed so given that these people could have been assured of its continuance, if your Majesty had taken their cause indeed to heart, they would have then yielded large contributions for any number of years, and no practices could have drawn them from you. But they now perceive how weary you are of them, and how willing that any other had them, so that your Majesty were rid of them. They would rather have lived with bread and drink under your Majesty's protection than with all their possessions under the King of Spain. It has almost broken their hearts to think your Majesty should not care any more for them. But if you mean soon to leave them, they will be gone almost before you hear of it. I will do my best, therefore, to get into my hands three or four most principal places in North Holland, so as you shall rule these men, and make war and peace as you list. Part not with Brill for anything. With these places, you can have what peace you will in an hour, and have your debts and charges readily answered. But your Majesty must deal graciously with them at present, and if you mean to leave them, keep it to yourself. Whatever you mean really to do, you must persuade them now that you mean sincerely and well by them. They have desperate conceipts of your Majesty."

ROBERTUS DUDLEUS COMES LEICESTRIÆ
Nomine Ordinum Foederatorum ab anno 1586 ad
annum 1588 regimini præfuit .

Cum Privilegio Sad Ima

The implied reproaches of this letter were not undeserved. Elizabeth, though there had been some sincerity in her intention of being "an aiding friend," had greatly deceived the faith reposed in her. She had not only betrayed the confidence of the Hollanders by entering into secret negotiations for a peace, and by a sudden command, in the midst of earnest warfare, that only defensive operations must be undertaken, but she had abused the confidences of her own subjects, by leaving her soldiers unpaid, unfed, and unclothed. On several occasions the States had to advance money, quite outside of their bargains, to pay the English troops. And not only Leicester, who was eloquent enough in appeals on their behalf, but all the English captains and emissaries (including Sir Thomas Heneage and Lord Buckhurst) were constantly beseeching Her Majesty to show more pity for her starveling army. It would not appear, however, from the Queen's letter to her Favourite on 19th July (1586) that she had no care for the health and equipment of her defenders. Characteristically, she imputed the blame of their condition to some other than herself. Her affectionate letter to Leicester, now once more playing her game and foregoing any possible part of his own in life, has its interests and revelations in every line.

" ROB,—I am afraid you will suppose, by my wandering writings, that a midsummer's moon hath taken large possession of my brains this month ; but you must needs take things as they come in my head, though order be left behind me. When I remember your request to have a discreet and honest man that may carry my mind, and see how all goes there, I have chosen this bearer [*Thomas Wilkes*] whom you know and have made good trial of. I have fraught him full of my conceipts of those country matters [*the affairs of the Low Countries*], and imparted what way I mind to take, and what is fit for you to use. I am sure you can credit him, and so I will be short with these few notes. First, that Count Maurice and Count Hohenlo find themselves trusted of you, esteemed of me, and to be carefully regarded if ever peace should happen, and of that assure them on my word, that never yet deceived any." Oh, rare Elizabeth ! " And for Norris and other captains that voluntarily, without commandment, have many years ventured their lives and won our nation honour, and themselves fame, let them not be discouraged by any means, neither by new - come men nor by old trained soldiers elsewhere. If there be fault in using of soldiers or making profit by them, let them hear of it without open shame, and doubt not I will well chasten them therefore. It frets me not a little that the poor soldiers that hourly venture life should want their due, that well deserve rather reward ; and look, in whom the fault may truly be proved, let them smart therefore. And if the treasurer be found untrue or negligent, according to desert he shall be used. But you know my old wont that love not to discharge from office without desert. God forbid! I pray you let this bearer know what may be learned herein, and for the treasure I have joined Sir Thomas Shirley to see all this money discharged in due sort, where it needeth and behoveth.

"Now will I end, that do imagine I talk still with you, and therefore loathly say farewell one hundred thousand times, though ever I pray God bless you from all harm, and save you from all foes. With my million and legion of thanks for all your pains and cares,—As you know, ever the same   E. R.

" *P.S.*—Let Wilkes see that he is acceptable to you. If anything there be that W. shall desire answer of be such as you would have but me to know, write it to myself. You know I can keep both others' counsel and mine own. Mistrust not that anything you would have kept shall be disclosed by me, for although this bearer ask many things, yet you may answer him such as you shall think meet, and write to me the rest."

In the business-like directions, calm authority, and luxuriant sentimentality of this letter, we see the executive Queen and the doting woman in the blend which constituted Elizabeth at her best. Pity it is this blend is not all there was of Elizabeth. And pity also that the dash, the discernment, and the daring which enabled Leicester to start with happy auguries his rule in Holland, are not all there was of Leicester. But among other bad and questionable qualities, the Favourite of Elizabeth had a propensity as great as that of his Queen for vituperative language. He could swear oaths and call names as round and as hard as could Elizabeth. And he did not possess in the same degree as she did the virtue of loving not to discharge from office without desert.

After the collapse of his hopes of vice-regality, he became implacable against many. The bolts of his wrath fell about rather promiscuously, but he certainly believed the accusation he brought against Norris, the Treasurer of the army and uncle of Sir John, of keeping back part of the soldiers' pay. This peculation was peculiarly galling to one who had poured out all his living on the expedition, and who experienced such terrible difficulty in obtaining the most necessary supplies for his troops.

He was virulent also against England's first fighting-man, Sir John Norris. He disliked all the "bunch of brave brethren" that constituted the Norris family.

"His brother Edward is as ill as he," wrote the Earl on an occasion, "but John is right the late Earl of Sussex's son;" [How much Leicester must have disliked the nobleman!] "he will so dissemble and crouch, and so cunningly carry his doings, as no man living would imagine that there were half the malice or vindictive mind that plainly his words prove to be." And Leicester vowed he would hang Sir John Norris, and "his patience and slyness should not serve him."

For a man "infamed by the death of his wife," Leicester was curiously reckless in his threats against those who offended him. He called Wilkes "a villain, a devil, without faith or religion." And he referred to the inexpertness of Count Maurice and his "base brother," Admiral Justinus de Nassau, in preventing the loss of Sluys, as "the vile, lewd dealing of these men that have so naughtily carried themselves in this matter."

The number of wordy quarrels Leicester managed to enter into while in Holland, did more than anything else to make him unpopular. As the months went on, he who had been acclaimed as a god, and worshipped as a redeemer, came to be regarded with suspicion and dissatisfaction. But Leicester's recklessness was not all. Elizabeth crowned the sins and follies of her "friendly aid" to the Dutch by withdrawing from the States, at the thickest of their fight with Parma, the only man they acknowledged as a chief.

It is true that Leicester himself, impulsively, and in eagerness for some relief from the anxieties of his office, was for a sudden return home, without establishing any kind of regency in his absence, and that by the direction of Elizabeth, he remained until the arrival from England of a deputy. The state of his health, and the real shock of the death of Sir Philip Sidney, had added to his desire for a short rest.

But, having got her Favourite back in England, the Queen followed up a reception of him, in which pomp and affection were mingled, by making as if she never intended to part from him again. Leicester, for all the impetuosity of his self-grant of leave, was more conscious than Elizabeth of the mistake of his absence, and more anxious, when in England, to retrace his false step. He found himself on his return, as Sir Walter Raleigh had written to assure him he would, "agayne her sweet Robyn," and she had allowed his leave for a weighty and tremendous cause.

The uncompromising objects of the famous Babington conspiracy made it imperative that the activities of Mary Stuart should be finally suppressed.

So long as the captive could see the daylight of a restored and extended regality at any hole —no matter how small a one—of her prison-chamber, she would continue to act and to plan in view of that regality. And she would never cease to conspire against her chief gaoler —Elizabeth. To set Mary free had long been a political impossibility. Scotland did not want her. Her son James did not want her. France did not want her. To Philip of Spain, she would have been useful. He might, with a show of right, have conquered England in her name. Her existence was a constant invitation to him to launch against England the Invincible Armada that, boat by boat, and fleet by fleet, had long been building and assembling in Spanish ports. But the grandiosity of Philip made him almost equally satisfied to claim the throne of England for himself. He was a descendant of John of Gaunt, and as heir of his second wife, Mary Tudor, he had a further title that, to himself at least, justified any assault upon the power of Elizabeth. Mary Stuart, free, would have found herself a decided fifth wheel to the European coach which was, to be sure, borne along on the Hapsburg, Bourbon, Tudor, and Stuart dynasties. Only James, and not his mother, now represented the family of Stuart. Yet Mary Stuart, in prison, was the motive-force of many of the disagreements between the Royal houses of Europe, and of nearly all the disaffections, disputes, and miseries of the Kingdom of England.

Every Minister on Elizabeth's Council in whom remained any loyalty to England—and there were but few who, in their final thoughts, had no devotion to their native land—told Queen Elizabeth that the " Daughter of Debate " must die. Leicester, as has been shown, had long been calling for her dispatch. Yet, in this hour of awful decision, Elizabeth required her

Favourite at her side, chiefly to advise of a manner of freeing England from a danger-spot that would leave the English Queen guiltless of a sister's blood.

To the Queen herself, rather than to her Favourite, belongs the responsibility of endeavouring, when judgment and verdict had formally been given, to get "justice" executed upon the prisoner secretly. But the craft and the force in Elizabeth that could prevail upon a Sir Francis Drake to lead against a foreign power, expeditions of aggression and spoliation, of which she would share the profit while denying the responsibility, could not extort from men of condition and character fit to be entrusted with such a service to their Queen, a consent to take away the life of the Queen of Scots.

The mind of Leicester was perhaps too full of anxieties about the critical affairs of the States to have left in it any vindictiveness against an enemy whose fate was sure, although it was being deferred because Elizabeth wished "by God" that Mary's execution "could be done in some way that would not throw blame on her." In any case, Leicester's part in the final act of the tragedy of Mary Stuart was that of being one of the ten councillors— Lords Burghley, Howard, Hunsden, Cobham, and Derby, with Sir Francis Knollys, Sir

Mary, Queen of Scots, prepared for execution.

Francis Walsingham, Sir Christopher Hatton, and Secretary Davison, were the others—who, when the Queen at last signed the warrant of execution, saw to the fulfilment of its order. He was not present at the final horrifying scene at Fotheringay.

The only step towards hastening Mary's end Leicester can be said to have taken personally, was his urging his Queen, upon his return from Holland, to proceed fast in the great cause. But it was his anxiety for the Council to get at the discussion of the Netherlands' cause that made him insistent to have the barrier to the advancement of all other political business removed.

"Touching the Low Country cause," he wrote to Wilkes in Holland in December 1586, "very little is done yet, by reason of the continued business we have had about the Queen of Scots' matters."

That business over, and the rash, beauteous Queen removed finally from all association with England's political desperadoes, the affairs of the Netherlands received the attention of which they were in need.

Unfortunately for Holland, for England, and for Leicester himself, the Governor-General, sick at heart over the failure of plans which, however grandiose, had been in a great measure disinterested, betrayed the weakness and the

villainy that were in him by fiercely turning
on a number of colleagues and assistants in
the great enterprise of the Netherlands, and
attributing to insufficiencies, to spites, and
to delinquencies in them, the failures brought
about by his own arrogance and *entêtement*, and
by his Queen's double-dealing and parsimony.

Poor Davison was the first upon whom the
wrath of the chief fell. This Secretary had
certainly counselled the Earl's assumption of
the Governorship, but then he had never been
told of the Queen's prohibition of his accept-
ing such an office. In his audiences with Her
Majesty, in which he presented Leicester's
formal intimation of the rank awarded him,
Davison had been loyal to the Governor-
General, to the States, and to the principles
of Reform and Independence signified by the
Expedition. His manner had not lacked
respect; but he had argued stoutly, and told
the Queen to her face that in his own hearing
she had expressed, or allowed to be expressed
for her, her agreeableness to the acceptance of
any authority the States might choose to offer to
any Lieutenant-General she should elect to send.

It was a mistake to remind a woman, whose
postures of feeling and intention were so constantly changing, of past attitudes of mind.
Leicester would never have committed a folly
like unto that. Yet Davison most certainly

did not deserve the letter in which the Governor - General railed at the "negligent carelessness, whereof I many hundred times told you that you would mar the goodness of the matter, and breed me her Majesty's displeasure." The implications of the letter's valedictory were also unmerited. "Thus fare you well, and except your embassages have better success, I shall have no cause to commend them."

And Leicester's denunciation of the unfortunate Davison, in a letter to Walsingham, was even more emphatic and meaner spirited than the incriminations hurled at Davison himself.

"And I must thank him only for my blame, and so he will confess to you, for I protest before God, no necessity here could have made me leave her Majesty unacquainted with the cause before I would have accepted of it, but only his so earnest pressing me with his faithful assured promise to discharge me, however her Majesty should take it. For you all see there she had no other cause to be offended but this, and by the Lord, he was the only cause. . . ."

Vanity makes simpletons of the wariest, but it is difficult to believe that the crafty Leicester was ever so completely a fool as to hold that any other man than himself could discharge him from the consequences of disobeying the Royal Elizabeth. Paltry is the spirit of Leicester's vindications of his honour, but his chagrin over his project's failure, and over the Queen's commissions to other officers of hers, to oversee and report upon the conduct of himself the greatest of them, was intense. "I am too, too weary of the high dignity," is a real heart-cry. "Whatsoever become of me, give me leave to speak for the poor soldiers," is a nobler utterance. Leicester was ever genuinely concerned for the right treatment of his troops. "If they be not better maintained, being in this strange country, there will be neither good service done, nor be without great dishonour to her Majesty." There is less of sincerity perhaps in the announcement that the Queen's disregard of the wants of her army "is one cause that will glad me to be rid of this heavy high calling, and wish me at my poor cottage again, if any I shall find." Kenilworth, Kew, and Wanstead, could certainly be considered cottages only in a manner of speech, that, to say the least of it, was self-conscious and self-commiserative.

Leicester's attacks, after his final visit to the Netherlands, on Lord Buckhurst, Sir John Norris, and Sir Thomas Wilkes, were even more determined and virulent than those on Davison. Against these gentlemen and their activities during his absence in England, he caused the Queen in Council to make accusations of gross mismanagement. The records of the charges brought against the three on the whole successful and altogether loyal servants of England and of Elizabeth, together with the answers of those servants and Leicester's rejoinders, are instructive, if somewhat tedious reading. Whatsoever the specific complaints lodged against each one, their dignified denials of the faults attributed to them, and Leicester's detailed and pictorial affirmations of their misdemeanours, leave the impression that the one certain offence of their committing was that of their taking Leicester to be only a man of like passions with themselves.

Yet many letters of the Favourite at this time, as earlier, reveal to us other Leicesters than the pettish, vindictive, clamorous one. Passages from only three of these letters may be quoted to exemplify not only his admirable epistolary style, but his courage, enthusiasm, devotion, kindliness, and pity.

We take first, part of a letter written to Mr Secretary Walsingham, from Holland, on 6th October 1586.

"Sir, I thank God he hath given us this day a very happy success of the two principal forts here. We have taken one by a gallant and a thorough-fought assault, and for a quarter of an hour we did look for a very furious resistance, yet so it pleased God to daunt their hearts, and to animate these worthy soldiers who attempted it, as it was entered, and the enemy, as many as did abide, killed, the rest fled to the other fort. There was one gentleman whom we all present did behold, that had the leading of all the rest that went to the assault, which was Mr Edward Stanley, lieutenant to Sir William Stanley. Since I was born, I did never see any man to behave himself as he did. First climb the breech a pike-length before and above any person that followed him, so did he alone maintain the fight, first with his pike, then with the stumps of his pike, and afterwards his sword, against at the least nine or ten, and every man either brake his pike upon his breast or hit him with the shot of their musket, yet would he not back a foot, but kept himself in this sort without any one man to get up to him, the ground was so false, being all sandy, insomuch as we all gave him for lost if he had a hundred lives, for I was within twenty-eight yards and less, myself, and V^m [*five thousand*] saw it beside, being all in yellow saving his cuirass. When he had long thus dealt most valiantly and worthily, and none of his company easily could come to him, at length they all came so fast together as one bare up another even to the top of the breech, where that gentleman got a halberd and leapt among the enemies, and then the rest with him, in so resolute manner as they speedily dispatched the enemy, and in the sight of all the town, both placed their ensigns and made this fight. A place they little looked to be won so soon, and in all troth, it is one of the strongest places for sure fights within, that ever I saw in all my life. But this gentleman shall I never forget if I live a hundred years, for if he had fainted and tarried for his fellows, as many one would have done, we had been like enough to have made a new battery for the rest; but even so worthily he did by

God's goodness, as he was the chief cause of man's work, of all the honour of this day, and he shall have part of my living for it as long as he lives. And I would God her Majesty had seen this enterprize, for it was worthy her sight to see the willingness of her subjects, their valour in performing, and with how little loss of them it was achieved, notwith-standing that we had all the artillery of the town against them on the one side, and the other fort on the other, yet was there not slain five persons in all, nor above six hurt, whereof an honest proper young gentleman of my brother of Warwicks is one, called Cooke, who even at the first attempt was by the shot of a cannon thwart his belly stricken so strangely as I never saw ; his armour broken with a hole as big as a bullet, himself with a piece of the armour cut along his belly, two inches deep, and yet his bowels whole, and I am in hope of his life.

.   .   .   .

"Lastly, and that will not like you least, your son and mine [Sir Philip Sidney] is well amend-ing as ever any man hath done for so short time. He feeleth no grief now but his long lying. His wife is with him, and I to-morrow am going to him for a start. But for his hurt, that Thursday may run among any of our Thursdays, for there was never a more valiant day's service seen this hundred years by so few men against so many, and the most of them such men as those were, lords, knights, and gentlemen among others. . . . Here will be many worthy men as ever England had. Mr Norris is a most valiant soldier surely, and all are now perfect good friends here. . . ."

Another, also to Walsingham, on 23rd December 1586, refers to the sad tale of Sir Philip's death and his widow's serious illness.

"I cannot be quiet till I know how my daughter doth amend, wishing her even as to my own child, which God willing, I shall always esteem her to be. I would gladly make a start to you, but to - morrow King Antonio" [*of Portugal, and an opponent of Spain*] "comes hither, but my heart is there with you, and my prayer shall go to God for you and for yours. There is a letter come from the Scottish Queen that has wrought tears, but I trust shall do no further harm, albeit the delay is so dangerous."

This letter went from the Court at Greenwich during the time Leicester spent in England between his two commands in Holland. The effusion to the Queen that follows, is assigned by the editor of the *State Papers Addenda* for Elizabeth's reign, to the year 1587, but by 8th October—the date the letter bears—Leicester was away again in the Netherlands and certainly not at Kenilworth, where it was written. It seems to indicate that a portentous storm had burst over London on a day when some act of Royal "justice" was being executed. The "we who lately felt the punishment of your stormy clouds" suggests the year 1585 as a more likely date than 1587.

"A grievous accord it has showed the heavens had made for so sharp a scourge to light upon poor earthly travellers, my gracious lady, but more bitter was it when it appears they have fulfilled your displeasure, procured from your own sweet self, whose nature has always abhorred so sore revenge; but if you it were that hath borne that high sway to cause the celestial places to obey your will, we may not wonder to see all earthly creatures so far at your devotion. No doubt, they have prepared a blessed place for you, but cursed should they be if they would seek to bereave you from those that here hold you so dear. Well pleased I am that they strive who love you most, so they let you dwell still with them that I believe will never be weary of your continuance among them, with which we, who lately felt the punishment of your stormy clouds, would gladly suffer a greater smart to have again the fair show of our blessed sun, whose beams giveth both life and light; and so appealing from the old hag's prophecy, I will pray for this felicity, that we may only enjoy this our shining joy to be our lasting light. Amen.

" For sending so far, most sweet Lady, to know how your poor *eyes* doth, I am unworthy to give thanks, only as you have sent to a creature wholly of your own making, so are you to have your full offer of him that is a double bondman; and no longer will he have life than it shall be found most true; which having offered already once for all, have no more sacrifice left, but the due obligations which shall never fail, and I trust will be acceptable in the sight of the Highest, to whose most gracious goodness I humbly and most faithfully recommend both life and service."

CHAPTER XIX

LEICESTER'S second administration in the Low
Countries, if a government of the limited
character the States finally allowed, can be
called an administration, was marked by certain
acts of severity and by many projects of
duplicity he certainly did not mean to descend
to, when he first set foot in the Netherlands.
He, whom an almost co-temporary historian—
Osborne — designated a "terrestrial Lucifer,"
never fell from the outward greatness of the
rank and favour to which Elizabeth raised
him, though, so curiously, some chroniclers of
the generation immediately succeeding his seem
to consider that he did. But his decline was
sharp and considerable from the moral attitude
to which, in the periods of England's danger
from the Catholic conspiracy, he attained under
the influence of his own intelligences and per-
ceptions, and of the Puritan ideas and Protestant
principles of the associates and followers of his
official and family life. The deeds of harshness
and practices of meanness he resorted to as

counter-stays of his languishing reputation, and in substitution of his lost authority during the months of his last stay in Holland, were the crowning sins of a career that had never been free from designs of guilt and deeds of pettiness.

But if his exemplary punishments of cowards and traitors were severe, he had the support of the States in inflicting them, and his orders to avoid bloodshed if possible were frequent and unusual in the age he lived in. It is true his devices for the seizure of over-zealous patriots bore a close resemblance to the plots which the rebels from the rule of English Elizabeth had formed under the guidance of Scottish Mary, but he never went so far in disloyalty to the aims he had professed, as to play directly into the hands of Spain. He compromised with principle, and betrayed Holland to the extent of seeking advantages for his Queen that would enable her, when the opportunity arose, to dictate terms of peace to the Hollanders. But Leicester was guiltless of designs attributed to him by some disappointed patriots among the Dutch, of gaining possession of Leyden and other of the principal towns of Holland, for the purpose of delivering them treacherously into the hands of Philip. His plan was to hold them for Elizabeth, so that, when the period for a general reconciliation came, she might have an actual and not only a sentimental authority in the affairs of the States.

Leicester never deceived himself, as did Elizabeth, concerning the ultimate intentions of Spain. He was far less surprised than she, when at last the Invincible Armada set sail for the English coast.

In the supreme hour of her country's danger, the call of the Queen of England was to the same Lieutenant - General she had sent forth with her first challenge to the enemy. Perhaps the advance of the foe Elizabeth had had the fatuity to think she could repel with blandishments and paralyse with coquetries, caused her to repent of the machinations that had contributed to the disasters of Leicester's first command.

In any case, the Favourite was now made Commander-in-Chief of the army assembled for the protection of London and the mouth of the Thames, and not a man in England disputed the fitness of his appointment. The shock of the common danger made every patriot know his fellow. The opportunity for a legitimate activity and the occasion for valour and for chivalry brought all that was best in Leicester into play. Not only the show of war appealed to him. The practical and mathematical Leicester came to the fore. The literary and imaginative one—the name of the Leicesters was legion—bided his time.

On 22nd July 1588, he wrote to Walsingham that he had talked with one, Peter Pett, "about the lighters and chain to stop the river at Tilbury, which are not sufficient unless strengthened with a competent number of masts placed before them." And not content with the inefficiency of talking, Leicester went "down the river with Pett to view the place." The following day, he reported to the Council on the fortifications at Gravesend and Tilbury, and pointed out that Tilbury was much out of order, but could be made impregnable. He requested the immediate dispatch of powder, ordnance, and other fighting implements, and was insistent that each fort should be sufficiently provisioned for a siege.

On the 26th July, Leicester at Gravesend gave further account to Walsingham of the situation of affairs in his command. The 4,000 men of Essex were assembled at West Tilbury, and "were as forward and willing men as ever he saw." It is delightful to find once more in Leicester the freshness of enthusiasm, and to note that true sympathy with the needs of his men which is such a human feature of his character. He deplored the great want of victuals—"Some one had blundered." After a march of twenty miles, the Essex stalwarts had "not a barrel of beer nor a loaf of bread" among them. To avoid an extension of famine, Leicester promptly sent orders to the 1,000 Londoners on the march to join forces with their comrades of Essex, to halt where his message met them, "except they had provisions with them." And the literary Leicester, whose existence could never be wholly suppressed, gave forceful expression to the thought of wisdom :—" Though it has pleased God to begin graciously, it will not do to be too secure. *Great dilatory wants are found upon all sudden hurly-burlies.*" Falling back into instant practicalities, the difficulty of getting men together from long distances owing to the dearth of vehicles was considered by Leicester, the mathematician. The chivalrous anxiety of the Favourite was exhibited in his urging that a strong force should be about the Queen. His letter closed with the comment: "If the Navy had not been strong at sea, what peril England would now have been in."

And on 27th July and 5th August there went forth from the busy general in camp two letters to his Sovereign, which showed the "Eyes" of Elizabeth in his proper character of watchman of England and sentinel of his Queen.

The letter of 27th July opened with the prayer that a most just God that beloveth the innocency of heart and the cause she is assailed for, will assist and bless her with victory. According to her request, Leicester offered

Elizabeth his advice. First, at once to gather an army about her in the strongest manner possible, some special nobleman to be placed at the head of it, to be officered with the oldest and best assured captains. Second, for her own person—"the most dainty and sacred thing we have in this world to care for"—he could not consent that she should proceed to the confines of her realm to meet the enemy, but advised her to go to her home at Havering, with the army round about her there, and to spend two or three days at the camp at Tilbury, "there to rest in her poor lieutenant's cabin." Thus far, but no further, could he consent to the adventure of her person. Lastly, for himself, for her gracious favour to him, he can only yield the like sacrifice he owes to God, which is a thankful heart, and to offer his body, life, and all to do her service.

On 5th August, Leicester had received in secret the news that pleased him most, next the well-doing of her sacred person, that she intended to behold the poor company now in the field, ready to die for her. "Good sweet Queen!" he urged, "alter not your purpose if God give you good health." The lodging prepared for her was a proper, sweet, cleanly house, the camp within a little mile of it, and her person as sure as at St James's.

Elizabeth — every inch a Queen — went to

Tilbury and rode through all the squadrons of
the army gathered there, 23,000 strong—22,000
being foot and 1,000 horse. On either side of
her, as she reviewed this force, rode the two
men whose names for good or for ill are
immortally associated with her own. The
General on the one hand was Robert Dudley,
Earl of Leicester, and on the other, Robert
Devereux, Earl of Essex. Was the riding there
of these three an omen for England? If so, the
portent was not read. No one who saw the
upright and active, yet florid and grizzled
Favourite pass by in all the magnificence of his
bearing and his office, could have guessed how
soon — how very soon — the mantle of his
favourdom must fall from his shoulders on to
those of his dashing, splendid stepson.

Essex is sometimes regarded as a more certain
favourite of Elizabeth than was Leicester. But
Essex had no part in forming the mind or in
influencing the character of his Queen. He
was for Elizabeth always a graceless boy, on
whom she fondly doted, as mothers and grand-
mothers dote on babes they have dandled,
grown to years. The grandmother of Essex
(the mother of Lettice) was first cousin of
Elizabeth. Leicester was the stepfather of
Essex. Undoubtedly, the younger favourite
copied many of the tricks by which the elder had
kept his hold upon the extraordinarily coquettish

Queen. But Essex had not served that early apprenticeship to misfortune which made Leicester ever careful of overstepping certain bounds of audacity, and his self-control was inferior to his stepfather's.

Behind the mounted "Excellencies" and their Sovereign at Tilbury, there came afoot Sir John Norris, the Lord-Marshal. That fine soldier, with whom Leicester had refused to serve any longer in the Netherlands, was welcomed as a coadjutor when their common country was assailed. Then every Englishman was a hero to his neighbour. No petty hates, no paltry jealousies divided any to whom the integrity of their native land was dear.

And for Leicester, there must have been satisfaction enough in that hour of hours. What could patriot or Queen's favourite desire more than to hear, delivered in his presence, the stirring speech in which Elizabeth displayed her own enthusiasm for Queenship and her just title to England's Sovereignty, and whereby she commended the worthiness of her Favourite to stand before her people in her stead.

"My loving people," cried the Queen, on the camping ground at Tilbury, "we have been persuaded by some that are careful of our safety, to take heed how we commit ourselves to armed multitudes, for fear of treachery; but, I assure you, I do not desire to live to distrust my faithful and loving people. Let tyrants fear, I have always so behav'd my self, that, under God, I have placed my chiefest strength and safeguard in the loyal hearts and good will of my subjects; and therefore I am come amongst you, as you see, at this time, not for my recreation and disport, but being resolved, in the midst and heat of the battle, to live or die amongst you all; to lay down for my God, and for my kingdom, and for my people, my honour and my blood, even in the dust. I know I have the body but of a weak and feeble woman; but I have the heart and stomach of a King, and of a King of *England* too, and think foul scorn that *Parma* or *Spain* or any Prince of *Europe*, should dare to invade the borders of my Realm; to which, rather than any dishonour shall grow by me, I myself will take up arms, I myself will be your General, Judge, and Rewarder of every one of your virtues in the field. I know already, for your forwardness you have deserv'd rewards and crowns; and, we do assure you, on the word of a Prince, they shall be duly paid you. In the meantime, my Lieutenant-General shall be in my stead, than whom never Prince commanded a more noble or worthy subject; not doubting but by your obedience to my General, by your concord in the camp and your valour in the field, we shall shortly have a famous victory over those enemies of my God, of my Kingdoms, and of my People."

But the "famous victory" had already taken place, though confidence that danger was over could not yet be felt. The victory was one of tides and tempests rather than of "concord in

the camp" and "valour in the field," though
the Navy Leicester had pronounced to be
"strong at sea" had a proud share in the defeat
of the Armada. The military arm, no less
ready for the fight than the naval, was only
raised to strike. Yet the conceit of Leicester
had been inflamed by the Sovereign's praises of
her Lieutenant-General, and by the obedience
rendered by the massed forces under him.
He had the ear of the Queen. She was in the
mood to do him honour. It is impossible to
determine the exact end she had in view—
whether recompense to Leicester for depriva-
tions of his authority in the Provinces, or
reward to him for his prompt and effective
gathering of an army at the Thames mouth—
but she certainly consented to the drawing of
Letters Patent creating him Lord-Lieutenant
under her in the government of England and
Ireland. This was to constitute him a Viceroy
indeed! But Lord Burghley, Sir Francis Walsingham and Sir Christopher Hatton, though
all friends of Leicester, had the courage to
prevent the fatal step Elizabeth, in an excess
of that delirious emotion that follows the
removal of strains of anxiety, especially that
greatest of all strains for heads of governments,
the fear of an armed invasion of their country,
had assented to. Undoubtedly, she felt at the
moment that she could not do enough for any

one to whom could be attributed the salvation of her Kingdom and the safety of her person. Not that her serenity was ever disturbed by a sense of gratitude. But Leicester had been her deputy in the field; he was that *creature of her own* she had always singularly favoured; and there was no further dignity left for him but this. He was not to receive it.

About the 20th of August, the last onslaught of Spain's might was known to have been utterly repelled. On 29th August, Leicester was already on his way to "the Bath" to take the cure for the complaint he had long suffered from, and which had been probably made worse by the strains and activities of his military service. The "Bath" he aimed at may have been Leamington. He died at Cornbury in Oxfordshire, on his way to Kenilworth, on the 4th of September 1588. Six days before, he had written the letter, now exhibited as a national treasure in the museum of the Record Office, and here reproduced in *facsimile*.

Being deciphered, it runs thus:

"I most humbly beseech your Majesty to pardon your pôôre old servant" [*note the symbol*] "to be thus bold in sending to know how my gracious Lady doth and what ease of her late pain she finds, being the chiefest thing in this world I do pray for, for her to have good health and long life. For my own poor case, I continue still your medicine and find it amend much better than with any other thing that hath been given me. Thus hoping to find perfect cure at the bath with the continuance of my wonted prayer for your Majesty's most happy preservation I humbly kiss your foot, from your old lodging at Rycott this Thursday morning, ready to take on my journey, by your Majesty's most faithfull and obedient servant,

"R. LEYCESTER."

" Even as I had wrytten thus much I received your Majesty's token by young Tracy."

One wonders what was the fantastic trinket Elizabeth sent at this time as a " token " to the man who had been as her brother! Whether or not a mere trifle, we may believe its symbology was terrific and immense. Leicester addressed his missive of tenderness and sentiment " To the Queen's most excellent Majesty." Underneath the superscription, in the elaborate hand of Elizabeth herself, are the words,

" HIS LAST LETTER."

In early womanhood, she had kept the miniature of Lord Robert Dudley in a casket, as one of her most precious treasures. She had drawn it thence to show to Sir Robert Melville when she proposed to him her favourite as a husband for Mary, Queen of Scots. In later life, Elizabeth preserved among her "jewels" the last letter of the Earl of Leicester.

The quiet and quick snuffing out of the most brilliant luminary of Elizabeth's Court, the most bewildering light of her Council, and the chief sun of her grandeur and her state, impressed the most poetic mind of the age with a sense of curious blankness.

Of the passing of the Favourite, Edmund Spenser sang:

> "I saw him die, I saw him die, as one
> Of the meane people, and brought foorth on beare;
> I saw him die, and no man left to mone
> His dolefull fate, that late him loved deare:
> Scarse anie left to close his eylids neare;
> Scarse anie left upon his lips to laie
> The sacred sod, or requiem to saie.

> "He now is dead, and all is with him dead,
> Save what in Heaven's storehouse he uplaid:
> His hope is faild, and come to passe his dread,
> And will men (now dead) his deedes upbraid:
> Spite bites the dead, that living never baid.
> He now is gone, the whiles the fox is crept
> Into the hole, the which the badger swept.

> "He now is dead, and all his glorie gone,
> And all his greatnesse vapoured to nought,
> That as a glasse upon the water shone,
> Which vanisht quite, so soone as it was sought:
> His name is worne alreadie out of thought,
> Ne anie poet seeks him to revive;
> Yet manie poets honoured him alive.

> "Ne doth his Colin, carelesse Colin Cloute,
> Care now his idle bagpipe up to raise,
> Ne tell his sorrow to the listning rout
> Of shepheard groomes, which wont his songs to praise:
> Praise who so list, yet I will him dispraise,
> Untill he quite him of this guiltie blame:
> Wake, shepheard's boy, at length awake for shame.

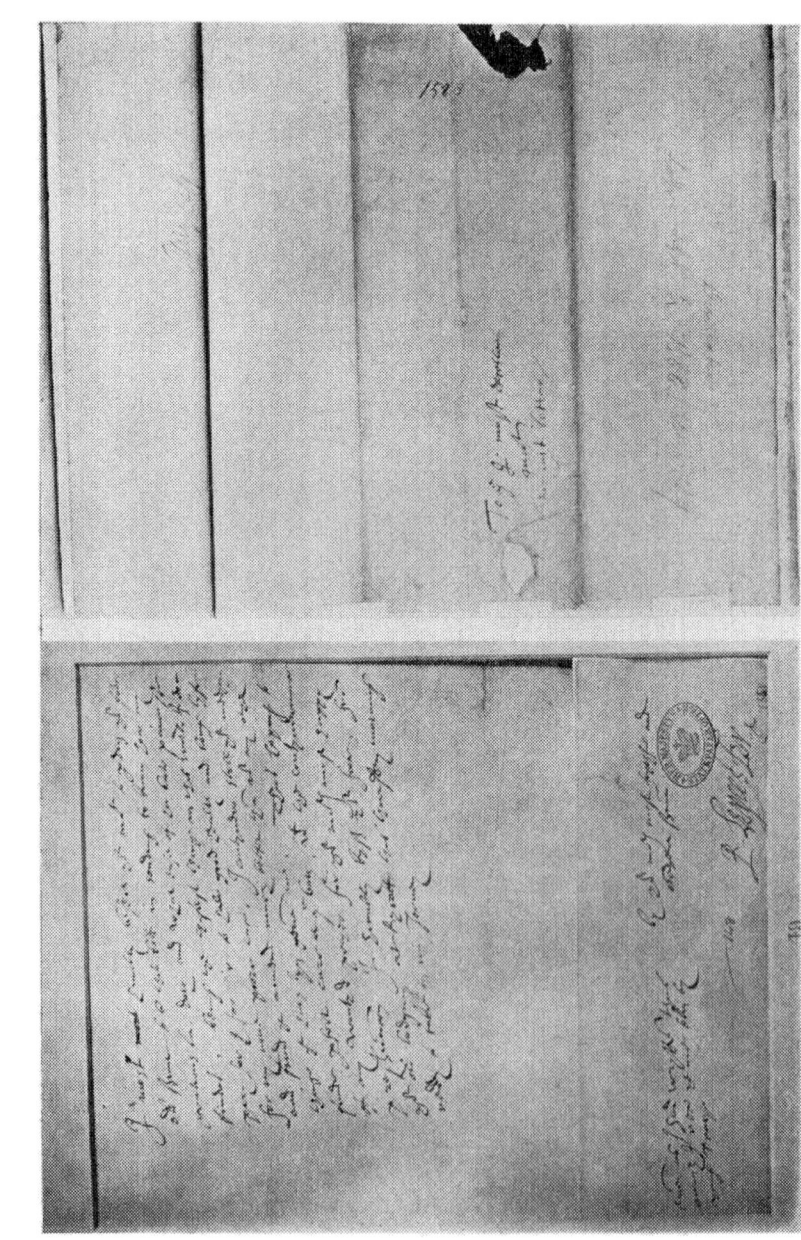

"And whoso els did goodness by him gaine,
And whoso els his bounteous minde did trie,
Whether he shepheard be, or shepheard's swaine,
(For manie did, which doo it now decrie)
Awake, and to his song a part applie :
And I, the whilest you mourne for his decease,
Will with my mourning plaints your plaint increase."

Indeed, the flaring torch of Leicester's greatness was very suddenly put out.

We may not doubt the Queen of England dropped a tear upon that folded paper, across which she wrote the phrase that carries its note of tenderness,

"HIS LAST LETTER."

But her mood of sentiment quickly passed. It was a speedy concern of the Royal spinster to obtain repayment from the estates of Leicester of all monies he did actually owe and that she conceived he owed her.

His Countess too—left in straits through the Queen's prompt claims on her husband's property —was not long in consoling herself for the loss of her "Illustrious Prince." Shortly after his death, she married Sir Christopher Blount, who had been Gentleman of the Horse to Leicester. But she composed the Latin epitaph on the gorgeous tomb of Leicester, in the Lady Chapel of the Church of St Mary, Warwick. For years she sought in vain a reconciliation with the Queen. She died on Christmas Day, in the year 1634, in the ninety-fifth year of her age,

2 B

and was laid to rest beside her second husband. The stone effigies on the tombs of the Earl and Countess of Leicester have their hands lifted in prayer, and their feet extended. Both figures are crowned and robed as peer and peeress.

Leicester wrote his will while in Holland. Its dispositions are numerous, and by it he provided liberally for his "most dear, well-beloved wife, the Countess of Leicester," and for his "base son." But because of his "charges" in the Low Countries, and the action taken by the Queen upon his death, there was, for all the possessions in his name, very little estate to divide. His bequest to his Queen memorialised his devotion to her.

"And first of all and above all Persons, it is my duty to remember my most dear and most gracious Sovereign, whose Creature under God I have been, and who hath been a most bountiful and most princely Mistress unto me, as well as in advancing me to many Honours, as in maintaining me many Ways by her Goodness and Liberality. And as my best Recompense to her most excellent Majesty can be from so mean a Man, chiefly in Prayer to God, so whilst there was any Breath in this Body, I never failed it, even as for mine own Soul. And as it was my greatest joy in my Life Time to serve her to her Contentation, so it is not unwelcome to me, being the Will of God, to die, and end this Life for her Service. And yet, albeit I am not able to make any

Price of Recompense of her great Goodness,
yet will I presume to present unto her a Token
of an humble, faithful Heart, as the least that
ever I can send her, and with this Prayer
withal, that it may please the Almighty God,
not only to make her the oldest Prince, that
ever He gave over England, but to make
her the Godliest, the Virtuousest, and the
Worthiest in His sight, that ever He gave
over any Nation. That she may indeed be a
blessed Mother and Nurse to this People and
Church of England, which the Almighty God
grant for His Christ's Sake. The Token I do
bequeath unto her Majesty is the Jewel with
three great Emeralds, with a fair large Table
Diamond in the Midst, without a flaw, and
set about with many diamonds, without flaw,
and a rope of fair white Pearl, to the Number
of Six Hundred, to hang the said Jewel at;
which Pearl and Jewel was once purposed for
her Majesty against a coming to Wanstead,
but it must now thus be disposed, which I do
pray you, my dear Wife, see performed, and
delivered to some of those whom I shall hereafter nominate and appoint to be my Overseers
for her Majesty."

As overseers, and to "help, assist, and
comfort" his "dear and poor disconsolate
wife," whom he had named as his executrix,
Leicester appointed "Sir Christopher Hatton,
Lord - Chancellor of England, my loving
brother, the Earl of Warwick, and my very
good Lord and Friend, the Lord Howard,
High-Admiral of England."

Among the State Papers of the reign of

Elizabeth is a note of Instructions bearing date 31st May 1589, from which it appears that after the death of the "Noble Imp," Leicester revived his project of the marriage of his son by Lady Sheffield to the Lady Arabella Stuart. For in this paper an agent in England of the Scottish Government is directed to ascertain "what party Arabella and her favourers adhere to, and how they mean to bestow her in marriage, seeing Leicester's intention to match his bastard with her is by his death made frustrate."

So perished with him his last scheme for appropriating the crown of England. His name lives ever and only as the Favourite of a Queen. Yet there were in him parts and abilities that made him something more than the mere worm in the dust Elizabeth, in her hateful moods, loved to see wriggling before her throne.

Motley, in his severe yet sympathetic analysis of the Favourite's character, describes him as "that luxuriant, creeping, flaunting, all - pervading existence which struck its fibres into the mould, and coiled itself through the whole fabric of Elizabeth's life and reign." No picture of the Great Parasite could be more complete. Yet the creeper was not satisfied to be a vegetable. By sheer force of a natural tenacity he clung to the prop of his honour—Elizabeth

— and choked many higher existences that crossed his trail. But on occasion he reared his head and struck with a fury that was evidence of an autonomy. He had the wisdom of the serpent, but there was in him sufficient of the brute as well as of the reptile, to leave no doubt as to his being a man.

Besides the Queen herself, three women loved him; made sacrifices for him of favour, fame, or life. And from Leicester himself shot forth at times beams of a magnanimity, of a compunction, and of a zeal for service that revealed a soul in him, and proclaimed him not wholly unregenerate. The pity is that the man who could say to the envoys of the Netherlanders, who first came to plead in England their holy cause: "For my own part, I am ready to stake my life, estates, and reputation, upon this issue," and who did indeed make the cast of his whole fortune and his every energy, was also the man who declared openly in his camp that he would hang Sir John Norris, and who railed at the Hollanders when they refused to become his tools, for "tinkers, boors, devils, and atheists," while he threatened some among them with hanging!

Yet in Holland, as in England, his courage never faltered, and the character lost in the Netherlands was redeemed at Tilbury. There, his energy, intelligence, and consideration for others saved him from the curse that else would surely have followed his name and reputation: "Upon thy belly shalt thou go, and dust shalt thou eat all the days of thy life."

For all his dependencies and his treacheries, Leicester rose times and again to the erect attitude of a man. And those who condemn his failings, insufficiencies, and vices — of which he had very many—should pause to enumerate his accomplishments, capacities, and virtues, of which there were in him not a few.

Undoubtedly, he had qualities that may be designated religious and moral, as well as many that were intellectual, literary, and artistic. His nature was a mass of contradictions, as was proper to a son of the Renascence, to a disciple of Macchiavelli, to a champion of the Protestants, and to the FAVOURITE OF QUEEN ELIZABETH.

INDEX

CPSIA information can be obtained at www.ICGtesting.com
Printed in the USA
LVOW04s0304031014

406967LV00006B/321/P